Blechingley and The Grange

Blechingley and The Grange

A Pictorial and Social History of a Quintessentially English Village

David John McCleave

Second edition published by Shakspeare Editorial, UK, May 2024
ISBN 978-1-7392549-9-5 (hardback)
ISBN 978-1-7384422-4-9 (paperback)

First edition published by Shakspeare Editorial, UK, April 2023
ISBN 978-1-7392549-2-6 (hardback
Copyright © 2023 David John McCleave

The right of David John McCleave to be identified as the author of the work has been asserted by him in accordance with the Copyright, Designs and Patents Act 1988.

The content of this publication, including text, photos, illustrations, maps, newspaper articles, graphics etc. are copyright the author, or are used with permission or under licence from copyright holders. A small number of photos/illustrations are in the public domain. Some items have been reproduced from original artefacts owned by the author. Most of the unattributed modern photos are by and are copyright of the author. The author has worked diligently to obtain permissions to publish images, if any copyright holder believes that this is not the case, the author would be pleased to be informed for future editions. No part of this publication may be reproduced, stored in a retrieval system, or transmitted, in any form or by any means mechanical, electronic, photocopying, recording or otherwise without the prior written consent of the publisher; nor be otherwise circulated in any form of binding or cover other than that in which it is published and without a similar condition being imposed on the subsequent purchaser. This book is not published as a commercial venture.

Design and typesetting www.ShakspeareEditorial.org

Cover illustration – Line and wash sketch by Don Coe Hon. FSAI of The Grange stable yard in the late 1800s, commissioned by the author from old photographs and records. Cover design – Sarah Clarkson (née McCleave) © *David John McCleave.*

Contents

A Selection of Headlines in Chronological Order vii
Forewords xxi
Introduction 1

Blechingley | A Brief History 5
    Blechingley | Pictures and Stories from Yesteryear | Pubs | Garages | Wren Blacksmiths | Shops |
    Businesses | Transport 15
    Court Lodge Farm 46
    Blechingley | A Selection of Notable Past and Present People (and a Pigeon) 49
    Blechingley | Pictured Today 63

The Grange | Tudor to Victorian Overview 70
    The Grange 1841 | Farmhouse on Town Farm 84
    The Grange 1861 | From Farmhouse to Home and Medical Practice 85
    The Grange 1866 | The Blechingley Auction and Black Friday 89

The Grange | Edward VII to Charles III 95
    The Grange 1906–20 | The New Domesday Book Entry 95
    The Grange 1971 | A Bird's-Eye View 99
    The Grange 1987–2023 | From One Home to Eleven 100

The Grange | Connected Properties and Institutions | Businesses 102
    Blechingley Farm/Town Farm | Town Mead 102
    Grange Meadow | Bowls | Quoits | Blechingley Amateur Dramatics |
    Cricket | Hevers Pond | Ivy Mill 107
    Grange Cottage 121
    The Outwood Lane Story | The Dewdney Cottages | Seven and Nine |
    Post Offices | Postmen | Engineers 126

The Grange Farmhouse | Owners and Tenants – 1586–1867 144
    The Hoskins Family | Owners 1586–1767 144
    Henry Lovell and Family | Tenants circa 1618–25 144
    The Perkins Family of Pendell, Blechingley | Owners 1808/9–55 146
    William Judson and Family | Tenants 1849–57 155
    John Henry Sharp and Family | Tenants 1859–62 156
    The Birkbeck Brothers | Bankers/Owners/Mortgagees 1861–67 157

The Grange Home and Doctor's Surgery | Owners and Tenants – 1865–1987 . 159
    Surgeon-Major Leslie and Family | Tenants/Owners 1865–1924 |
    Elizabeth Mary Leslie's Mission Work and Emigration 159
    Doctor Charles Edmund Oldman and Family | Tenants 1877–1904 |
    Godstone Union Workhouse 173
    Doctor Charles Allen Robinson and Family | Tenants 1904–09 180

    Doctor Frederick William Robertson OBE and Family | Tenants/Owners 1909–52 | Robertson Whisky Business | Blechingley Isolation Hospital 181
    Doctor FW Robertson's work in WWI Soldiers' Hospitals | Red Gables | Castle Relief 201
    Doctor Mark and Mrs Philippa Marshall and Family | Owners 1952–87 |
    Gay Kindersley | The Mid Surrey Farmers Draghounds 228

Other Blechingley Medical Practices 235

Local people and their Homes (with some Grange connections) 238
    Edmund William Blessig Esq. | Garston Park 238
    The Denny Family | Brick Kiln Farm | Mount Pleasant Dairy Farm | Kennels Dairy Farm 250
    The Smith Family Photo Gallery, early 1900s 256
    Herbert Smith's WWII Diary 262
    The Lambert Family | South Park | Cuckseys Farm | Sandhills 267
    Jarvis Kenrick IV | Pendell House 278

The Lordship of the Manor of Blechingley | 1066–2023 281

Interesting Facts | Events | Statistics | Local Families 300

Grange | Summary of Owners and Tenants 307

Acknowledgements 309

Bibliography 312

About the Author 319

A Selection of Headlines in Chronological Order

Event	Page no
Earthquake in Blechingley – 1551	302
Duke executed for plotting treason in his Blechingley palace – 1521	282
Henry VIII stops for a beer at the Red Lion – circa 1521	16
Anne of Cleves ex-Queen of England and local resident, borrows altar bell from St Mary's Church and fails to return it – circa 1543	12
Guy Fawkes stores his gunpowder in basement of local mill – 1604	120
Grange resident imprisoned in the Tower of London for election meddling – 1624	145
Rector ordered by Parliament to confess his sins and promise repentance to his congregation from his pulpit at St Mary's – 1624	145
Blechingley Palace/Place demolished – 1670	14
Charles Hoskins Esq. and consortium re-build The Grange – 1739	73
Man 'continued sensible till within an hour of his death in his 104th year' at the workhouse – 1768	174
Man dies in his 107th year at the workhouse – 1778	174
Travelling woman of unknown name and age buried at St Mary's – 1806	302
John Hassell watercolour artist records seven buildings in Blechingley, including The Grange – 1822	71
Lord Palmerston MP for Blechingley and later prime minister delivers election speech in front of the town hall – circa 1831	39
Murder, man shot on his cart driving home from Epsom Market to Blechingley – 1834	147
Bletchingley sold for £11,000 – 1835	300
John Perkins Esq., Lord of the Manor of Pendell, buys Blechingley Manor for £540 – 1835	147
Death after altercation in a Blechingley public house – 1836	24

Fire at Town Farm Bletchingley – 1851 ....80, 104

Farmhouse, The Grange, converted to medical practice for
  Surgeon Major Leslie – 1863/5 ....71, 85

Henry Thomas Lambert JP takes over Sandhills farm, the first
  of the Lamberts to reside in the village – 1866 267

Bletchingley man scores the first ever goal in an FA Cup Final – 1871 ....50, 278

Elizabeth Leslie, formerly of The Grange, arrives in Foochow City, China,
  to work as a missionary – 1891 161

Joint founder of Denver & Rio Grande Railway and the towns of Colorado
  Springs and Manitou Springs, settles in Blechingley mansion – 1891 .....50, 152

Miss Drews thrown from pony and cart in Blechingley High Street – 1893............235

Local gentleman gifts cricket pitch to village and free use of
  convalescent home – 1896..116, 209

Doctor's wife at The Grange advertising for cook: 'beer supplied – must be
  churchwomen' – 1899 179

Barclays Bank and new post office opens in the High Street – 1900 133

Local ladies stand in protest at the planned demolition of the
  Dewdney Cottages – early 1900s 128

Helen D'Oyly Carte, widow of Richard D'Oyly Carte, takes country
  home with her new husband in Blechingley – 1902...................................51, 242

Mystery of Blechingley gentleman found drowned in the Thames – 1903 236

Surrey Foxhounds meet at White Hart Inn on Boxing Day – 1905...........................17

Jarvis Kenrick gives lectures warning of Germany's rapid
  military expansion – 1909 278

Hard labour sentence for 10 Blechingley workhouse inmates – 1910......................174

Caretaker/Fuller's Earth digger inherits his employer's house and estate – 1912......57

Legg Family post office tenure ends after 100 years – 1912 131

Motor omnibus arrives in Blechingley – 1912 44

Red Gables and Castle Hill Relief WWI military hospitals open – 1914.........201, 205

Georgiana Grace Quinlan, sub-postmistress, publishes letter on 'beauties'
  of Blechingley – 1918 135

Ivy Mill burns down – 1920s 118

Performance of Gilbert and Sullivan's Patience – 1925 115

A Selection of Headlines in Chronological Order

Snow drifts of 20 feet – 1927 260
Postman William (Bill) Lord clocks up 300,000 miles on his bicycle – 1927 137
Recreation ground for children gifted to village – 1929 107
Grange Meadow Sports Ground gifted to village by local Esquire – 1929 107
Cawley Bakers taken over after 200 years trading in the village – 1935 .... 36, 37
Doctor Robertson marries the nurse he met at The Grange – 1937 195
Grange Doctor builds battery-powered electrocardiograph in loft – 1938 194
Bill Brandt, photographer, comes to town – 1939 218
Head Parlourmaid Dorothy Pratt becomes a national star – 1939 218
Herbert Basil Smith starts writing a diary for son, missing in action – 1944 262
Flying Bomb kills young mother, house and chapel destroyed – 1944 273
Community of St Mary the Virgin Convent opens old people's home
    at Pendell Court – 1947 153
Cricket legends play in the village – 1946–1964 116
Man refuses a free mansion and estate in Blechingley – 1950 245
Jump jockey champion Gay Kindersley recovers from a broken back
    at The Grange – 1955 231
'James Bond' spy, pirate, and smuggler of WWII Enigma cypher
    machine settles in Blechingley – 1957 58
Desmond Tutu, new curate at St Mary's 1964 54
Fire at The Grange – 1970s 81
Gay Kindersley steals Oliver Reed's girlfriend – 1976 230
Hero WWII pigeon with secret code found in chimney – 1982 61
Bletchingly-born Hilda Wren dies three months before her 108th birthday – 1993 ... 28
Dame Judi Dench comes to town – 2016 54
Last curtain call for Bletchingley Players after 56 years – 2019 .... 54, 111
Marriage proposal captured on the steps of Norfolk House – 2022 42
Phil Carson, record executive and bass guitarist for Dusty Springfield,
    Led Zeppelin, AC/DC, takes second home at The Grange – 2022 55
Local man becomes UK prime minister – 2024 48

Illustrations

Allen, George, driving the isolation hospital fever van – early 1900s ... 188
Allom, Maurice James Carrick, Surrey and England Cricketer ... 53
Anne of Cleves, Queen of England, January–July 1540 ... 282
Ashdown, Benjamin, Oddfellows Grand Master and Clerk to the Parish Council ... 52
Bagnall, Ethel Hope, and Doctor F W Robertson OBE, memorial in St Mary's ... 193
Baker, Josephine – 1940 ... 59
Bank Buildings – 1906 ... 133
Bank Buildings, enlarged section showing post office ... 133
Bank Buildings under construction – 1899/1900 ... 134
Battling with snow in December 1927 ... 260
Bell, 'Archie', 21st-birthday fancy dress party invitation, Pendell Court – 1904 ... 30
Bell, Dr. William Abraham (1841–1921) full portrait ... 50
Bell, Dr. William Abraham (1841–1921) portrait extract ... 152
Biffy, see Dunderdale ... 58
Bird, AJ, fishmonger, fruiterer and greengrocer at Forgeside ... 31
Birkbeck, Edward, 1st Baronet of Horstead Hall – 1885 ... 158
Black Horse Coach House and Stables, The former – August 2022 ... 25
Blechingley auction catalogue page – 1866 ... 94
Blechingley auction catalogue plan – 1866 ... 93
Blechingley from Castle Hill and from Castle Meadow, looking towards the North Downs – 2024 .. 317
Blechingley from the north, looking south – 2024 ... 318
Blechingley High Street looking east – 1905 ... 181
Blechingley High Street looking west – 1909 ... 15
Blechingley Isolation Hospital ... 186
Blechingley Isolation Hospital aerial view – 1971 ... 189
Blechingley Isolation Hospital nurses' home ... 189
Blechingley Isolation Hospital porter's lodge – 1914–20 ... 188
Blechingley Isolation Hospital, the old porter's lodge – 2021 ... 190
Blechingley Parish Magazine cover – 1878 ... 302
Blechingley Place – from a 1622 map ... 12
Blechingley village aerial view from the south, looking north – 2020 ... 103
Blechingley village centre – 1903 ... 179
Blechingley village looking east – c. 1965 ... 234
Blechingly ancient castle ground plan – 1809 ... 11
Blechingly, map of ... xxii
Blessig, Edmund William, age 66 ... 238
Blessig, Edmund William, at Garston Park, age 89 ... 239
Bletchingley Amateur Dramatic Society, curtain call of *My Three Angels* – March 1964 ... 113
Bletchingley Amateur Dramatic Society, curtain call of *The Book of the Month* – October 1963 ... 112
Bletchingley Amateur Dramatic Society, publicity stunt for *When We Are Married* – October 1964 114

Illustrations | xi

Bletchingley Castle Relief Hospital, group of wounded soldiers – 1914 207
Bletchingley House –2000 222
Bletchingley Players AGM – 2016 114
Bletchingley Players Chairman John Tomlin presenting a bouquet to
    Dame Judi Dench at the AGM – 2016 114
Bletchingley tithe map – 1841 76
Bletchingley village sign.. 5
Bletchingly village looking east – c. 1910 20
Bletchingly, village scene – c. 1909 200
Boulter family photo in front of the tennis lawn at Garston Park – 1911 243
Boulter, Stanley Carr and family in Brighton 241
Boulter, Stanley Carr JP 240
Bowling at Blechingley – 1929 109
Brandt, Augustus Philip (1871–1952).. 215
Brandt, Bill, five photos featuring Head Parlourmaid Dorothy Alice Pratt 219
Brandt, Bill, photo, 'Cocktails in a Surrey Garden' – 1930s 217
Brandt, Bill, photo, 'Parlourmaid and Under Parlourmaid Ready to Serve Dinner' – 1939 218
Brandt, Henry Bernard and Dorothy Alice Pratt, Capenor nursery – 1939 223
Brandt, Jean Champion, née Garmany (1867–1950)... 216
Brewerstreet Tudor Farmhouse.. 66
Buck, Marian and John – 2022 115
Campo Tosto (Campotosto), Henry, *The Primrose Gatherer* 57
Campo Tosto (Campotosto) insignias (HC and OC) on the gateposts at Snatts Hill House – 2022....... 57
Capenor, as built for Hudson Taylor Esq. – 1887 222
Carson, Phil with Robert Plant... 55
Castle Cottages in Castle Street – 2021 140
Castlefield, the 'real' James Bond's house... 59
Castle Hill and surroundings, map of – 1934 225
Castle Hill/Bletchingley Castle, west end 207
Castle Hill, entrance gate to the former stables – 2021 226
Castle Hill Farm, disused cow sheds – 2021 227
Castle Hill Farmhouse – 2021... 227
Castle Hill mansion, front 206
Castle Hill mansion house/Bletchingley Castle rear.. 209
Castle Hill map showing remains of Blechingley Castle – 1935.. 10
Castle Hill, west gate in Castle Street – 2021 226
Castle Place, front of, formerly Castle Hill/Bletchingley Castle – 2020 224
Castle Relief Hospital, group of wounded soldiers – 1914 208
Cawley advertisement – 1935... 37
Cawley Bakers, rare Blechingley photo postcard, – c. 1908 37
Cawley, Old, The Rat Catcher, wearing a Surrey smock – c. 1870 36
Chuchill, Winston, signature on War Office certificate –1920.. 211
Church Lane, Forge Cottage and Wren's Forge, The corner of – 1920s 27
Church Walk – 1941 35
Church Walk –2021 64

Church Yard – 2021 64
Cinderhill Cottage, Cuckseys Lane – 2024 302
Clayton estate map of Blechingley – 1761 293
Clayton monument in St Mary's Church – 2020 286
Clayton, Robert junior on monument – 2020 286
Clayton, Sir Robert 283
Clive House – 2021 61
Cockburn, Sir Alexander, Lord Chief Justice – 1866 92
Coe, Don, line and wash drawings .... Front cover, 23, 126
Colin, Jean, with Tommy Trinder – 1941 52
Congregational chapel, The old – December 1960 21
Coppard, Derrick and Ann – 2022 305
Copstick, Gill, at The Punchbowl, Dorking, Surrey – 1976 230
Cossor Robertson Portable Electrocardiograph 194
Court Lodge Farm farmhouse – 2024 47
Court Lodge Farmhouse – c. 1948 46
Cuckseys Farm – 1930s 259
Cuckseys Farm – c. 1934 259
Cuckseys Farm from the air – 2024 277
Cuckseys Farmhouse – 2021 277
Cuckseys Farm, watercolour – 1880 276
Davies, 'Teddy', postman – c. 1912 137
Dench, Dame Judi and David Mills – 2016 54
Dench, Dame Judi, at Bletchingley Players AGM – 2016 114
Denny, Albert and his son Walter, advertisement – 1935 254
Denny, Albert and Kate with their first child, Dorothy Emma – late 1800s 251
Denny, Albert, known in the family as the Guv'nor – late 1800s–1930s 252
Denny, Ezekiel and Emma – late 1800s 250
Denny, Kate and Albert, memorials in St Mark's Chapel – 2022 255
Denny, Kate, and Herbert Smith on a pony and trap – 1927 261
Denny, Kate Frances – late 1800s 252
Descent of the Manor of Blechingley, Table 1 297
Descent of the Manor of Blechingley, Table 2 298
Descent of the Manor of Blechingley, Table 3 299
Dewdney Cottages, 7–9 Outwood Lane – early 1900s 128
Dower House, The – 1914–20 210
Dower House, The, foundation stone – 1896 212
D'Oyly Carte, Helen 243
D'Oyly Carte, Helen, and Stanley Carr Boulter, younger days – c. 1875 51
D'Oyly Carte Island, Eyot House and D'Oyly's Cafe, River Thames, Weybridge, Surrey ... 242
Dunderdale, Biffy and Debbie 60
Dunderdale, Biffy in uniform 59
Dunderdale memorial in St Mary's Church 60
Dunderdale, Wilfred Albert, a younger Biffy (1899–1990) 58

East Surrey Traction Company bus – c. 1918	45
Eddolls, George, butcher at 5 Outwood Lane – early 1900s	142
English, Thomas, business card	128
Faber, Leslie (1880–1929)	51
FitzClarence, Geoffrey, The 5th Earl of Munster (right, 1906–75) with General Metcalfe	53
Foochow, China, school group	163
Forge, The, and Forgeside – early 1900s	30
French, Chris and Sacha of Brewerstreet Farm	304
Garage, Bletchingley – 1927	19
Garage, Bletchingley, and Captain Harry Thomas Molyneux	19
Garage, Bletchingley, and St Mary's Church – c. 1955	20
Garston Park aerial view – 2021	249
Garston Park, former lodge – 2021	249
Garston Park gardens– early 1900s	245
Garston Park House, front of – 2021	248
Garston Park House, front of – early 1900s	247
Garston Park House, lounge hall – 1950	246
Garston Park House, rear of – early 1900s	241
Garston Park, Princess Patricia's Canadian Light Infantry	249
Garston Park top of the Clock House– 2021	248
Gayler, Alan , with Sir Geoffrey Howe and Lady Elspeth – 1980s	54
Gilbert and Sullivan's *Patience* – 1925	115
Glenfield House, High Street – 2021	64
Goad, Dame Sarah Jane Frances, née Lambert, DCVO, JP	56
Goad, Timothy Francis, High Sheriff of Surrey – 1994	55
Godstone Rural District, list of trades – 1911	187
Godstone Union Workhouse – c. 1908	176
Godstone Union Workhouse – c. 1915–20	174
Grange Cottage, 1 High Street – 2021	88
Grange Cottage in its original smaller form – c. 1920	123
Grange Cottage, original front chimney stack	125
Grange Cottage, snow scene – 2021	125
Grange Cottage, view from Grange Meadow – 2021	121
Grange Meadow event – early 1900s	124
Grange Meadow Sports Ground commemoration	110
Grange Meadow Sports Ground, opening day ceremony – 1929	109
Grange, The, aerial photo – 1971	99
Grange, The – c. 1920	98
Grange, The, close-up of brick bond on the north chimney – 1979	75
Grange, The, coach house – c. 1915	81
Grange, The, coach house/coal house after the 1970s fire – 1979	82
Grange, The, collage of inscriptions on bricks at the front	73
Grange, The, commemorative rose garden at rear – late 1930s	197
Grange, The, deed of conveyance –1924	170

Grange, The, French doors – 2020 87
Grange, The, from the southeast – 2020 77
Grange, The, front of – 2020... 2
Grange, The, front of – 2024... 4
Grange, The, galleting in the stonework of the former scullery – 2020 80
Grange, The, inscribed date on the front – 23 June 1739 73
Grange, The, north chimney – 1979 74
Grange, The, north chimney – 2020 75
Grange, The, old boundary wall – 2021 88
Grange, The, old plinth of the south-facing wall – 2019 79
Grange, The, plan – 1866 93
Grange, The, plan – 1987 79
Grange, The, rear of – 2017 83
Grange, The, rear of – 2021 100
Grange, The, south courtyard – 1979 78
Grange, The, south courtyard – 2019 78
Grange, The, stables – 1983 83
Grange, The, stables/coach house block – 1979 82
Grange, The, Surrey County Council plaque on front 76
Grange, The, Town Farm and Grange Cottage: view from the south – c. 1920 81
Grange, The, watercolour of the rear – 1982 232
Grices Bakery – 1951.. 140
Groom, Mary – late 1800s 252
Guinness, Oonagh, at The Punchbowl, Dorking, Surrey – 1976 230
Harris, Doctor Nathaniel, memorial to in St Mary's Church 145
Hermitage, The.. 203
Herring, Thomas (1693–1757)... 49
Hevers Pond – 2016 117
High Street – 1948 31
High Street – 1951 35
High Street, east end – c. 1956 33
High Street looking west – c. 1880 132
High Street on a sunny day – 1951 32
High Street showing Camden House – 2022 236
High Street, south side – c. 1909 38
Holman, Robert and his wife Ann (née Brereton) – 1600s 150
Hope Chapel, Redhill– 2021 255
Houghton, Douglas, Baron Houghton of Sowerby CH, PC 52
Howard, Charles, 2nd Baron Howard of Effingham, Lord High Admiral (1536–1624) 283
Howe, Sir Geoffrey, Baron Howe of Aberavon, CH, PC, QC (1926–2015)
 and his wife, Lady Elspeth, Baroness Howe of Idlicote, CBE (1932-2022)................................ 54
Huashan, China, sketch of houses.. 165
Inland Revenue Survey Map – 1911 96
Inland Revenue surveyor's field note book – 1915... 95
Ivy Mill, a poem by Alfred Uvedale Miller Lambert – 1918 119

Ivy Mill House, Ivy Mill and Mill Pond – early 1900s	118
Ivy Mill, remains of, and Ivy Mill House – 2020	120
James, Brigadier-General Alfred Henry Cotes DSO, MVO, JP (1873–1947)	111
Jekyll, Sir Joseph (1663–1738)	49
Jenner, Margaret (1878–1964) and Horace Albert (1875–1938)	204
Kennels Farm – 1930s	257
Kennels Farm – c. September 1943	261
Kennels Farm, haymaking– 1930s	257
Kenrick II, Jarvis	294
Kenrick IV, Jarvis, early photo (1852–1949)	50
Kenrick IV, Jarvis, in later years	280
Kenrick IV, Jarvis, memorial in St Mary's Church	280
Kenrick IV, Jarvis, self-portrait	278
Kindersley, Gay, at The Punchbowl, Dorking, Surrey – 1976	230
Kucheng Massacre, dedication of the monument to the martyrs of	166
Kucheng Massacre, photo taken before	165
Kucheng Massacre, scene of	164
Lambert, Alfred Uvedale Miller JP, FRHS	270
Lambert family memorial in St Mary's Church and Chapel dedication – 1952	276
Lambert, Michael Uvedale LVO – 2022	304
Lambert, Roger Uvedale MBE	269
Lambert, Sir Henry Charles Miller KCMG, CB	269
Lambert, Uvedale Henry Hoare	270
Lambert, Uvedale Henry Hoare and his second wife Melanie at a hunt meeting – 1952	275
Lambert, Uvedale Henry Hoare High Sherriff of Surrey, 1961	53
Lambert, Uvedale Henry Hoare in front of South Park	295
Lamingtons Tea Room and Gift Shop (The Cobbles) with Mark – 2021	63
Lenoir, Helen, at her desk in the Savoy Theatre – 1884	244
Leslie, Elizabeth Mary	161
Leslie, Elizabeth Mary, at a missionary exhibition in Napier, New Zealand	168
Leslie family, New Zealand – 1906	169
Leslie family tea party in New Zealand – early 1900s	169
Library and Post Office at 32 High Street – 1930s	141
Longhurst Post Office and Store, High Street – 2021	64
Lord, Bill, postman – c. 1912	137
Lord, Bill, postman with his bicycle – early 1900s	137
Macleay, Sir George, KCMG	294
Maddison, George, Coral Pritchard-Gordon and Doctor Mark Marshall	232
Marden Park – 1874	288
Marden Park before the 1879 fire	290
Marden Park – c. 1679	287
Marden Park, the new, now Woldingham School – 2020	292
Maribel, Mother General	153
Marshall, Doctor Mark and Mrs Philippa	233

Marshall, Doctor Mark, George Maddison and Coral Pritchard-Gordon 232
Marshall, Dr. Mark, at The Punchbowl, Dorking, Surrey – 1976 230
Marshall, Philippa Margaret 228
Marsh, Sam and Son advertisement – 1914 44
Marsh, Sam and Son advertisement – 1918 45
Martin, Ann and David with pigeon NURP 40 TW 194 – 2022 62
Martin, Caroline and Chris of Henhaw Farm – 2022 305
Martin, Chris and his father Frank 305
Mayers, Lieutenant-Colonel John Perkins JP 294
Mayers, Lieutenant-Colonel John Perkins JP, tomb and inscription – 2023 151
May, Peter, England and Surrey cricketer, playing at Grange Meadow – 1964 116
McCleave, David John – 2022 319
Melbourne, Lord (1779–1848) 49
Melrose Cottage, High Street – 2021 64
Middle Row, High Street –2021 64
Mid Surrey Farmers Draghounds (MSFD) meet at Warlingford – 1955 231
Mid Surrey Farmers Draghounds (MSFD) meet at Wiremill – c. 1950 229
Miles, Christopher Richard (1928-2015) and Jean Mary (1930-2021) 48
Miles, Richard, of Court Lodge Farm – 2024 306
Mill Cottage model 52
Millett, Edward Tracey Fletcher and Elizabeth Mary Leslie 171
Millett, Towers Trevorian (1852–82) 167
Molyneux, Captain Harry Thomas, at Bletchingley Garage 19
Moore, Derek, The Boss – 2023 305
Mount Pleasant – c. 1930 254
Mountrath – 2017 255
Munster, 5th Earl of – see FitzClarence 53
Napier, New Zealand, missionary exhibition in a court 168
Norfolk House marriage proposal re-enactment – 2022 42
Norris and Partridge family memorials, Blechingley Cemetery 214
Obberds in Church Walk – 2021 65
Obberds, rear – 2021 65
Old Brick Kiln – 2020 253
Old Brick Kiln – early photo 253
Old Butchers Shop, Church Walk – 2020 67
Old Forge, The, and Forgeside – 2022 34
Oldman, Doctor, Front page of medical report – 1898 177
Oldman, Doctor, memorial plaque in St Mary's Church 178
Old Rectory, Sandy Lane – 2020 65
Omnibus, motor, first day outside the White Hart Inn – June 1912 44
Omnibus, Redhill and Reigate horse bus – late 1800s 43
Ottaway, The Rt. Hon Sir Richard PC 56
Outwood Lane, an original colour construction plan for 7 and 9 – c. 1906 130
Outwood Lane, looking north – 1906 97

| Illustrations | xvii |

Outwood Lane, looking south – 1912/13 142
Outwood Lane, looking south from the High Street – 1911 97
Outwood Lane, looking south from the High Street – 1951 143
Outwood Lane, looking south from the High Street – 2021 127
Outwood Lane, north end, c. 1740 – artist's impression by Don Coe 126
Outwood Lane (The Square), looking south from the High Street,
 a gathering around the baker's cart in – 1900/06 129
Overend, Gurney and Company Limited share certificate 92
Overend, Gurney, 'The assault on the bank of Overend Gurney,
 in Lombard Street, London' – 1866 91
Palmerston, Lord (1784–1865) 49
Parish magazine advertisements for The Old Forge – 1954 and 1965 33
Parkgate Cottages, Outwood Lane – 1930s 258
Partridge and Norris family memorials, Blechingley Cemetery 214
Pendell Court – 1773 149
Pendell Court – 1810 148
Pendell Court – 2021 154
Pendell Court, party invitation – 1904 50
Pendell Court rear view – circa 1914–20 152
Pendell Court (The Hawthorns School), front – 2021 155
Pendell House – 2021 279
Perkins and Scullard families at Pendell Court 150
Perkins, John George Wilson Esq. and Mrs Mary 146
Pigeon NURP 40 TW 194, The famous Blechingley – WWII coded message and remains ... 62
Place Farm – 2020 13
Place Farm – early 1900s 12
Plant, Robert with Phil Carson 55
Plough Inn, The – 1908 16
Plough, The, quoits team 110
Post office, enlarged section of High Street looking west – c. 1880 132
Post office staff at 7 Outwood Lane – c. 1912 131
Post office when it was at Bank Buildings – early 1900s 134
Pound Hill Kennels – c. 1915 258
Pratt, Dorothy Alice and Henry Bernard Brandt, Capenor nursery – 1939 223
Pratt, Dorothy Alice's childhood home 222
Princess Patricia's Canadian Light Infantry at Garston Park – 1940–41 249
Pritchard-Gordon, Coral, George Maddison and Doctor Mark Marshall 232
Public houses, the three remaining: Red Lion, Whyte Harte, Bletchingley Arms – 2020–24 .. 63
Quinlan, Georgiana Grace, advertisement and letter from the parish magazine – 1918 135
Quinlan's Photo Series postcard – 1917 135
Red Gables. group photo at – 1915 202
Red Gables, nurses and sisters 204
Red Gables soldiers' hospital – c. 1915 203
Red Gables, wounded soldiers on the terrace during WWI 203
Redhill Bowling Club, newly built in 1931 193

Red Lion, The, parish magazine advertisement – 1959	16
Reed, Oliver, at The Punchbowl, Dorking, Surrey – 1976	230
Rice Brothers advertisement – 1911	37
Rice Brothers at Forgeside	39
Risbridger advertisements – 1935 and post-WWII	138
Risbridger, Gerry and Barry	306
Risbridger petrol pump patent – 1934	20
Risbridger, William (1859–1942) and Emma (née Burbery, 1861–1947)	139
Risbridger, William Arthur (1894–1969)	139
Risbridger workers in front of the factory during WWII	139
Riste, H. P., post office advertisement – 1944	141
Robertson, commemorative rose garden – late 1930s	197
Robertson, Dick and Betty's wedding	195
Robertson, Dick, Lieutenant-Colonel	195
Robertson, Doctor Andrew and Rosemary's wedding at St Mary's – 1964	196
Robertson, Doctor Frederick William OBE (1866–1937)	182
Robertson, Doctor Frederick William OBE and his wife Hope – 1921	197
Robertson, Doctor F W OBE and his daughter Ethel Hope Bagnall, memorial in St Mary's	193
Robertson, William Alexander (1833–97)	182
Robertson, William Alexander, The twelve surviving children of, Savoy Hotel – 1921	184
Russell, Thomas, signature and seal – 1750	74
Sandhills – 1911	271
Scullard and Perkins families at Pendell Court	150
Scullard, George (1725–76) and Mrs Hester Wade (d. 1799)	150
Selmes Butchers – 1911	67
Selmes Butchers advertisement – 1959	67
Smith, Derrick and his brother David in front of Kennels Farm – 2023	304
Smith, Dorothy Emma, née Denny (1888–1968)	256
Smith, Flying Officer Derrick Albert John, DFC, and colleagues in front of a Halifax	267
Smith, Frank, age 18 –1916	211
Smith, Herbert, and Kate Denny on a pony and trap – 1927	261
Smith, Herbert Basil and Smokee	262
Snatts Hill House – 2022	58
Southern Diocese Church Army van – 1914	22
South Park and St Mark's Chapel – 2019	274
South Park from the gardens – 2019	274
South Park, remaining wall of seventeenth-century farmhouse – 2023	273
South Park, seventeenth-century farmhouse and St Mark's Chapel – c. 1920	273
South Park, south flank wall	273
SS *Tunisian*	168
Stilgoe, Sir Richard OBE	55
St Mark's Chapel, exterior – 2020	68
St Mark's Chapel, interior – 2020	69
St Mark's Chapel, Tudor west door –2024	68

St Mary's Church from the southeast – 2024	9
St Mary's Church interior – 2020	284
Stratton Brook	120
Taylor and Bristow advertisement – 1884	40
Taylor and Bristow delivery boy setting off on his bicycle – 1951	43
Taylor and Bristow, Norfolk House, 80 High Street – c. 1904	39
Thompson, Flora, at her typewriter – 1921	6
Thresh's Steam Disinfector – 1909	189
Tithe map for Blechingley, section – 1841/3	84
Tobitt, George of Castle Hill Farm – 2022	304
Tobitt, George's father, Walter Hubert, in front of Sandhills	304
Tobitt, John, The Dairy, 9 Outwood Lane, advertisement – 1940s	254
Tower Cottages, High Street –2021	64
Town Farm and Hevers Pond from the south – c. 1915	104
Town Farm (ex-farmhouse) from Outwood Lane – 2020	106
Town Farm farmhouse (The Grange) watercolour by John Hassell – 1822	70
Town Farm, viewed across Town Meadow – 1983	105
Town Mead dew pond – 2020	106
Tutu, Archbishop Emeritus Desmond Mpilo (1931–2021)	54
Victorian traffic jam in the village – c. 1880	41
Victorian warehouse – 2022	41
Village centre looking east – c. 1910	18
Village scenes – 2021	64
Village Stores, High Street –2021	64
War memorial – c. 1921	187
Water pump, remains of	237
Wetter-Sanchez, Henrik Uvedale Hans Hoare, incumbent Lord of the Manor in 2024	295
Wheelwright's shop – pre-1870	21
White Hart Inn, The, chimney corner – 1906	17
White Hart Inn, The, Surrey Foxhounds meet – 1905	17
Wideways, 100 High Street – 2023	51
Wolmer, Nicholas, House and St Mary's Church – 2019	8
Wolmer, Nicholas, House in Church Walk – 1951	18
Wolmer, Nicholas, timber-framed house in Church Walk – 1914	7
Workhouse, Godstone Union Workhouse – c. 1908	176
Workhouse, Godstone Union Workhouse – c. 1915–20	174
Wren Brothers advertisement – 1813	23
Wren, Hilda chatting to Governor-General Massey – 1957	28
Wren's Corner – 2022	34
Wren's Forge and Forge Cottage, 1906 scene – by Don Coe 2021	23
Wren, William Henry, advertisement – 1832	24
Wren, William Thomas, advertisement – c. 1920/30	30

Forewords

The history of Blechingley is briefly documented – by William the Conqueror's Domesday book, then by my grandfather in 1921, and now by Dave McCleave who has written a stirring and accessible modern-day account of the buildings and inhabitants, lavishly illustrated with colour photos. Enjoy!

Dame Sarah Jane Frances Goad, née Lambert, DCVO, JP – Lord-Lieutenant of Surrey from 1997 to 2015

My wife and I have lived in Bletchingley for many years. Throughout we have thoroughly appreciated its diversity and history. This book portrays in carefully researched detail the rich tapestry of a village at the heart of Britain. Historians in the years to come will find much in these pages.

Rt Hon. Sir Richard Ottaway PC

David McCleave's *Blechingley and The Grange* was a groundbreaking contribution to local history when it appeared last year. The profusion and quality of the images embraced modern publishing techniques to an astonishing degree. David worked tirelessly in pursuing the history of a very special parish and the result was a triumph. I welcome this updated version as a testimony to the author's industry and passion for incomparable Blechingley.

Roger Packham, author and Chairman of The Bourne Society, Surrey, regarded as the largest local history society in England

This book is the result of many hours research and interviews with local people. It is an accurate and fascinating account of this historic village, once a borough with two members of parliament. Bringing the history up to date with stories about WWII secret agents and a pigeon which made its last flight on D-Day 1944, carrying a secret coded message. Read the book for an insight into history.

David Martin, past chairman Bletchingley Parish Council, Bletchingley Conservation and Historical Society and Bletchingley United Charities

Map of Blechingly

Introduction

Living in part of The Grange near Blechingley (Bletchingley) village centre in Outwood Lane, Surrey, I had always been curious about its past, and why there was the nearby Grange Meadow, Grange Cottage and Grange Close. I heard rumours that a surgeon had once lived here, and that its outbuildings had equestrian or other uses. The equestrian and surgeon stories are true, but I doubt there was ever an operating theatre with archaic surgery taking place involving saws and knives, as some folks have imagined.

I started researching in September 2019 with a plan to write a few pages for the benefit of my fellow residents. Three years later I was still researching and writing and had ventured far beyond the borders of The Grange. The book evolved and expanded due to the many (sometimes tenuous) connections that The Grange has with this ancient village. Starting life as *The Grange and Bletchingley*, later changed to *Bletchingley and The Grange* as it became more about Bletchingley, centred around The Grange. My only qualification to produce this book, perchance, is a fondness for the days of old, when life moved at a gentler pace, before the motor car's reign, and smartphones did not compete for society. When greetings were exchanged with a tipped hat, a graceful bow or a respectful curtsy.

The Grange site dates from Tudor days, and the current house, or at least most of it, was rebuilt in about 1739. Landed gentry once owned this farmhouse, 'the capital messuage', with lands spreading out over a large part of Blechingley. Around 1863–5 it was separated from its farm (Town Farm) and for the next 120 years it was a doctor's home and surgery. Town Farm continued independently and a later owner built a new farmhouse around 1866–70. In the 1980s Town Farm yard was turned into a residential site (Town Mead). The stature of The Grange diminished further in 1987 when the house, outbuildings and gardens were sold to a developer. A new road (Grange Close) with five large houses was built in the main garden, and High Bank Cottage was built on the western garden plot in Outwood Lane, directly opposite the front of The Grange. The eight-bedroom house – with its drawing room, dining room, consulting room and so on – and the outbuildings were divided and converted into five homes. Thankfully the conversion left most of the original external features of the main house intact. The former attached coach house and stables, which had already been repurposed as garages and had suffered a fire in the 1970s, were more extensively altered and renovated, but retained a period charm and many original features. The front of the main house is now partly hidden by a tall hedge and can easily be missed by passers-by but, as I will reveal, it has an interesting history, as does Blechingley.

Front of The Grange – 2020
On the far left is 1 Grange Close, one of five houses built in the garden in the late 1980s. On the right is the former stable yard, coach house and stables. Not the grandest house in the village, but one of the more elegant, still looking as it did over 200 years ago.

An early resident at The Grange (an earlier house on the site) was Henry Lovell, who was locked in the Tower of London in 1624 for his involvement in Blechingley election irregularities. Some later residents include Surgeon-Major Leslie in 1866, whose daughter Elizabeth inherited The Grange, or held it in trust. She was a missionary to China from 1891 and settled in New Zealand in 1905. She remained the owner/trustee of The Grange until 1924. Doctor Oldman was resident from 1877. He was the Godstone Rural District medical officer for health, medical officer to the local workhouse/poorhouse and chair of the committee to set up the new Blechingley Parish Council in 1894. There is a plaque commemorating his medical work inside St Mary's Church.

Doctor Frederick William Robertson also has a memorial plaque in St Mary's. He was awarded the OBE (Order of the British Empire) for his military medical work from The Grange during WWI. One of his sons went on to be a heart specialist and inventor-pioneer in electrocardiography while living at The Grange. From 1952 Doctor Mark Marshall lived and practised in The Grange for over 30 years. His wife Philippa was related to the Guinness and Kindersley families, was master of the Mid Surrey Farmers Draghounds, and used parts of the garden for equestrian purposes. A full list of the owners and tenants at The Grange can be found on page 307.

The first part of this book focuses on The Grange and connected properties/lands. The later sections cover some interesting owners and tenants, along with other local people, families, properties, businesses and institutions. During my research I collaborated with a number of current and former residents of Blechingley, to whom I am most indebted. I have endeavoured to write this as a story based on written records, the recollections of local people and various experts. Records have been diligently researched and cross referenced, using primary sources where possible. Historical information can be inconsistent, and it is often impossible to pinpoint exact dates, so, to keep the narrative honest, terms such as 'about' or 'probably' are used, or I have made an educated guess. I have also very occasionally indulged in speculation and fiction, which I trust will be obvious to the reader.

I have written this book with the help of many esteemed history writers who have gone before me. I often quote Alfred Uvedale Miller Lambert (1870–1928), 'The father of Blechingley local history',[1] and his son, Uvedale Henry Hoare Lambert (1909–83). Confusingly they are both usually referred to as Uvedale Lambert, so for clarity I refer to Alfred as Uvedale Lambert Snr, and to his son as Uvedale Lambert Jnr.

I must also acknowledge the help of the Blechingley Conservation and Historical Society, in particular the most eminent Derek Moore, president and former chairman. During my research around the village, Derek's name came up time and time again, and he is thought of as the 'Blechingley History Guru'. He kindly loaned me some of his research material and articles going back to the 1990s, which have given me a huge head start. Also thanks to Richard Fowler, current chairman and secretary, archivist Daphne Constable and webmaster/technician Bill O'Brien. For more on the Lambert family, and their involvement in the village, see page 267.

---
1 Borrowed from Juliette Jaques' *Bygone Godstone*, 1992, which she dedicates 'To the memory of Uvedale Lambert, the father of Godstone local history'.

My young granddaughter once wonderfully and very logically surmised that 'everything was black and white in the old days'. Perhaps we imagine the 'old days' as rather drab, whereas things were as colourful as today. With this in mind, I have converted some of the black and white photos to colour. Each photo has been partially processed with automated software and then painstakingly manually retouched. Colours for uniforms and clothing have been researched, so they are generally correct for the period. The converted photos are labelled as 'colourised by author' and some have been sympathetically restored.

This is the story of Blechingley and The Grange, with a glimpse into the life of some residents: artists, actors, airmen, soldiers, sailors, doctors, nurses, teachers, missionaries, matrons, masters, farmers, bailiffs, gentry, rectors, rat-catchers, sportsmen, postmen, postmasters, postmistresses, parlourmaids, publicans, photographers, painters, politicians, drapers, grocers, grainers, blacksmiths, wheelwrights, basket makers, builders, butchers, bakers and candlestick makers.[2]

The Grange with Town Mead (formerly Town Farm) in the background– 2024

---

2 Examples of people in these categories are all mentioned by name, except the candlestick maker, who was unnamed but listed in the Blechingley churchwardens' account of 1546–52.

Blechingley | A Brief History

Many accounts of the history of Blechingley have been written, so without wishing to repeat history and by way of an introduction, with some up-to-date information, here is an overview of the village. This is followed by three chapters covering some past and present landmarks, businesses and people. But first, some reminiscing.

Through talking with some older residents, studying and contemplating historical books, parish magazines and records, newspaper columns and looking through the lens of photographers of yore, I feel I have become friends with the bygone people of Blechingley.

I grew up between the late 1950s and the early 1970s on a Surrey council housing estate, built on farmland after the war. I remember the visits of the milkman, baker, coalman and chimney sweep, and I have a faint recollection of the rag-and-bone man with his horse and cart, ringing a bell to announce himself. We had a little row of shops at the end of our street: a greengrocer, butcher, newsagent (the sweet shop) and a post office that sold wool for knitting. Today there is a trend for tall garden fences for privacy and security, but in the old days we used to talk to our neighbours across the fence, and we knew everyone in the street, and their business. Technology such as smartphones, Alexa or Siri only existed in futuristic novels, films and TV shows. Younger readers might be shocked to hear that once we only had two TV channels, which were black and white, and we had to actually get out of the chair and walk across the room to change the channel – technology that was heralded at the time as 'at the touch of a button'. Later, remote-control colour TVs and push-button telephones were exciting new must-have commodities.

In the past, generation after generation stayed in the same area, and there were no strangers in a village. Blechingley families, such as Selmes, Legg and Cawley, lived, worked and traded in a continuous line for 200 years or more. The Wrens, blacksmiths and publicans, arrived in Blechingley in 1813; by 1926 Wrens were living at nine different addresses in the village. I have not carried out a full genealogy, but I suspect they were all related. Many of the Blechingley families of old have gone, but there are at least seven still here, with roots in farming and various trades, who can be traced back to the nineteenth or eighteenth centuries and probably earlier.

The village is surrounded by farmland, where around the mid-twentieth century there were some 17 dairy herds, ranging from 3 to 200 cows, now all moved away. Much of the land is now cultivated and planted with cereal crops and some maize and rapeseed, along with some grazing for sheep and beef cattle. Many of the old farmhouses and farm buildings are now wonderful country homes, or commercial-use buildings.

As I have intimated, I imagine, perhaps naively, that life was better, simpler and more relaxed in the old days; Flora Thompson portrays a similar narrative in *Lark Rise to Candleford*, a semi-autobiographical novel documenting the loss of close-knit rural life at the end of the nineteenth century. *The Oxford Dictionary of National Biography* entry for the book reads: 'Few works better or more elegantly capture the decay of Victorian agrarian England'.

Flora Thompson at her typewriter – 1921
(née Timms 1876–1947) *Photo courtesy John Owen Smith.*

She wrote:

> Most of the men sang or whistled as they dug or hoed. There was a good deal of outdoor singing in those days. Workmen sang at their jobs; men with horses and carts sang on the road; the baker, the miller's man, and the fish-hawker sang as they went from door to

door; even the doctor and parson on their rounds hummed a tune between their teeth. People were poorer and had not the comforts, amusements, or knowledge we have today; but they were happier. Which seems to suggest that happiness depends more upon the state of mind – and body, perhaps – than upon circumstances and events.

Passing through Blechingley on the A25 at thirty miles per hour takes about a minute, and one could be forgiven for assuming it was an unremarkable place. But many of the treasures of this charming village are set back from the main road and along the surrounding, winding leafy lanes. Many buildings in the village date from the 1500s or earlier, which is not always apparent as they are often cleverly concealed by later fronts and additions. Timber framing from the 1500s/1600s and earlier can be seen when walking off the beaten track, and glancing down alleyways; there are some good examples along Church Walk, which is the path between the war memorial and St Mary's Church.

Nicholas Wolmer's timber-framed house in Church Walk – 1914
Probably the most photographed scene in the village, and it still looks as it did when this print was published over 100 years ago. The similar house with the jettied (overhanging) front, to the left of the picture, is Obberds, which dates from the 1300s. Church Walk was the main road through the village until about 1800. *From a 1914 print in* A Pilgrimage in Surrey *by writer and artist, James S Ogilvy.*

Blechingley Parish is situated between Nutfield to the west and Godstone to the east, down south towards Outwood and up to the crest of the North Downs. It was once a bustling market borough, hence the wide areas each side of the main road in the village centre. Up until the electoral reform act in 1832, Blechingley was one of 56 'rotten boroughs' – rotten in the sense of politically corrupt and/or in decline. Only the burgage holders were allowed to vote in local elections. A burgage was a plot of land rented from the lord of the manor or patron; a typical plot had a 50-foot frontage, and was 300 feet deep. The elections were public affairs, where the burgage holders (tenants) voted publicly by a show of hands. The tenants were expected to vote for the patron or his preferred candidate; not complying with his wishes was risky, and would likely result in a rent increase or other repercussions. The tenants were thus in the pocket of the patron. Blechingley had two members of parliament before the electoral reform. After 1832 Blechingley ceased to be a borough. The current 'Welcome to the Historic Borough of Bletchingley' signs at each end of the village are a nod to the past, the initiative of Mr Martin, former parish council chairman – in case you were confused!

Nicholas Wolmer's House and St Mary's Church – 2019

Like most villages its name has been spelt in many different ways. In the 1086 Domesday Book it appears as Blachinglei, more recently it has been Blechingley or Bletchingley. The Map of the County of Surrey by John Rocque, circa 1762, used Bletchingley. The 1761 Clayton estate map used Blechingley. Mr Uvedale Lambert Snr objected passionately to 'the hideous t of Bletchingley', on which the official name has gradually settled. Many local businesses and institutions omitted the t until recently, as can be seen in the local advertisements throughout this book. A few loyalists still leave it out, for example: *Blechingley Magazine*; Blechingley Conservation and Historical Society; Blechingley Horticultural Society; and the Blechingley and Hathersham Estate Co Ltd (2023). Most local history books published to date have used Blechingley, as does this book (but the t has been retained in the title to help with internet searches).

St Mary's Church has a tower dating from Norman times (circa 1090), its ten bells and ancient hourly chiming clock (1787) can be heard across the village. The church is one of only a few in Surrey with ten bells. They are rung before church service on Sunday mornings, on special occasions, and for bell ringing practice on Wednesday evenings. Bellringing in Blechingley has a long tradition, with advanced ringing taking place here in the 1700s, when there were eight bells. Former Historic Buildings Officer for Surrey, Martin Higgins, tells me that 'the number and weight of bells was an indication of the wealth of the town or village in the past, which would put Blechingley in the top tier, dare I say, punching above its weight'. Much of the village was put up for sale by auction in 1835, when a newspaper reporter commented, 'to the ordinary observer the property had a most un-saleable aspect'. There are some interesting memorials inside the church and many of the characters in this book are buried in the church and graveyard, or in the newer cemetery, built around 1850, a quarter of a mile away in Godstone Road.

St Mary's Church from the southeast – 2024
For interior photos of St Mary's, see pages 284, 286.

There was once a workhouse behind the church, first opened in 1754, expanded in 1839, and known as the Godstone Union Workhouse, or the Guardians Institute. In the twentieth century it was Clerks Croft Hospital for the elderly. It was demolished in the 1980s and replaced with a development of houses called Clerks Croft. Workhouse Lane on the east side of the church has been sanitised with the new name of Church Lane. For more on the workhouse see page 173.

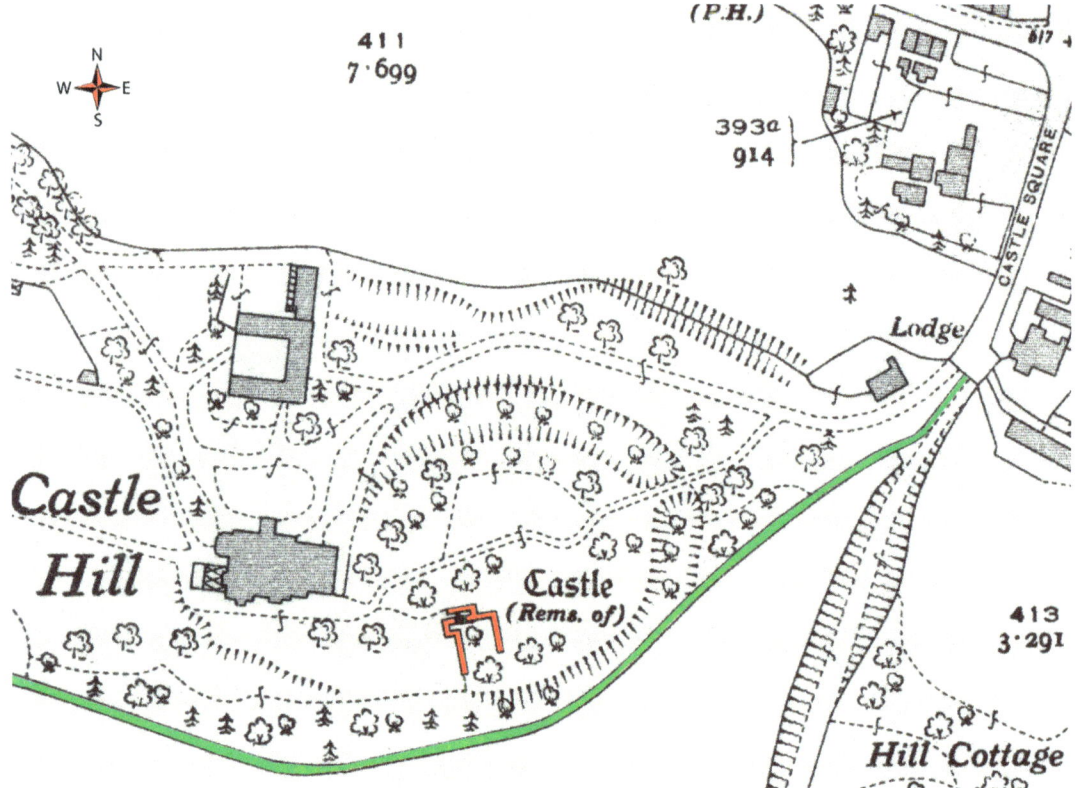

Castle Hill map showing remains of Blechingley Castle – 1935
Showing the old castle earthworks with the remains of its foundations, now a scheduled ancient monument. Some of the earthworks can be seen from the narrow public footpath (green on the map) which starts at the end of Castle Square. *Ordnance Survey Map of Surrey XXVII.14 Bletchingley, 1935, with author's annotations. Reproduced under a CC-BY-NC-SA licence with the permission of the National Library of Scotland.*

Blechingley Castle. William the Conqueror and his army are thought to have had a base here, or nearby along the Nutfield Ridge, after the 1066 invasion. The castle was built some time after the invasion and was owned by the De Clare family, relatives of William. It was sacked and largely destroyed by royalist forces after the Battle of Lewes in 1264. Some of the castle's stone foundations and the dry moat still exist, but the site is heavily overgrown, and the land is private. Manning, in 1809, says that the ancient castle was restored after 1264, but was long since left to ruin. He postulates that the moat could have been filled with water, pumped from a well by a windmill. Some of the moat was filled in when the 19-bedroom Castle Hill mansion house was built on the west end of the castle grounds in 1868. A section of the mansion remains, now called Castle Place (2023). An impressively deep section of the castle moat is visible along the southern edge of the private lane running from the end of Castle Square to Castle Place. The lane was built as one of two carriage drives for the mansion house and its associated buildings, such as stables, coach house and cottages, which are all now private homes. For more on Castle Hill, see page 205.

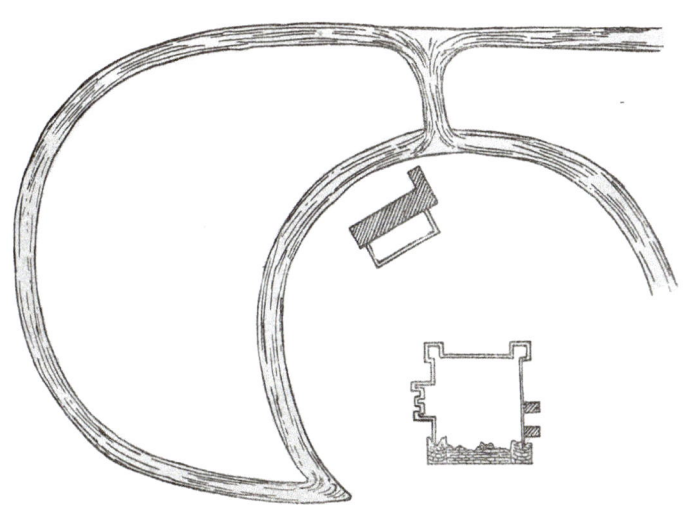

Blechingly ancient castle ground plan – 1809
Manning and Bray

Blechingley Palace/Place. As well as a castle, Blechingley once had a royal palace in the same league as Hampton Court Palace and Hever Castle, more commonly known as Blechingley Place. Edward de Stafford, 3rd Duke of Buckingham, was executed in 1521 by Henry VIII 'for plotting treason in the gallery of his palace in Blechingley'. The Place first appears in records in 1262, on a valuation of the Clare estates, which mentions a court-house or manor-house with a garden and parks. Major building works were carried out in about 1500 by Edward de Stafford, to create a very grand country residence. A later report on his lands refers to it as a 'newly bilded house'. The Place had inner courtyards and was believed to have had 32 fire hearths.

Sir Nicholas Carew KG, Master of Horse for King Henry VIII, was the next owner of The Place until his execution in 1539. King Henry then gave it to his fourth wife, Anne of Cleves, along with the Manor of Blechingley and the north and south deer-hunting parks, part of a generous divorce settlement after their marriage of six months was annulled. Anne spent much of her time at Richmond Palace but also stayed at her other main house in Blechingley. The parish registers record the deaths of some of her staff at Blechingley, and the churchwardens' accounts note that she once borrowed an altar bell from the church and failed to return it.

Blechingley Place – from a 1622 map
Rough sketch from the map of Pendell Manor. *From Uvedale Lambert Snr's 1921 book.*

Place Farm – early 1900s
Formerly part of the gatehouse to Blechingley Place, showing the Tudor archway with the off-centre door, designed to sit centrally between the windows when render was added in

Georgian times. Dairy farmer Charles Atkey was resident in the early 1900s; in 1911 he lived here with his wife Emily, two children Edward and Ellen, and servant Dorothy White. *From a Frith & Co Ltd postcard, with a postmark of September 1910.*

In 1547, King Edward VI's Privy Council asked Anne to exchange Blechingley Place for Penshurst Place, Kent (as per King Henry VIII's wishes), to make way for a new resident, Sir Thomas Cawarden. Up to this time Thomas had managed the estate for Anne. He was Master of the Revels (theatre entertainment), and Keeper of the King's Tents (managing military expeditions etc.). He lived in great state, with 100 servants in livery, and paid rent to Anne until her death in 1557, when ownership of the Place reverted to him. Thomas died in 1559 in the Tower of London, where he was serving as joint lieutenant for Queen Elizabeth. He is buried in a table tomb alongside the altar in St Mary's Church, Blechingley.

Place Farm – 2020
The Tudor arch would originally have been higher as the door and ground floor of the house are now about four feet up from Tudor levels. Royal visitors to the Place who may well have passed through this arch were King Henry VIII and Catherine of Aragon. While Queen Elizabeth I was welcomed by Charles Howard, 2nd Baron of Effingham, who lived here in the 1590s.

After Thomas' death, an inventory of the house and contents listed 63 rooms on two floors, which included: large private apartments on the first floor; a range of downstairs rooms consisting of the great hall, parlours, spicery, buttery, cellar and other rooms for food preparation; the kitchen; an armoury; a wardrobe; the glass-house; the new gatehouse; and agricultural buildings.

The hunting parks were split into farms around 1650, and Blechingley Place, which was said to be in disrepair, was pulled down, probably by the second Earl of Peterborough before he sold the Manor of Blechingley to Sir Robert Clayton in 1677. Part of the gatehouse survived and became a farmhouse. For the next 200 years or so it was occupied by tenants of the Clayton family. It is now a private home called Place Farm, in Place Farm Road. Following the de-parking, Blechingley expanded with the building or rebuilding of many houses and farmhouses, including The Grange, Cuckseys Farmhouse, South Park (Fields Farm) and Glenfield House, to name a few. New farmers, farm workers and tradesmen settled in Blechingley.

The gatehouse's internal roof timbers are of a 'scientific king post structure' and supported a diamond set tower with a bell. In 2010, the timbers were dendro-dated (measurement of tree growth rings) to 1547, making this king post roof the oldest in the country by 50 years. The date of 1547 ties in with the gatehouse being added by Thomas Cawarden. In about 1800 the end walls of the house were demolished and rebuilt in a slightly different alignment. The current doors and windows were added in Georgian times, along with render to the front, which was removed in 1900, revealing that the front door is off-centre to the Tudor arch. There is also a Tudor arch on the rear of the house.[3]

Mr Uvedale Lambert Snr says that a grand Tudor fireplace at Reigate Priory, five miles from Blechingley, was likely salvaged from Blechingley Place. Anne of Cleves' main residence, Richmond Palace, was demolished in the 1600s, and like Blechingley Place, the gatehouse survives. Penshurst Place, Kent, 15 miles from Blechingley, is still intact and open to the public, as is its nearby neighbour, Hever Castle, which was also part of Anne's property portfolio. Hever Castle was the former home of Anne Boleyn, Henry VIII's second wife, who lost her head.

---

3 Some of the up-to-date historical information for Blechingley Place is taken from Mary Saaler's *Anne of Cleves, Fourth Wife of Henry VIII* (1995), a former member of the Bourne Society Archaeological Group. Also from Mr Martin Higgins, former Historical Buildings Officer, Surrey County Council.

Blechingley | Pictures and Stories from Yesteryear | Pubs | Garages | Wren Blacksmiths | Shops | Businesses | Transport

Blechingley High Street looking west – 1909
By Irish illustrator Hugh Thomson (1860–1920), best known for his black and white pen-and-ink drawings. For accuracy he would go to the British Museum and the Victoria and Albert Museum to study period costume, furniture and decor. He illustrated reprints of books by Shakespeare, Dickens, Austen, Gaskell and others, and many of the *Highways and Byways* series of history books. He was the first of the Cranford School of illustrators. The black and white version of this drawing was first published in *Highways and Byways in Surrey*, Eric Parker, 1909. *From an original colour print*.

Over the years there have been about a dozen public houses in the village. After the closure of The Prince Albert at the north end of Outwood Lane in 2013, followed by the demolition of The William IV in Little Common Lane, three remain:

The Red Lion in Castle Street at the west end of the village dates back to Tudor days or earlier. Formerly called The Angel, and before that probably The Maid and/or The Flanders Mare. It is said that Henry VIII stopped here for beer, funded by the village, on a visit to inspect Blechingley Place, which was forfeited to him after the execution of its owner in 1521. This author is sceptical, but the Churchwarden's account mentions that the bellringers were given 2d to drink at The Maid at the time of the king's visit.

Parish magazine advertisement for The Red Lion – 1959
The pub was run by Mr and Mrs CVL Handley at the time.

The Plough Inn – 1908
As it had been known for about 300 years, until it was renamed The Bletchingley Arms after refurbishment in 2015. Located at the east end of the village, at No. 2 High Street, it is based around a late seventeenth-century timber-framed cottage with later extensions. This photograph was taken in June 1908 from the south, looking north across Grange Meadow (then probably known as Town Meadow). It shows a horse and cart at the front, the driver having stopped for refreshment on his way to deliver eggs and milk to Godstone.
Photographer Jarvis Kenrick, © Surrey History Centre. Colourised by author.

The White Hart Inn, Surrey Foxhounds meet – 1905
10.45am, 26 December (Boxing Day). The signs read: 'Good Stabling & Lock-up Coach House – Pagden's Epsom Ales – Barclay Perkins'. It is located in the High Street in the centre of the village and is mentioned in 1816 records as formerly the Swan, and a 1738 document states 'lately the Butcher's Arms' (ref. Derek Moore); it is now The Whyte Harte Hotel. It has a hanging sign outside displaying a date of 1388, but historians date it a little later, with many additions and alterations. It is thought to have been a house up to the early 1700s. Uvedale Lambert Snr comments: 'Perhaps once the Drakes House.' The village post office is in the building on the far left edge of the photo, part of Bank Buildings, which moved to No. 7 Outwood Lane a year or so later.
Photographer Jarvis Kenrick, © Surrey History Centre.

Chimney corner at the White Hart – 1906
The iron fireback with its date of 1613 is still there today. When the logs are blazing in the cold winter months it is the most coveted corner of the pub. *From a Frith's Series postcard with a postmark of September 1910.*

Village centre looking east – c. 1910
On the far right is Legg, Grocers and Drapers at No. 2 The Cobbles, now Lamingtons Tea Room and Gift Shop at 25 High Street (2023). In 1911 the Legg family were listed here and also at the 'post office and house', at 7 Outwood Lane, next door but one to The Grange.
From an unnamed postcard (some postcards do not display the publisher's name).

Nicholas Wolmer's House in Church Walk – 1951
Photo by Donald Ashley Birkinshaw (1922–88) who took over 15,000 photographs of English towns and villages between 1938 and 1953. Some of them were published through his postcard company, the Ashley Series. *From an original negative.*

Bletchingley Garage – 1927

It had been owned by the Rice brothers and managed by Harry Riste. Harry went on to run the adjacent village post office for 32 years (circa 1925 to 1957). In 1903 AE Waghorne Grocer and Draper and general store was trading here. *Photo by Dorothy Emma Smith, née Denny, courtesy of Derrick and David Smith.*

Bletchingley Garage, Captain Harry Thomas Molyneux

(1895–1968) OBE, MC (MIMT, AM, inst., BE), known as Tom, took over the garage in about 1923. In 1935 it was his AA appointed garage and Tecalemit Station. He married Euphie, daughter of Benjamin Ashdown, who was chairman of the parish council. He served with the Royal Fusiliers Hampshire Regiment in WWI and received the MC for gallantry. He was demobbed as a captain. In WWII Tom served in the Fleet Air Arm RNVR, and left the service as Lt Commander in 1946 with an OBE. In his time he drove his own taxi and ran a bus service to Redhill. He was also a flying instructor and had his own Tiger Moth at Redhill Aerodrome. *Photo courtesy Derek Moore.*

Bletchingley Garage and St Mary's Church – c. 1955
The fuel pumps were manufactured by the local Risbridger engineering company. The garage closed c. 1981 but metal fuel tank covers were still on the forecourt in 2023 when it was the Village Stores at 28 High Street. The building dates from the 1500s. © *The Francis Frith Collection. For more on the Risbridger family see p. 138.*

Risbridger petrol pump patent – 1934
notice of examination of patent number 750. Photo courtesy of Annie Risbridger Hind.

Bletchingly village looking east – c. 1910
The car in the foreground was 'pasted in', after the photo was taken, as was sometimes done in the day; the clue is that its shadows are pointing south and other shadows in the photo are pointing north. *From a Frith & Co Ltd coloured postcard.*

The old Congregational chapel – December 1960
On a foggy day (behind the lamp post in the centre), looking east. Built circa 1826, by Mr Charles T Smith of Reigate. The last service took place in the 1930s. At the start of WWII, the chapel became an infant school until it was requisitioned by Canadian and English troops and the WRVS (Women's Royal Voluntary Service). In later years it was an antiques showroom and a builders' store, until it was demolished in the 1960s to widen the road. The Victorian house behind the chapel, called Plummers or Hill Brow, was also demolished. The Manse (the minister's house), on the far left, dates from the 1600s and was believed to have originally been two cottages, which were combined into one in about 1894. The Manse is now a private home on the corner of Stychens Lane and Castle Street. *Photo taken by D Yellan, © Surrey History Centre. Colourised by author.*

Wheelwright's shop – pre-1870
At the west end of the High Street, next door (east of) the old Congregational Chapel. John Cawley (1796–1849) was listed as Blechingley's wheelwright in 1839. This building probably dates from around 1500. It was demolished in the 1800s and replaced by the house called Plummers or Hill Brow. *Photographer Jarvis Kenrick, © Surrey History Centre.*

Southern Diocese Church Army van – 1914
Photographer Jarvis Kenrick, © Surrey History Centre.

The Wrens were the village blacksmiths for over 110 years, and for much of that time they were also publicans. They were descended from blacksmith and wheelwright Henry Wren, who was born in nearby Lingfield in 1756, and lived for 93 years. His son William married Lingfield-born Elizabeth Burley by common licence in October 1805 at the church of St Peter and St Paul, Lingfield. Common licence was a faster way to get married if it was not convenient to wait for the reading of the marriage banns (church announcements) before the wedding, for example, if the bride was with child. The 22-year-old couple's licence was sanctioned by the Bishop of Winchester, with an affidavit/oath signed by William, testifying that there were no lawful impediments to the marriage. The document included a bond of £200 of 'lawful money', (equal to ten years' wages for a labourer). The extremely high bond value was a deterrent to marrying unlawfully; if the marriage was later proved unlawful, the bond would be payable to the rector. Their first child, William Henry, was baptised at St Peter and St Paul, three months after the wedding in January 1806. Their second child, Susannah, was born in December that year, followed by Charles in 1811.[4]

Wren's Forge and Forge Cottage, 1906 scene – by Don Coe 2021
View from Outwood Lane, the Forge is to the right at 22 High Street with a two-horse cart parked at the front. The blacksmith's house, Forge Cottage, is to its left, with gates between leading to the yard at the rear. *Sketch commissioned by the author and Martin Cundey from a 1906 Francis Frith Collection photo. © Francis Frith Collection, Martin Cundey and David John McCleave. The original photo can be seen on page 97.*

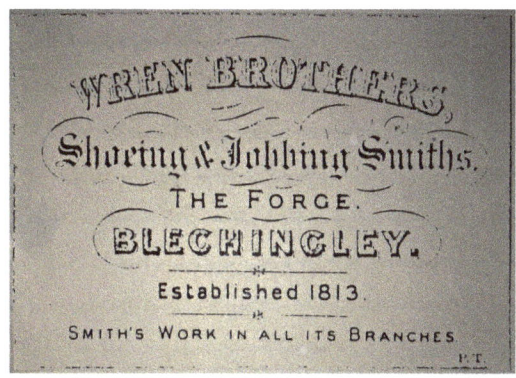

1813 William and Elizabeth Wren and family moved to Blechingley, where they established the business at the Forge. Their landlord up to 1816 was William Kenrick Esq., followed by Patrick Drummond Esq. William Wren died aged only 38 in 1821, leaving Elizabeth to run the business.

Wren Brothers advertisement – 1813

---

4 The total number of children in each of the families discussed throughout this book is often a considered approximation, based upon available records.

1832 William Henry took over the running of the business, aged 26, with 1841 records showing his mother Elizabeth owning: Forge Cottage (circa seventeenth-century building, now demolished); the Forge; a house adjoining to the east (today called Forgeside, at 22 High Street); plus yards/gardens. William Henry and his younger brother Charles jointly owned another cottage and garden at the rear of the site, tenanted by farm labourer James Parsons. The family probably purchased the properties via the 1835 Blechingley auction (lot number one). After the 1832 electoral reform act Blechingley lost its 'rotten borough' status with its two members of parliament. The village was now a less desirable asset for the gentry, and property was said to go at auction for a fraction of its former value.

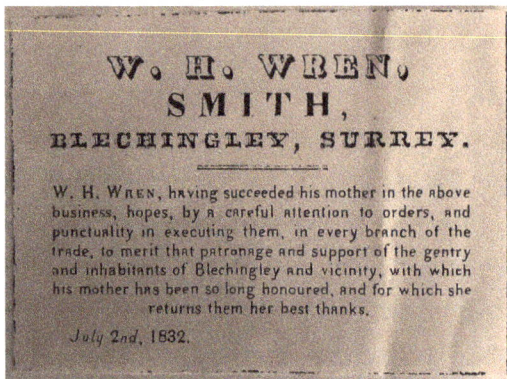

Wren, William Henry, advertisement – 1832

1836 Blacksmith Charles Wren was in court charged with the manslaughter of James Marsh after an altercation in a Blechingley public house:

> the deceased challenged the latter to fight, and that at length blows were exchanged between them, and after a scuffle the deceased was thrown to the ground violently by the defendant, and falling on his head injured his scull so severely as to cause his death in a very few hours.

After an inquest, and a manslaughter verdict had been reached, Mr Hoggins addressed the judge at the bail court:

> My Lord, the defendant, who is a blacksmith, and in humble circumstances, I hope will be allowed to enter into bail, without being put to the expense of coming to town [London].'

Charles was subsequently ordered to attend court about a week later when Justice Coleridge ordered him to enter into 'recognizances, himself 60/-, and four sureties in 15/- each [bound over to keep the peace]'. Having put in the required sureties, he was discharged from custody. James Marsh, aged 30, was buried at St Mary's, Blechingley, on 27 October 1836. From articles in *The True Sun*, London, 7 November 1836, and *The Sun*, London, 14 November 1836.

1851 William Henry, master blacksmith and employer of four men, lived with his mother Elizabeth and his nephew, apprentice blacksmith John Wren, aged 15. Elizabeth was the head of the household, her occupation was 'retired smith'. William Henry's widowed brother and master blacksmith Charles Wren (his wife, Elizabeth Wren née Chapman, died at only 36 in 1849), father of six children, was, from as early as 1849, publican at The Prince Albert, opposite the Forge, where William assisted him at the bar.

The former Black Horse Coach House and Stables – August 2022
At 55 Station Road, Gomshall, Surrey, last known as Tillings Cafe/The Lavender Goose. An adjoining brewery was pulled down in the 1920s, and this historic building was ruthlessly demolished shortly after this photograph was taken to make way for new flats and houses.

1861 William Henry Wren and his wife Sophia (née Bond) had moved away from Blechingley and were now innkeepers at the Black Horse Coach House and Stables, Gomshall, Surrey. They do not appear to have had any children, having married later in life in 1852. The 1852 London church marriage register lists William Henry's occupation as 'postmaster', residing in Blechingley. Sophia Bond was born in 1804 in Blechingley, and in 1851 was listed among the gentry, occupying a farm of 110 acres, near the Red Lion public house, employing three labourers. Twenty years earlier she was listed in land tax records as renting land and tenement (house) from William Russell Esq., who was a substantial landowner.

Sophia Bond's father, Edward (b. 1756), was a licensed victualler (innkeeper) at The Plough Inn, Blechingley (The Bletchingley Arms in 2023) from around the 1780s. He died in 1809 and his wife Ann took over. Her daughter, Ann Bassett Bond, and relative Elizabeth French, took over in about 1821.

In 1861 Charles was back in the role of master blacksmith, running the Forge with his four sons: John, 24; Charles T, 18; James, 16; and Christopher, 14. Matriarch Elizabeth Wren died in 1860, at 77, followed by Charles in 1868 at 57, and William Henry in 1875, at 70. All three were buried in Blechingley.

1871 James Wren (b. 1845), son of Charles, married a 25-year-old local girl, Anne Allingham. At 16 Anne was in service with Surgeon William Henry Sargent in Blechingley High Street, and at 24 she was a servant with solicitor William Pownall in Reigate. James and Anne had nine children, all born in Blechingley. Their son Claude, a draper's assistant, was involved in a bicycle crash in 1906 on the way to play a football match with two of his friends, Archie Legg and Tony Howard. Claude's knee was badly cut, which gave rise to lockjaw. Despite the constant care of Doctor Pratt and Nurse Oriel, he died two weeks after the accident, and was buried in Blechingley on 6 December 1906, aged 26.

Claude's death had a profound effect on the family, and shortly after his brother and sister, Horace and Elizabeth (Bessie), emigrated to Canada, where they were joined by their younger sister Hilda in 1908. Horace, a painter by trade, had served with the 1st Battalion of Scotch Guards for 12 years, and in Canada he served with the 5th Royal Highlanders of Canada. In 1915 he enlisted with the 42nd Battalion of the Canadian Army, and fought in Europe during WWI. He was injured when an enemy shell exploded in the trenches, killing six of his comrades. He died in a Belgian hospital two days later on 11 August 1916, aged 39. His name is listed on the village war memorial, the village hall, and inside St Mary's Church, along with Seaman Archie Legg (RNVR) and 36 others who gave their lives in the Great War.

The corner of Church Lane, Forge Cottage and Wren's Forge – 1920s
(then called Workhouse Lane) and the High Street. On the right is Wren's Forge, on the left is Forge Cottage. James Wren, fifth son of Charles Wren, was born in Forge Cottage in 1845, and James' daughter Hilda was born here in 1886. To the right of 'The Old Farm Teas' sign, is the Wren's sign. On the corner is a gas street lamp; Blechingley was lit by gas until the 1930s. The style of brick front entrance steps on Forge Cottage can still be seen on some of the old cottages around the village. Forge Cottage was ruthlessly demolished in the late 1960s to widen the road and improve the turning sight line for vehicles. *From a Walford and Sons Real Photograph and P.P.P.P. Postcards, courtesy of the East Surrey Museum, Caterham. Colourised by author.*

James and Anne Wren were still living at Forge Cottage in 1911, with their son Walter, and James' brother, Charles Thomas. All three men were blacksmiths. Doctor Frederick William Robertson's annual health report of the same year notes that there were 19 businesses in the Godstone Rural District comprising blacksmiths, wheelwrights and coach builders, employing a total of 56 men.

Hilda Wren relocated from Canada back to Blechingley in 1922 when her mother Anne died, aged 76, at Chestnut Cottage, Common Lane. However after six months, she became lonely for her work and friends at Ross Pavilion, Royal Victoria Hospital in Montreal, and returned to Canada. Starting out as a maid she went on to be in charge of housekeeping for some 50 years, and continued working into her eighties.

Hilda became a bit of a legend and appeared in various Canadian newspapers over the years:

> Her thoughtfulness of others and her pleasant smile have made this bright eyed little women a friend of patients and staff alike at the hospital - an energetic little woman from Surrey, England, her friendly manner and remarkable memory has endeared her to thousands of patients.

Her hearing and sight diminished in later years, but she remained quite healthy and alert, and was fully mobile up until her 106th year, when she fractured her hip.

Hilda chatting to Governor-General Massey – 1957
During a visit to the new gift and coffee shop at the Royal Victoria Hospital, Montreal. *Photo courtesy of The Montreal Gazette, a division of Postmedia Network Inc, and Steve Clifford – Doing Our Bit, Military and Family History, Canada.*

Hilda's father James died in 1925 at Forge Cottage, where he had been born eighty years earlier. Hilda lived to be almost 108 having lived through the Second Boer War and World Wars One and Two. She saw: six monarchs on the throne of England; the motor car replacing the horse and cart; England winning the football World Cup in 1966; the first man on the moon; the end of the Cold War; and the dissolution of the Soviet Union in 1991. She was the youngest child of James and Anne, born on 19 January 1886 at Forge Cottage, baptised at St Mary's, Blechingley, on 28 February 1886 and died on 29 September 1993 in Montreal, Quebec, Canada.

Hilda was in touch with some Blechingley people by letter from Canada between 1985 and 1991. She wrote:

> My father [James Wren] remembers being taken to the Blechingley railway tunnel in 1854 to see the Emperor of France's train pass by. [Commenting on the 1920s Walford & Sons photo postcard showing

Forge Cottage and The Forge] – It is like a voice from the past and brings back many fond memories, it was taken after my sister Ethel and her husband Joe Bagaley had renovated the cottage. How well I remember the red steps, I used to take a pail with hot water soap and cloth and clean them before breakfast. I polished the brass knocker on the door and we always knew the postman's raps. We used to grow Arum Lilies in the bit of garden in the front with the railing round. There was a street light on the pavement right outside the first floor bedroom and the lamplighter came round in the evenings turning on the gas. The window of the bedroom over the front kitchen looked right down Outwood Lane. Between the cottage and the blacksmith's shop there were gates and they were left open during business hours so that horses could come through to be shod.

I guess the three forges, bellows and anvils were taken away. I've seen many a horseshoe shaped red hot on the anvil – three holes for nails on the one side and four on the other. The long bars of iron used to be kept in the loft. The business did a good trade until motor cars came on the scene. The gentry kept hunters and carriage horses and tradesmen had to have them for delivering goods.

I spent a long time studying the picture, and I didn't sleep very well last night. Like the minstrel in Sir Walter Scott's poem 'And scenes long past of joy and pain, came wildering over his aged brain'.

From an article published in the parish magazine, February 1991 by Derek Moore.

William Thomas Wren (1862–1944), was the only son of blacksmith John Wren (1835–67), who was the eldest son of Charles Wren (1811–68). Both William Thomas' parents died young: Eliza (née Lambert) aged 31 in 1866, and John in the following year, aged 32. Their cause of death is not known; they were both buried in Blechingley. At age 8 William Thomas was living with his grandparents, William and Mary Lambert, at the Prince Albert, where William was publican. William Thomas married Mary Charlotte Hollands in 1884 in Croydon, and they had at least nine children. In earlier years the family lived in The Square (the north end of Outwood Lane, between the Prince Albert and The Grange). Later, they lived at The Mint (today, four cottages in Church Lane), then later at 16 Sackville Cottages in Outwood Lane. William was probably the last of the Blechingley blacksmith Wrens.

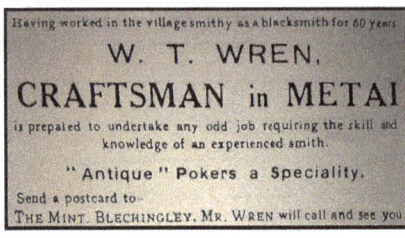

WT Wren advertisement – c. 1920/30
Courtesy Derek Moore.

The Wrens' name on The Forge had gone by 1927, and RJ Andrews was trading there as 'Shoeing and General Smith', who also sold and repaired lawnmowers and supplied farm and garden tools and so on. The Wrens or their relatives had run the Prince Albert since before 1850. Christopher Wren, who died in 1914, had run it for almost 34 years, and in 1926 Charles and Emma Wren were resident. That same year Wrens were living across nine different addresses in Blechingley. During the 1800s the Wren family line of blacksmiths and innkeepers were spread across various towns and villages, including: Copthorne/Crawley Downs and Felbridge in West Sussex; Chipstead near Sevenoaks in Kent; Gomshall, Reigate, Lingfield, Godstone, and Blechingley in Surrey. Eventually, more motor car tyres and fewer horseshoes were needed; the pioneering Rice Brothers, Risbridger Brothers and Harry T Molyneux, with their early motor car garages, effectively replaced the blacksmiths. In 2024 the Wren family name appears to have gone from the village.

The Forge and Forgeside – early 1900s
Both believed to have been built around 1800. Behind the pony and trap is the Cottage of Content public house, which existed from as early as 1881 and was still in business in the 1940s. *From an early 1900s postcard, courtesy of Blechingley Conservation and Historical Society.*

A J Bird, fishmonger, fruiterer and greengrocer at Forgeside
They were still trading in the village at a different location in the 1980s. In 1918 they ran a parcel-carrying service to Redhill: small parcels up to 7lbs were 3d (about 1p) and larger parcels from 28lbs to 56lbs were 9d (about 3p). The edge of the Forge can just be seen on the far left. Forgeside was purchased in 1920 by Sid and Raymond James Eddolls, descendants of George Eddolls the butcher, from William Thomas English and William Thomas Everett English. The English family were local builders in the 1800s and early 1900s. *Photo courtesy of Blechingley Conservation and Historical Society.*

High Street – 1948
Photo taken from near The Whyte Harte Hotel showing the single storey Forge in the centre, looking rather dilapidated, with Forge Cottage to its left. To its right is Forgeside, at 22 High Street, the right hand side of which had been used as a shop for many years. All three buildings were once owned by the Wren family. To the right behind the lamp post is the Cottage of Content public house, and on the far right is The Prince Albert, which by 1926 had been run by the Wren family and/or their relatives for over 75 years. *Photo by Donald Ashley Birkinshaw, from an original negative.*

High Street on a sunny day – 1951
Photo taken from alongside The Prince Albert public house, looking west. On the right is the corner of the Forge/Forge Cottage, showing some exposed timber framing; further left is Blechingley Garage, with its four pumps. The bus on the left is an RT-RLH series, built lower than the standard RT so that it could pass under low bridges on rural routes. Upstairs there were rows of bench seats on the left with the gangway on the right, rather than in the centre. Six of these were put into service at Godstone in 1950 for the 410 route. On the right is a standard RT, the 411 en route to West Croydon. *Photo by Donald Ashley Birkinshaw, from an original negative. Colourised by author.*

In the early 1950s the Forge was converted to a shop, with the three Georgian-style bay windows we see today. The proprietors changed a few times in the 1950s. In 1954 it was 'Perkins & Cheeseman Fishmongers and Poulterers High Class Fruiterers and Florists' who obtained planning permission to fry fish on the premises in 1955. They were succeeded by 'JW Burke, High Class Fishmonger, Grocer and Greengrocer'. 'J & P Agate Fishmongers & Fruiterers' took over in about 1958 and were still there in 1965.

From 1969 to 2018 the Old Forge was home to estate agents, first Maurice White, followed by Howard Cundey. Owner Martin Cundey commissioned Kents Builders to carry out extensive refurbishment in 1988/9, adding dormer windows and a mezzanine floor. In 2023 it had been leased for several years to Surrey Burners, who sell wood-burning and other stoves.

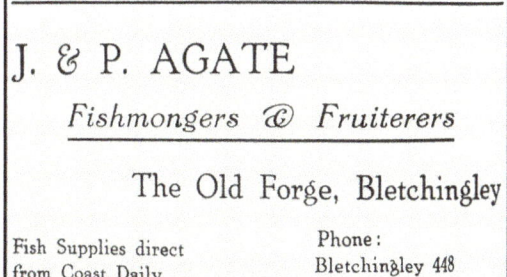

East end of the High Street – c. 1956
L–R: edge of Forge Cottage with its front steps and garden railings; JW Burke High Class Fishmonger, Grocer and Greengrocer in the recently refurbished Old Forge with its new Georgian-style bay windows; the sign on the roof is where the Wren's sign once was; Forgeside and the cottage to its right is where the Cottage of Content public house once was. A *section of a larger photo,* © *The Francis Frith Collection.*

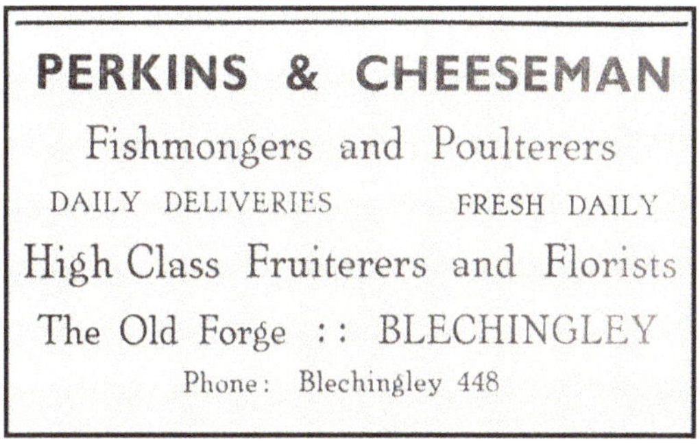

PERKINS & CHEESEMAN
Fishmongers and Poulterers
DAILY DELIVERIES   FRESH DAILY
High Class Fruiterers and Florists
The Old Forge :: BLECHINGLEY
Phone: Blechingley 448

J. & P. AGATE
Fishmongers & Fruiterers
The Old Forge, Bletchingley
Fish Supplies direct from Coast Daily
Phone: Bletchingley 448

Parish magazine advertisements for The Old Forge – 1954 and 1965

The Old Forge and Forgeside – 2022
The wooden bench on the far left marks the approximate position of the front steps of the demolished Forge Cottage.

Wren's Corner[5] – 2022
1) The Mint Cottages in Church Lane; 2) Horseshoe Cottage in Church Lane, built in the late 1980s by Kents builders, just to the rear of the demolished Forge Cottage; 3) The Old Forge at 24 High Street; 4) Forgeside at 22 High Street; 5) Cottages on the site of the former Cottage of Content public house; 6) The former Prince Albert public house, a sixteenth-century building. Pub closed in 2014 and (in 2024) was pending conversion to a home/homes.

5 Wren's Corner is the author's idea – send your vote on a postcard to Blechingley Parish Council to make it official!

High Street – 1951
Looking west from the top of Outwood Lane. *Photo by Donald Ashley Birkinshaw, from an original negative.*

Church Walk – 1941
Photo by Donald Ashley Birkinshaw, from an original negative.

"OLD CAWLEY," THE RAT CATCHER, *c.* 1870.

Old Cawley, The Rat Catcher, wearing a Surrey smock – c. 1870
Uvedale Lambert Snr comments: 'Mr Kenrick has preserved the picture of a well-known character, old Cawley, the rat-catcher, whom the writer can remember striding with his dogs across Sandhills Farm, a mysterious and rather alarming figure, to whom bad boys would certainly be given by their nurse over 40 years ago.' *Photographer Jarvis Kenrick, from Uvedale Lambert Snr's 1921 book.*

Cawleys lived in the village for over 200 years. Thomas Cawley (1781–1871), was listed in the 1841 Bletchingley census as a rat-catcher and in 1851 and 1861 as a vermin destroyer. They were related by marriage to the Wren blacksmith family. William Cawley married Ann Bassett Bond in 1832, the sister of Sophia Bond, who married William Henry Wren in 1852. William and Ann Cawley were witnesses at the 1852 wedding.

Blechingley Cawleys listed in 1839 were:

- William Cawley: baker, grocer and draper
- William Cawley: basket and chair maker
- John Cawley: wheelwright.

Cawley Bakers, rare Blechingley photo postcard, – c. 1908
On the hill in the background is Whitehill Tower, a folly built in 1862 for Jeremiah Long.
From the Roger Packham postcard collection.

Cawley advertisement – 1935 **Rice Brothers advertisement – 1911**
The Surrey Mirror & County Post advertisement © Mirrorpix/Reach Licensing

High Street, south side – c. 1909
The buildings to the left (with the three gable ends), are the White Hart Flats, next door to the White Hart Inn, 19–21 High Street, circa seventeenth century with later alterations. On the left is Rice Brothers, saddlers and hardware supplies; at some point they also had a shop on the north side of the village (now Forgeside, 22 High Street). In the centre is Edwin Cawley's bakers shop. Edwin was a baker in the village for almost 60 years, and was a well-known local cricketer. He died in 1917, aged 82. On the far right is Legg, grocer and draper, at 2 The Cobbles (25 High Street). *From a postcard.*

Rice Brothers at Forgeside
The five large black dots on the left at first floor level are metal patress plates, connected to internal metal tie-bars, a repair system installed to hold unstable walls in place. The house was rebuilt in the 1980s. *Photo courtesy of Blechingley Conservation and Historical Society.*

Taylor and Bristow, Norfolk House, 80 High Street – c. 1904
They traded here for some 100 years. Horse-drawn carriages once alighted in front of the elegant entrance steps. Lord Palmerston, MP for Blechingley from 1831 to 1833, who was later British prime minister, was said to have once stood on the steps to deliver an election speech. Proposals of marriage have also been made on these steps. The buildings on the right are the old almshouses – put up by Clara Matilda Charles Perkins, lady of the manor 1846–70 – sadly now demolished and replaced with modern flats. *From a Walford and Sons Real Photograph and P.P.P.P. Postcards, with a postmark of 1906, courtesy of the East Surrey Museum.*

Taylor and Bristow. The 1851 census lists Norfolk House as formerly the town hall, with William Saunders trading as grocer and draper. The Saunders family (Saunders and Son) sold the business to Edward Barcham in 1869. Later three generations of the Bristow family ran a business here, beginning with Frederick Bristow, who was born in 1851 in West Grinstead. In 1874 he married Annie King (b. 1851) at St Mary's, Blechingley. Annie was the daughter of James King, who was innkeeper at the White Hart Inn, Blechingley, and also a farmer. Frederick was trading at Norfolk House from about 1874, in partnership with Henry Taylor.

In a 1905 advertisement Taylor and Bristow claimed to be the largest cheddar cheese dealer in the county, and it was said that you could buy almost anything there. In 1940 they were trading as 'Taylor & Bristow – Wholesale and Retail Drapers, Grocers and Provision Merchants, Outfitters, Merchants. Furnishing and General Warehousemen'.

Norfolk House has been altered over the years and the Victorian front hides earlier building/buildings. Derek Moore noted a timber by an attic doorway bearing a date of 1597. The front sections are Grade II listed, but the huge Victorian warehouse attached to the rear is unlisted. Allan and Betty Bristow took on the village post office at Norfolk House around 1965, and Taylor and Bristow closed around 1970. The post office, which also sold coffee, continued until about 1984. Lawrences Auctioneers have traded here since 1964, and were still holding regular antiques auctions in 2023.

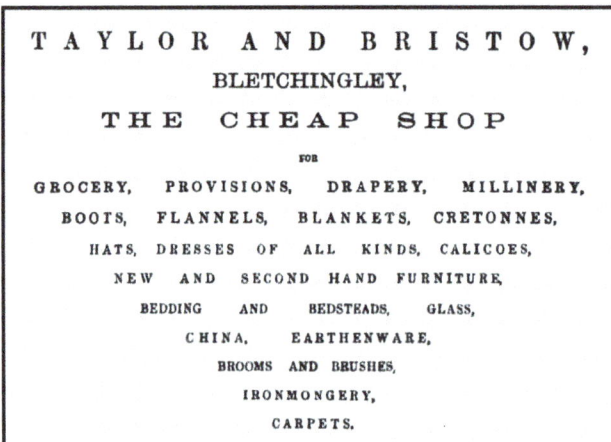

Taylor and Bristow advertisement – 1884
Surrey Mirror and General County Advertiser © Mirrorpix/Reach Licensing.

Victorian traffic jam in the village – c. 1880
Looking east across the front steps of Taylor and Bristow. The gentleman on the left wearing the overcoat and hat and facing away from us appears in another photo in this book, see if you can spot this mystery man. *Photographer Jarvis Kenrick, © Surrey History Centre.*

Victorian warehouse – 2022
Attached to the rear of Norfolk House. Some say it was built in anticipation of the railway coming to Blechingley, which never materialised.

David Hawkins recalls happy times in the late 1940s, when he was 11 or 12 and working for Taylor and Bristow as 'the boy'. His primary job was to deliver groceries on the trade bicycle, which was difficult to master, as the loaded bike was very heavy and the weight of groceries in the front basket could tip the bike over when dismounting. Another of his jobs was to spread sawdust on the shop floor under the watchful eyes of Mr Warren and Mr Laver. At the request of his mother he was allowed to take garments home on approval for her inspection. Each item was accompanied with a detailed, bright-orange approval slip, and he remembers the prices all seemed to end with 11¾d – much like today, when everything seems to end with 99p.

Norfolk House marriage proposal re-enactment – 2022
Our talented actors are Jennifer and Jason, who were well qualified for the job, having got engaged in September. They created quite a spectacle on the day this photo was taken, with at least one kind passer-by taking a photo on their phone and offering it to the couple. *Colour photo converted to black and white; some of the untidy street furniture has been edited out!*

David's most enduring memory was when he proposed to Ottilie Agate on the steps at the front of the shop. She accepted and by 1993 the marriage had lasted over 30 years. Ottilie's sister's husband also proposed on the steps, and that marriage had lasted over 40 years. The front of Norfolk House and the steps look a bit untidy these days, but perhaps it was once the place for marriage proposals. David Hawkins' recollections were published in the *Blechingley Magazine* in 1993. Ottilie E Agate and David WJ Hawkins were married in 1959.

Taylor and Bristow delivery boy setting off on his bicycle – 1951
Perhaps David Hawkins? *Photo by Donald Ashley Birkinshaw, from an original negative.*

The first horse drawn omnibus (bus) service was apparently introduced in Blechingley in 1878. Sam Marsh & Son later claimed to be the original omnibus service provider, but an article in the Reigate, Redhill, Dorking & Epsom Journal, dated 15 October 1878 read:

REDHILL & BLETCHINGLEY Introduction of Omnibus Traffic. On and after Monday, the 28th, Mr Stafford, of Ladbroke-road, will run daily (Sundays excepted) a pair-horse omnibus from that town to the Plough at Bletchingley. The times of starting, as at present decided upon, are from Bletchingley at 8.45 and 11.20 a.m. and six p.m. The fare will be one shilling each journey.

Omnibus, Redhill and Reigate horse bus – late 1800s
The Blechingley service probably looked similar. *Photo courtesy of Blechingley Conservation and Historical Society. Colourised by the author.*

Parish magazine advertisement – 1914
At this time Sam & Son were still competing with the motor omnibus, perhaps hoping that these new noisy contraptions would never catch on.

The first Blechingley motor omnibus was introduced in 1912 with an hourly service from Redhill to Blechingley. Sam Marsh & Son continued to operate their established horse-drawn omnibus service alongside the motor bus, with a route from Redhill to The Plough Inn (The Bletchingley Arms since 2015). Sam also supplied carriages for weddings and events and in 1904 he provided for Alfred Uvedale Miller Lambert's wedding at St Nicholas' Church, Godstone.

Omnibus, motor, first day outside the White Hart Inn – June 1912
This is a single deck Leyland S.30.T of The East Surrey Traction Company, with a Leyland 30 horse power petrol engine and worm driven rear axle, 4-speed 'crash' gearbox and top speed of about 22mph (legal limit 12mph). It had a Liversidge body and was built in 1912. By about 1914 the service had expanded with routes from Reigate to Sevenoaks via Blechingley. *Courtesy Blechingley Conservation and Historical Society.*

East Surrey Traction Company bus – c. 1918
Double decker Daimler Y, registration number P 8697, heading towards Blechingley on the Bletchingley Road at Godstone Green, on route 23 from East Grinstead to Reigate. *From a Frith & Co Ltd postcard, from the Roger Packham postcard collection.*

Parish magazine advertisement – 1918
The unequal struggle with the motor bus had come to an end and by March 1918 Sam Marsh and Son were running livery stables in Redhill. In 1935 Sam Marsh was advertising his riding school in Redhill.

Court Lodge Farm

Court Lodge Farm, opposite St Mary's Church in Church Lane, is reckoned by historians to have originally been where manorial court proceedings were held, going back many hundreds of years. The manor court building was typically adjacent to the church. The west side of the current farmhouse has external timber framing from the 1600s, with many beautiful period features inside, including doors, exposed beams and three inglenook fireplaces. The official listed building entry has it as C1700, grade II listed. Sir Robert Clayton is thought to have inherited it from his brother, Thomas Clayton, shortly before his own death in 1707. Uvedale Lambert Snr said: 'When the Rev. Matthew Kenrick acquired the manor [Blechingley Manor in 1799] the Courtlodge was still Clayton property, and courts were held at the White Hart'. So it was probably converted from manor court house to farmhouse around 1800. On a side note, The Grange was described as Manor Court House of Bletchingley by artist John Hassell in 1822 (see page 70) so the court may well have been held there at some point.

Sir William Robert Clayton Baronet owned the house and farm in 1841, and Sir Benjamin Vincent Sellon Brodie Baronet owned it in 1892. In 1881 Court Lodge was a farm of 175 acres, farmed by twenty three year old Arthur Dawe, with his wife Mary Hannah, who was born in Ohio, USA. Seven men and three boys were employed on the farm.

Court Lodge Farmhouse – c. 1948 Looking north down Church Lane from the High Street. The timber structure on the left may be holding up a building after bomb damage, possibly the old Fox and Hounds. *Photo by Donald Ashley Birkinshaw, from an original negative.*

Court Lodge Farm farmhouse – 2024
The farmhouse on the left has timber framing from the seventeenth century on the right side. The house is on about four acres of land. The old farm buildings are on the right with St Mary's Church just across Church Lane in the background. The cottage to the right of the church is called The Old House.

Christopher Miles, great grandson of Sir Walpole Lloyd Greenwell, bought Court Lodge Farm with the farmhouse in 1963 and farmed it along with the adjoining farms, North Park and Place Farm, which he had farmed since 1950. Christopher extensively modernised the farmhouse and added a new wing to the east side. He had a pedigree Jersey herd based at North Park, orchards in Blechingley and arable land in between. When Christopher retired in 1992, the Court Lodge farmland was developed into Bletchingley Golf Club.

Sir Walpole Lloyd Greenwell was the founder of W. Greenwell & Co, one of the largest stockbrokers in the City of London, and owner of the Marden Park estate, Woldingham/Godstone, from 1906. The Marden estate extended from Woldingham to Tandridge and included North Park Farm. Sir Walpole Lloyd's son, Sir Bernard Eyre Greenwell (1874–1939) inherited the estate in 1919, followed by his only son and heir, Peter

McLintock Greenwell. Peter was captured at Dunkirk at the beginning of WWII, and remained prisoner for the duration of the war. The local Greenwell estates were sold during and after the war to pay off death duties. Peter relocated to Butley in Suffolk, where the family had bought land in the 1920s, and where his son, Edward Bernard, the current baronet, still lived in 2024.

Miles, Christopher Richard (1928-2015) and Jean Mary (1930-2021)
They lived at Court Lodge Farm from 1963 to 1994, and then in a cottage opposite (a converted farm building). *Photo courtesy of Richard Miles.*

Christopher's son Richard remembers, 'Court Lodge was an active farmyard in the heart of the village, with the noise, dirt and disruption of tractors, combine harvesters, grain dryers, lorries, right up to 1992. Hard to imagine now.' Richard was born at North Park Farm in 1957 and has lived in Blechingley on and off since then. He has owned and lived at Court Lodge Farmhouse, with his wife Juliet and family, since 1992. He is the last descendant of the Greenwell family in the area.

Sir Keir Starmer KCB KC, UK prime minister in 2024, has a connection with Marden Park. His great-grandfather, Gustavus Adolphus Starmer, served as a gamekeeper at Marden Park for Sir Bernard Greenwell. Keir's great-uncle, Gustavus Edward (known as Gussie), worked for Christopher Miles in the 1960s. Richard Miles remembers Gussie as a farm manager, a fine man, war hero and someone of notable kindness. Kier was brought up in Oxted, five miles from Blechingley.

Blechingley | A Selection of Notable Past and Present People (and a Pigeon)

Sir Joseph Jekyll (1663–1738)
KS PC, was a very active British MP, and for a time was Lord of the Manor of Reigate. In 1713 he owned and lived at Garston Park, Blechingley. Jekyll Island in the Province of Georgia, USA, was named in his honour following his financial assistance in founding the colony. *By and published by George Vertue, after a Michael Dahl engraving, 1731. © National Portrait Gallery.*

Thomas Herring (1693–1757)
Archbishop of Canterbury from 1747 to 1757. He served as rector at St Mary's, Blechingley, from 1731 to 1737. *Portrait by Thomas Hudson, © National Portrait Gallery.*

Lord Melbourne (1779–1848)
William Lamb, 2nd Viscount Melbourne, PC, PC (Ire), FRS, was MP for Blechingley from 1827 to 1828. He went on to be prime minister. Melbourne in Australia was named after him. *© National Portrait Gallery.*

Lord Palmerston (1784–1865)
Henry John Temple, 3rd Viscount Palmerston, KG, GCB, PC, FRS, was MP for Blechingley from 1831 to 1833. He was foreign secretary and went on to serve twice as prime minister. *© National Portrait Gallery*

William Abraham Bell (1841–1921)
MA, MB, Cantab, is famed (with his business partner, General William Jackson Palmer) for establishing the Denver & Rio Grande Railway, along with the towns of Colorado Springs and Manitou Springs in the USA. He was a Fellow of the Royal Geographical Society and a doctor. He went to the USA in 1867 to study homeopathy and was later the official photographer for an expedition of the Union Pacific Railway, when he became friends with General Palmer. The portrait can be seen in the entrance to the village hall, where it was placed in 1922. *Painting by Sir Hubert Herkomer, photographed by HP Robinson and Son of Redhill.*

In 1891 William returned to England and purchased Pendell Court (with the Lordship of the Manor of Blechingley), where he lived with his wife Cara and family. He had married Cara (née Scovell) in London in 1872. In 1903 he largely financed the building of the Blechingley village hall on land given by Jarvis Kenrick. The hall was rebuilt in 1985/6. He was known for his hospitality at Pendell Court, with fancy dress and 'servants dances' starting at 9pm and going on to 3am.

Pendell Court, party invitation – 1904
Believed to have been for 21st birthday fancy dress celebration of William Bell's son 'Archie'. *Courtesy Blechingley Conservation and Historical Society.*

The 1905 Primrose League garden party was hosted there with entertainment provided by the Blechingley Brass Band and the popular Caterham Gypsies. The event was described as a mix of music, politics and bohemianism culminating with a firework display. His daughter Margaret married Sir Montagu Frederick Montagu-Pollock, at St Mary's, Blechingley, in 1899, and became Lady Pollock. His daughter Hyacinth married Patrick James Boyle, Viscount Kelburne, at St Mary's in 1906, becoming Viscountess, then Countess of Glasgow.

Jarvis Kenrick IV (1852–1949)
A solicitor, footballer, cricketer, croquet player and prolific photographer, among many other things. He scored the first-ever goal in an FA cup final in 1871. As a cricketer he made a first-class appearance for Surrey. He lived for a time at Pendell House. *For more on Jarvis Kenrick and Pendell House, see page 278. Photo courtesy of Roger Packham.*

Leslie Faber (1880–1929)
Leslie (far left) was a celebrated West End and Broadway actor. He lived at Wideways, 100 High Street, from about 1912 to 1920. The gentleman on the far right is Sir Charles Hawtrey (1858–1923). The British actor from the *Carry On* series of comedy films took Charles Hawtrey as his stage name. His real name was George Frederick Joffre Hartree (1914–88). *From an article in 'The World of the Theatre' section of the* Illustrated London News, *13 April 1921. © Illustrated London News Ltd/Mary Evans.*

Wideways, 100 High Street – 2023

Younger days: Helen (D'Oyly Carte) and Stanley Carr Boulter – c. 1875
Stanley in his cricket outfit. *Photos courtesy of Alex Askaroff, great-great-grandson of Stanley Carr Boulter.*

Helen D'Oyly Carte (1852–1913), widow of Richard D'Oyly Carte and heir to the Savoy Theatre and Hotel empire, married Stanley Carr Boulter JP in 1902. Impresario Richard was famed for producing the Gilbert and Sullivan comic operas, but some have described Helen as being the real founder of the Gilbert and Sullivan era. Stanley was a businessman and founder member of the Law Debenture Corporation. The couple lived in London and at their country home at Garston Park, Blechingley, from around 1902 to 1911. For more on Helen, Stanley and Garston Park, see page 240.

Jean Colin with Tommy Trinder – 1941
Jean (1905–89) was a comedy actress who appeared in many films, including: *The Mikado* (1939); *Laugh it Off* (1940); and *Last Holiday* (1950). Jean lived at Mill Cottage for about 25 years from 1940, which is down a lane round the back of Pendell House. Derek Moore, president and former chairman of the Blechingley Conservation and Historical Society, lived there with his wife Valerie in the 1980s for about eight years. *Photo taken during the making of the film* Communal Kitchen: Eating Out With Tommy Trinder, *for the Ministry of Information in 1941. Public domain image.*

Mill Cottage model
Grade II listed, timber framed, dating from the seventeenth century. There was once a mill and mill pond here; the small mill stream remains. *Scale model owned by Derek Moore.*

Benjamin Ashdown, Oddfellows Grand Master and Clerk to the Parish Council
He was Grand Master in 1926 and Clerk from 1899 to 1937. He is remembered for rescuing the local historical parish records from the trash. He lived for a time above Barclays Bank, at Bank Buildings on the corner of the High Street and Outwood Lane. *Photo courtesy of David Martin.*

Douglas Houghton, Baron Houghton of Sowerby CH, PC
He was born in 1898 and fought in the Battle of Passchendaele in 1917 during WWI. Among his many roles he was a Labour MP, and served under Prime Minister Harold Wilson. From 1941 he presented the BBC wireless (radio) programme *Can I help you?* It was a popular show, which ran for 23 years, and Douglas became a household name. He was president of the Blechingley Horticultural Society for 30 years. He lived with his wife, Lady Vera Houghton CBE, at Becks Cottage, Whitehill Lane, which dates from about 1650. Vera was a women's health and family planning campaigner. Douglas died in 1996, aged 97. Vera died in 2013, aged 99. *Photo licensed from and © the BBC.*

Maurice James Carrick Allom (1906–95)
Lived at Glenfield House (see p. 64) in the High Street from around the mid 1930s up to the early 1970s. He was a Surrey and England cricketer and one of only three players to take a hat-trick on a Test cricket debut. He was also the first Test player to take four wickets in five balls. He was almost six and a half feet tall, and his son Anthony was reckoned to be one of the tallest first-class cricketers, at up to six feet ten and a half inches. Maurice was President of the MCC 1969/70, President of Surrey CCC 1970; he was also a skilled jazz saxophonist. *Photo courtesy of Roger Packham. For more on Maurice and cricket in Blechingley see page 116.*

Uvedale Henry Hoare Lambert (1909–83)
Of South Park, as High Sheriff of Surrey in 1961. He was Lord of the Manor of Blechingley from 1970 to 1983 and wrote a number of local history books. *Photo courtesy Dame Sarah Goad. For more on the Lambert family see page 267*

The 5th Earl of Munster (right, 1906–75) with General Metcalfe
Woking, Surrey, 12 July 1963. The Earl was presenting new colours to the 3rd and 4th Queen's Surrey Battalion (TA). Geoffrey William Richard Hugh FitzClarence, KBE, PC, was Lord-Lieutenant of Surrey from 1957 to 1973. He was a peer and a Conservative politician. He owned and lived at Sandhills (house and farm), off Outwood Lane. He served under a number of prime ministers, including Sir Winston Churchill. The earl was a descendant of King William IV and would often have a pint at the William IV in Little Common Lane. The pub was demolished and replaced with four new homes called the William IV Cottages not long before 2023. © *Surrey History Centre.*

Sir Geoffrey Howe, Baron Howe of Aberavon, CH, PC, QC (1926–2015) and his wife, Lady Elspeth, Baroness Howe of Idlicote, CBE (1932–2022)
They had a weekend retreat at Henhaw Farm on the outskirts of Blechingley. Sir Geoffrey was a Conservative MP and served as Deputy Prime Minister from 1989 to 1990. Lady Howe was the half-aunt of Queen Camilla. Seen here in front of Longhurst Post Office at 46 High Street circa 1980s. Standing in the doorway is Alan Gayler, postmaster and chairman of the parish council. *Photo taken by Alan's wife, Lesley, courtesy of Blechingley Conservation and Historical Society.*

Archbishop Emeritus Desmond Mpilo Tutu (1931–2021)
He was an honorary curate at St Mary's Church while he was studying at King's College, London, from 1965 to 1967. He was a leading anti-apartheid and human rights activist in South Africa and received the Nobel Peace Prize. He was the first black African to hold the posts of Archbishop of Cape Town and Bishop of Johannesburg. During his time in Blechingley he lived at The Clerk's House, adjacent to the war memorial in the High Street. *Copy of a portrait on display in St Mary's Church.*

Dame Judith Olivia Dench, CH DBE FRSA, is a long-time resident of Outwood, on the southern border of Blechingley. Outwood was formed from parts of the parishes of Blechingley, Burstow, Horley, Horne and Nutfield in 1870. Dame Judi was patron of the Bletchingley Players amateur dramatic group until its closure in 2019.

Dame Judi Dench and David Mills – 2016
During a visit to the Bletchingley Players headquarters at Grange Meadow. *Photo courtesy of the Bletchingley Players, photographer Doris Parker.*

Sir Richard Stilgoe OBE
Musician, songwriter, lyricist and broadcaster, lived in North Park Lane in the old North Park farmhouse from 1981. In 1997 he founded the Orpheus Centre Trust for young disabled adults at North Park. He was High Sheriff of Surrey in 1998. He now lives in Oxted with his wife Lady Annabel OBE, but comes to Blechingley each year to open the village fete at Grange Meadow. © *Surrey History Centre*.

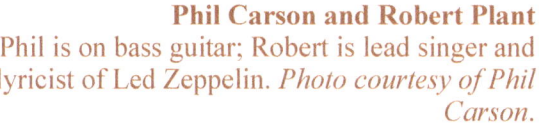

Phil Carson and Robert Plant
Phil is on bass guitar; Robert is lead singer and lyricist of Led Zeppelin. *Photo courtesy of Phil Carson.*

Phil Carson is an English former record label owner and was London-based Executive Vice President of Atlantic Records from 1969 to 1985. He lives in the USA and part-time at The Grange. Among his signings are Yes, AC/DC and Twisted Sister. He started his musical career as a bass guitarist, most notably alongside Dusty Springfield. He spent a great deal of time on the road with bands under his purview, especially Led Zeppelin. He is one of only a handful of people to have jammed onstage with them and the only person to appear onstage with both Led Zeppelin and AC/DC. In 2023 he was managing Foreigner and Dee Snider.

Timothy Francis Goad
Of South Park, as High Sheriff of Surrey in 1994. He was Lord of the Manor of Blechingley from 1995 to 2013. *Photo courtesy Dame Sarah Goad.*

Dame Sarah Jane Frances Goad, née Lambert, DCVO, JP
She was Lord-Lieutenant of Surrey from 1997 to 2015, the first female to serve in this role in Surrey. She supported a number of charities and organisations and, in recognition of her service as Lord-Lieutenant, was appointed Dame Commander of the Royal Victorian Order by Queen Elizabeth II in 2012. Dame Sarah is the daughter of Uvedale Henry Hoare and Diana Mary Lambert, and lives in Blechingley with her husband Timothy. *Photo courtesy of Dame Sarah. For more on the Lambert family see page 267*

A Lord-Lieutenant's original sixteenth-century role was to organise the county's militia for the king. Today the duties include assisting the Royal Household in any matters it requires in relation to the county of Surrey, the arrangement of programmes for royal visits to organisations in the county, and the presentation of medals and awards on behalf of the monarch.

The Rt. Hon Sir Richard Ottaway PC
He has lived with his wife, Lady Nicola, at Snatts Hill House, Blechingley, since 1992. He served as an officer in the Royal Navy and later was a solicitor, specialising in maritime and commercial law. He was Conservative MP for Nottingham North from 1983 to 1987, and Conservative MP for Croydon South from 1992 to 2015. Nicola has been a magistrate and a TV producer. *Photo courtesy of Sir Richard.*

Snatts Hill House, Rabies Heath Road, has an interesting history. It was built around 1890, with a studio, by Belgian-born artist Henry Campo Tosto (often written Campotosto, b. 1833). Part of an earlier building is believed to have been incorporated into the new house. Henry came to London around 1870 and was resident at Kensington Garden Square in 1875. His younger sister Octavia, also an artist, joined him there at some point and they obtained British citizenship in 1883. They lived together at Snatts Hill House and collaborated on projects, often exhibiting at prestigious art institutions, including the Royal Academy, London. Henry painted a portrait of Pope Pius IX in 1875, for which he received the Order of St Sylvester (Knighthood). Spinster Octavia Campo Tosto died of heart disease and dropsy (oedema) in 1909, aged 63, and was buried in Blechingley.

Henry was greatly affected by the death of his sister, whom he referred to as the 'sweet angel that has left me'. He became somewhat reclusive and was said to be drinking more than usual. He was well respected and liked in the village and was said to be a very interesting man. He died a bachelor the following year and was buried alongside Octavia. Controversially, he left the house and contents to his caretaker/personal assistant, Michael William Turk (known as William, 1866–1947) who was once a local Fuller's Earth digger. The will was contested by some of Henry's Belgian relatives, but the probate court jury decided in favour of William. Some of the witnesses were Ethel Legg, Benjamin Ashdown and Dr Pratt. William and his wife Alice (1871–1945) had seven children, lived in the house for thirty-odd years and are recorded on memorial boards inside St Mark's Chapel at South Park, where it is stated that William worked as an expert hedger. His death was registered in 1947 at 4 Crescent Road, Barfields, Blechingley, with effects of £926. One of the family descendants was still living in a detached cottage in the grounds of Snatts Hill House in the 1990s.

The royal-looking insignias of Henry and Octavia can still be seen on the gateposts at the entrance to Snatts Hill House. The original gates also had insignia but these were stolen. The artists left some sculptures built onto a wall of the house.

The Primrose Gatherer, **Henry Campo Tosto** *Public domain image Wikipedia.*

Campo Tosto (Campotosto) insignias (HC and OC) on the gateposts at Snatts Hill House – 2022

Snatts Hill House – 2022

'THE NAME'S DUNDERDALE, BIFFY DUNDERDALE'

Commander Wilfred Albert Dunderdale, nicknamed Biffy for his boxing prowess, settled in Blechingley with his wife Dorothy shortly before his retirement in 1959. They built 'Castlefield' on a two acre plot with spectacular views over the Kent Weald. The land was purchased from local architect and land owner, Felix McCredy. The total cost of the house, land and tennis court was £10,000. Neighbour Felix built his own similarly styled, much larger house 'Castle Hill House'. Due to Biffy's secret service background, police protection was put in place at the house.

A younger Biffy, Wilfred Albert Dunderdale (1899–1990)
Courtesy and © Paul Biddle, owner of the Dunderdale Archive

Biffy was born in 1899 to English parents in Odessa, Ukraine and spoke fluent Russian, French and German. He joined MI6 from the navy in 1921, initially to work in

Constantinople (Istanbul), and was an agent for 38 years. He spent 1921 to 1940 in Paris. From 1926 he was Britain's principal link to the Deuxième Bureau (the French secret service), dealing with intelligence on the Soviet Union and counter-espionage against the German armed forces. There are various versions or embellishments of his story but, in summary, he was said to have been a rather stylish character who wore handmade suits with gold cufflinks, was chauffeured around Paris in a Rolls-Royce, which some say was bulletproof, and that 'a bottle of vintage champagne was never far from one hand, a cigarette held in a long holder in the other'. James Bond author Ian Fleming. worked in British Naval Intelligence during WWII and the inspiration for his 007 character came from Biffy and other military personnel he knew.

Castlefield, the 'real' James Bond's house
Photo from 'A view from every window', Country Life, 13 November 1958. © Country Life Archive. Colourised by author.

Biffy took delivery of a German Enigma cipher machine from Polish exiles in Paris in 1940. A British Naval destroyer was laid on to bring him back to England with the machine. The cipher was eventually cracked at Bletchley Park (Buckinghamshire, UK), under the project codenamed Ultra, which gave the Allies an advantage over the Germans. At the outset of the war, he recruited and was the handler for the American-born, French naturalised, world superstar singer and dancer, Josephine Baker, who undertook espionage duties for the Allies in France. In recognition of his service during WWII he was appointed Companion of the Most Distinguished Order of St Michael and St George (CMG).

Biffy in uniform
Courtesy and © Paul Biddle, owner of the Dunderdale Archive

Josephine Baker – 1940
Studio Harcourt France, public domain image

Friend and neighbour Averil Trott recalls that Biffy didn't drive. He told the following story, often repeated:

'I was at a huge military display in the Middle East [Constantinople] and accidentally reversed over a goat, which was the regimental mascot, and never drove again.' So James Bond's exploits in Aston Martins don't quite fit with Biffy in this respect!

David and Ann Martin, who have lived in Blechingley since 1970, were friends with Biffy and recall him talking about his many exploits and bringing an Enigma machine back to England: 'I did not let it out of my sight and kept it on my lap for the whole journey.' In 1919, aboard a naval vessel in the Black Sea, Biffy was made aware of an imminent mutiny by the crew, who were sympathetic to the Bolshevik cause. The plan was to throw Biffy and two other naval officers overboard, with weights on their feet. For his part in thwarting the mutiny he was awarded the MBE. Later he was the representative observer for England in the investigation of the murder of the Russian Romanov Imperial Royal Family at Ekaterinburg. In 1922 he accepted the task of paying off (with gold sovereigns) and repatriating those foreign members of the deposed Sultan Mohammad VI of Turkey's harem. He was known for recounting his stories and could tell a good tale. Biffy gave David and Ann a gift of a mahogany toilet seat, which they still have to this day. He said he'd wanted to wear it around his neck on the five-minute walk to their house, but thought better of it because it was awkward with the lid!

Biffy's second wife Dorothy died in 1978. In 1980 he married an American lady – Debbie. He died aged 90 in November 1990 at his home in New York. Some of Biffy's story was provided by The Sun/News Licensing, from his obituary in *The Times* of 16 November 1990, which ends with:

> All who knew Biffy remember him with great affection. He never lost a friend and he scorned convention to the end: a genuine romantic and a pirate.

Dunderdale memorial in St Mary's Church

Biffy and Debbie Dunderdale
Photo courtesy of Averil Trott.

The Famous Blechingley Pigeon. David and Ann Martin recalled another interesting story. In 1982 they purchased Clive House in the High Street and did most of the extensive renovations themselves. Clive House dates from 1690, built on the site of an earlier house, a burgage tenement, which is a house on a rectangular plot, typically 50 feet wide and 300 feet deep.

Clive House – 2021

During the work they discovered the remains of a pigeon in a disused fireplace (its chimney is on the right hand side of the house pictured above, and behind Ann and David on the next page). It was a WWII messenger pigeon, with a small red canister attached to its leg containing a coded message. It received a lot of media attention, from the likes of the BBC, ITV and CNN, who came to film and interview David and Ann. GCHQ, the UK's intelligence and cyber agency, analysed the message but, after six weeks, concluded that it could not be decoded. Biffy Dunderdale saw the message and commented, 'You should back off, it will never be published.' David and Ann still have the original message, which was partially decoded by Gord Young in Canada in 2012.

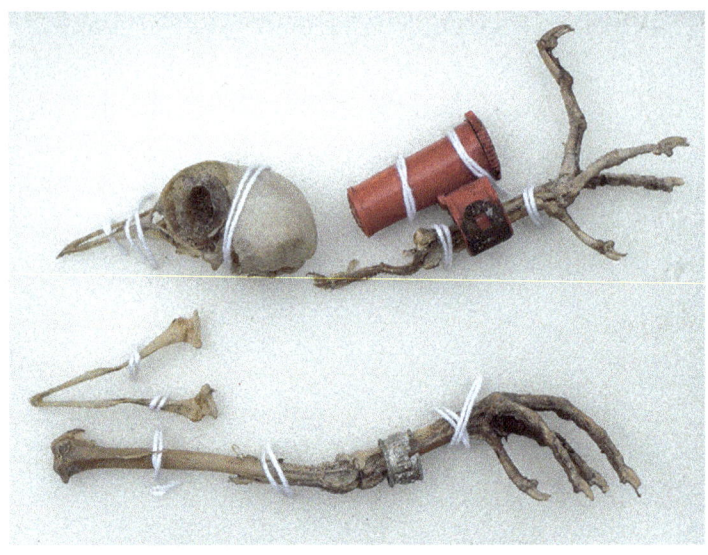

The famous Blechingley Pigeon NURP 40 TW 194 – WWII coded message and remains

The same message was sent via two pigeons around D-Day, June 1944; our valiant pigeon was NURP 40 TW 194 (National Union of Racing Pigeons and 40 was its date of birth, 1940). Hopefully the other, more experienced pigeon, NURP 37 OK 76, born in 1937, made it home, delivered the message and helped to win the war.

Ann and David Martin with pigeon NURP 40 TW 194 – 2022
David has held many roles in the village, including chairman of Blechingley Parish Council and of Blechingley Conservation and Historical Society.

More notable people are covered in the Lordship of the Manor section, page 281.

Blechingley | Pictured Today

The Whyte Harte Hotel

The Red Lion

The Bletchingley Arms

Three village pubs – 2020–24

Lamingtons Tea Room and Gift Shop (The Cobbles) with Mark – 2021
25 High Street, famous for home-made quiche and cakes. Originally, the buildings each side of Lamingtons were separate, with jettied (overhanging) fronts, dating from circa 1500. No. 25 was built in between them at a later date. The buildings are historically known as 1, 2 and 3 The Cobbles and have housed various businesses over the years, including: grocers and drapers, bakers, wool sellers, antique dealers, home interiors, bridal wear and the post office.

Longhurst Post Office and Store in Middle Row | The Church Yard and the Village Stores
Glenfield House – Melrose Cottage – Tower Cottages | Church Walk

Village scenes – 2021

Many of these buildings date back to the sixteenth century, including Longhurst (post office, newsagent and convenience store) at 46 High Street; some of its rear timber framing can be seen from Church Walk. It has been known as Longhurst since the 1940s. The Village Stores at 28 High Street is also an ancient building; the road between it and the red telephone booth leads up to St Mary's Church, known locally as the Church Yard or Square. The shop to the left of the telephone booth was the village post office from about 1914 to the 1960s. Church House is located at the end of Church Yard, an attractive building erected in 1905 and very recently renovated, with function rooms for hire. Glenfield House is the most imposing building in the High Street, it is seventeenth-century and Grade II listed. Many affluent people have owned and lived in this house over the years; in the early 1800s it was the home of Surgeon Robert Webb, and in the mid-1900s was home to Surrey and England cricketer Maurice James Carrick Allom. Melrose Cottage, the pink building to the right of Glenfield House, was said to have been Robert Webb's surgery, and was the village post office in 1832. Church Walk, once the main road through the village, is lined with ancient timber-framed buildings.

Obberds in Church Walk – 2021
Probably the oldest house in Blechingley, with a date of 1380 over the front door.

Obberds, rear – 2021
with its wobbly timber framing.

Old Rectory, Sandy Lane – 2020
This is a Grade II listed building with some parts dating from around the 1500s. It was rebuilt and extended by the Rector of Blechingley, Mathew Kenrick, between 1775 and 1803. There are two rainwater heads with the initials MK and dates of 1786 and 1800, which may be the dates of two stages of the rebuilding/alterations. Since then it has had further alterations. Today the house and gardens are used for weddings, events and as a media location for photography, film and television. Two notable productions were Jane Austen's *Emma*, and a *Vogue* photo shoot with Victoria Beckham.

Brewerstreet Tudor Farmhouse

The picture on the left is a print from A Pilgrimage in Surrey, 1914, by writer and artist, James S. Ogilvy, with a signed date of 1912. The cart bears the name of the Thomas King, Bletchingley, who was the widowed 70-year-old resident farmer at the time. The other two pictures were taken very recently. The building is a 1491 timber-framed, Wealden hall house, Grade I listed, the frame is of oak construction, with a Horsham stone roof. It has been owned by the French farming family since 1920, who carried out major restoration work between 1969 and 1971. The Tudor fireplace in the dining room has a date of 1601 scratched on the left. It was principally a 450-acre dairy farm with over 200 milking cows; the cows were sold in 2000 and a field was converted to host weddings and events, where up to 10 weddings a year have been hosted. Current owner Chris French describes Brewerstreet as a diversified farm, with some of the old farm buildings repurposed for various commercial activities.

Many buildings in the village centre are hundreds of years old and Peter Grey has covered them in great detail in: *Blechingley Explored* (1975) and *Blechingley Village and Parish* (1991).

Old Butchers Shop, Church Walk – 2020

Behind Longhurst village post office and store, adjacent to the war memorial. The shop front, added in the 1800s, hides an older building. The Selmes family were butchers here from the 1700s until 1973. Mrs Mary Selmes was listed as the village butcher in 1839 and 1855. In 1841 she owned and occupied some eight pasture and arable fields between Sandhills Farm and Town Farm and near Barfields and Stychens Lane. Livestock were slaughtered at the rear of the shop and carcasses were hung on the rail and hooks under the front canopy.

Blechingley had two butchers' shops in the early 1900s, the other being Eddolls in Outwood Lane.

Selmes Butchers advertisement – 1959

Selmes Butchers – 1911

© *The Francis Frith Collection*

St Mark's Chapel, exterior – 2020
St Mark's Chapel was converted from a seventeenth-century carthorse stable by Alfred Uvedale Miller Lambert JP in thanksgiving for the birth of his only child, Uvedale Henry Hoare, who was born on St Mark's Day 1909. The west door (left of the statue of St Mark), came from Hever Castle, Kent, and no doubt Henry VIII would once have passed through it. Mr AE Swan (of Seale, Swan and Seale of Oxted) designed the alterations and JT Williams and Son of Oxted carried out the work. It was dedicated for public worship by the Bishop of Woolwich. The chapel survived a fire in 1912 and a German flying bomb in 1944.

St Mark's Chapel, Tudor west door –2024

St Mark's Chapel, interior – 2020
St Mark's is a private chapel in the Southwark Diocese Church of England, but it is open to all. A Holy Communion service is held on Fridays. The chapel is an interesting place to visit, with records, coats of arms, details of the owners of the land since the Norman conquest and the ecclesiastical history. The names of some former parish residents and farmers are also displayed. A notice inside gives a short history of the chapel and ends with: 'So this is briefly the story of this place, once a stable, now a house of God, where his people meet their Lord and Saviour who was himself born in a stable for our salvation.'

The Grange | Tudor to Victorian Overview

Town Farm farmhouse (The Grange) watercolour by John Hassell – 1822
Annotated: 'Manor court house of Bletchingley called town or Tan house farm Surrey J Hassell 1822'. John George Wilson Perkins Esq. was the owner of Town Farm at the time but he lived at Pendell Court, about a mile away. The painting shows only one chimney on the nearest (north) end of the building, a second north chimney was added at a later date. It is possible that there was formerly one large ground-floor north room (nearest side of painting), which was split into two rooms (drawing room and dining room) at the time the second chimney was added. The ground-floor window to the left of the north chimney is absent today. The wooden single-storey extension seen attached to the house on the south side (right in the painting) was later replaced with a brick building (the single-storey south extension, a former doctor's waiting room and pantry/larder). © *Surrey History Centre, annotations enhanced by the author.*

The Grange first appears in records in the 1500s, but was not listed by name. In the 1600s it was identified as a house with six hearths. A tax was levied on the number of fire hearths in a house and was known as the chimney tax, chimney money or hearth money. The system was eventually abandoned and a 'window tax' was introduced, where a house was taxed on the number of windows it had. The system proved unpopular and residents bricked up windows to avoid the tax; it was repealed in 1851. In the early 1700s The Grange was mostly rebuilt on the site or extensively renovated with new facades. There are many houses in the village dating from the 1500s that are now hidden behind newer facades; for example, the Georgian front of The Clerk's House by the war memorial is hiding an earlier building. The Grange was a farmhouse in the 1700s and 1800s – and probably before that. Uvedale Lambert Snr refers to The Grange from the 1500s to 1866 as being 'the capital massuage', the main house in which the owner/tenant of the estate/farm lives. The house was separated from its farm in 1863/5, and became a doctor's home and surgery.

I believe Mr Martin Higgins first identified the John Hassell watercolour as The Grange and it is the earliest depiction we have. Hassell was an English watercolour painter, engraver, illustrator, writer, publisher and drawing-master. He produced at least 750 watercolour views of Surrey, and he published several works on the techniques of drawing and painting in watercolour and some illustrated travel guides. The Grange was one of only a few Blechingley properties Mr Hassell painted, the others being: Pendell House; Little Pendhill (alias the Manor House); The Old Rectory; Brewerstreet Farmhouse; the Almshouses (now demolished); and St Mary's Church.

An 1867 abstract of title document for the sale of a meadow on Town Farm (later to be Grange Meadow) from Robert Birkbeck to Reverend Charles Fox Chawner, rector at St Mary's, mentions that The Grange was farmhouse to Blechingley Farm in the 1700s, and that the farm name was changed to Town Farm around 1800. Abstract of title was a document produced by solicitors when a property was sold, giving some 50 years of history with details of owners, tenants, mortgages, deaths, wills and usually a plan. Outwood Lane is the location of the house and farmyard but it was called Blechingley Lane on the 1761 Clayton estate map. In the late 1800s The Grange and other properties at the north end of Outwood Lane were often listed as The Square, Blechingley. To confuse things further, it has also been called Outwood Road in the 1900s.

Some owners of an earlier version of the house on the site were identified by Mr Uvedale Lambert Snr as: the Sackville family in 1540 when William Sackville was a substantial landowner in Blechingley and was joint MP for Blechingley with Thomas Cawarden in 1542; the Sackvilles sold to the Gavells in 1546; who in turn sold to the Hoskins in 1586. Mr Lambert wrote in 1921, 'Charles Hoskins, gent., £20 in land, appears in the ley subsidy in 1593 in the borough, and from his house there, which is now the Grange, doubtless, Mr Thomas Coxe and Mary Hoskins, his daughter, were married on February 6th of that year' (the marriage is in St Mary's Church records). On the death of Charles Hoskins in 1597, his son, Thomas, inherited the Blechingley properties along with the manor of Oxted and Barrow, and from this time the Hoskins lived at Barrow (near Oxted), while retaining their Blechingley properties until about 1767.

A 1704 quit-rental record shows Sir William Hoskins, Knight, renting the house and farm lands to John Russell (house 6s, farmland £3 6s 8d)[1]. Around the time The Grange was rebuilt, Thomas Russell was renting it in 1738 at £99, tithe £9 18s, followed by John Russell in 1748. So it may be that three generations of the Russell family occupied Town Farm. James Collins was tenant from 1766 to 1774 and his rent in 1766 was £120 a year. Quit-rent was a fee paid by a tenant which released them from feudal obligations and guaranteed them exclusive use of the land. For example, nobody could hunt on the land without the tenant's consent.

In earlier days, farms and houses were often unnamed in records, as was the case with Town Farm in 1704. However the quit-rent which John Russell paid in 1704 stayed the same for over 100 years. The manorial court roll rent record of 1810 shows Mr John George Wilson Perkins of Pendell Court as owner of Town Farm: 'John Perkins acknowledged to hold freely of the lord a burgage messuage, farm and lands, 206 acres called Town Farm at yearly quit-rents of £3 6s. 8d. and 6s. relief when it happens, and duly paid the customary 1d. fine on entry.' Thus adding more evidence for John Russell's tenancy at Town Farm in 1704.

Mr John George Wilson Perkins had purchased the house and farm at auction (Garraways) in 1808/9 from the executors of the estate of Benjamin Booth Esq. (1732–1806) of Lincoln's Inn Fields, London. Benjamin was a director of the East India Company and an art collector. For more on the Hoskins and Perkins families, see page 144 onwards.

---

1 £3 6s 8d is three pounds, six shillings and eight pennies (translated as £3.33p in decimal coinage).

The Grange | Tudor to Victorian Overview | 73

Inscribed date on the front of The Grange – 23 June 1739
With the letters A M. It was discovered during renovation work in 2013 by contractors and Mr Martin Higgins. It can't easily be seen from the ground as it is near the top of the house. *Photo courtesy of Mr Martin Higgins.*

Collage of inscriptions on bricks at the front of The Grange

Charles Hoskins was the owner, and T • R is presumed to be Thomas Russell, who was a tenant to Charles Hoskins in 1738. The initialled bricks appear across the front ground floor wall of the house in a seemingly random fashion. They perhaps commemorate the rebuilding of the house and those who had an involvement or shares in the project. There is another letter alongside the single letter 'E', currently partially obscured by the flange of a boiler flue. Early photos of the front of the house indicate that the inscriptions had probably been hidden from early local history writers by climbing ivy, who made no mention of them. The Russells occupied other local properties and lands in the 1700s and they were, at times, churchwardens at St Mary's. There was more than one Thomas Russell in the 1700s.

Signature and seal, Thomas Russell – 1750
From the last will and testament of a Blechingley Thomas Russell, spelt 'Rufsell'.

The Tudor Chimney at The Grange, on which Uvedale Lambert Snr comments in 1921:

> The Hoskins' house, which was thus Town farm house, is now the Grange, and at its northern end still stands a fine external chimney built of firestone [or Reigate stone], strongly indicative of spoil taken from the remains of the castle, though the plinth and mason's work generally is too much weathered to retain any Norman adze marks [adze is a tool, similar to an axe]. Above the first floor this chimney has been rebuilt in two-inch mellow brick in English bond, doubtless as a casing to the mouldering firestone, in the early seventeenth-century days, while the whole top of the stack naturally dates from far more modern repairs and alterations, which have effectively disguised the antiquity of the chimney as seen from the road. But this chimney quite possibly dates back to Sackville ownership of Henry VIII's time, while the oak panelling, which was found some years ago in the room behind it, was no doubt put up by the Hoskins owners in early Stuart days. [The Stuart period was 1603–1714. English bond is the oldest form of brick bonding in England, popular until the late 1600s, consisting of alternate rows of headers and stretchers].

The Grange, north chimney – 1979
The newer Victorian chimney on the left has a much smaller stone plinth, built in a soft crumbly stone, probably firestone, no doubt added to complement the older one. © *Surrey History Centre*.

Today the old chimney's stone plinth (base) section is rendered over with cement. Oak panelling and an inglenook fireplace are listed in the 1915 Inland Revenue Valuation Office Survey of The Grange. In 2023 there was plywood on the walls in the room behind this chimney, which may be hiding the inglenook and the oak panelling. The lower section of this chimney certainly appears to be older than the rest of the house and the old oak panelling suggests there might be other remnants of an earlier house. Mr Martin Higgins commented, 'If the fire hearths to the chimney were opened up, more evidence might be found to confirm its antiquity.'

The Grange, north chimney – 2020
Its plinth rendered over with cement. The newer Victorian chimney, squeezed in on the left, cuts slightly across the lower corner of the top-floor window.

Close-up of brick bond on the north chimney – 2023
Showing the two-inch mellow bricks in English bond. Vertical galleting stones can be seen in the corner cement joint between the brickwork and tiles on the right.

Town Farm is a common name for a farm near the centre of a town or village. John Hassell labels the farmhouse in 1822 as 'Manor court house of Blechingley called town or Tan house farm Surrey'. There were once fields called Tanners Field and Tanners Shaw, and it is likely that the manor court was held here at one time. Before 1800 the court was held at what is now Court Lodge Farm (p. 46) near St Mary's Church in Church Lane. The White Hart Inn was also host to the manor court at a later date.

The dictionary definition for Grange is generally 'a large house in the countryside with farm buildings connected to it, from grain, grain house, granary'. Buildings with the name

Grange often have ecclesiastical connections. The official listed buildings entry for The Grange dates it circa 1700, Grade II listed, first listed in 1984.

Surrey County Council plaque on the front of The Grange

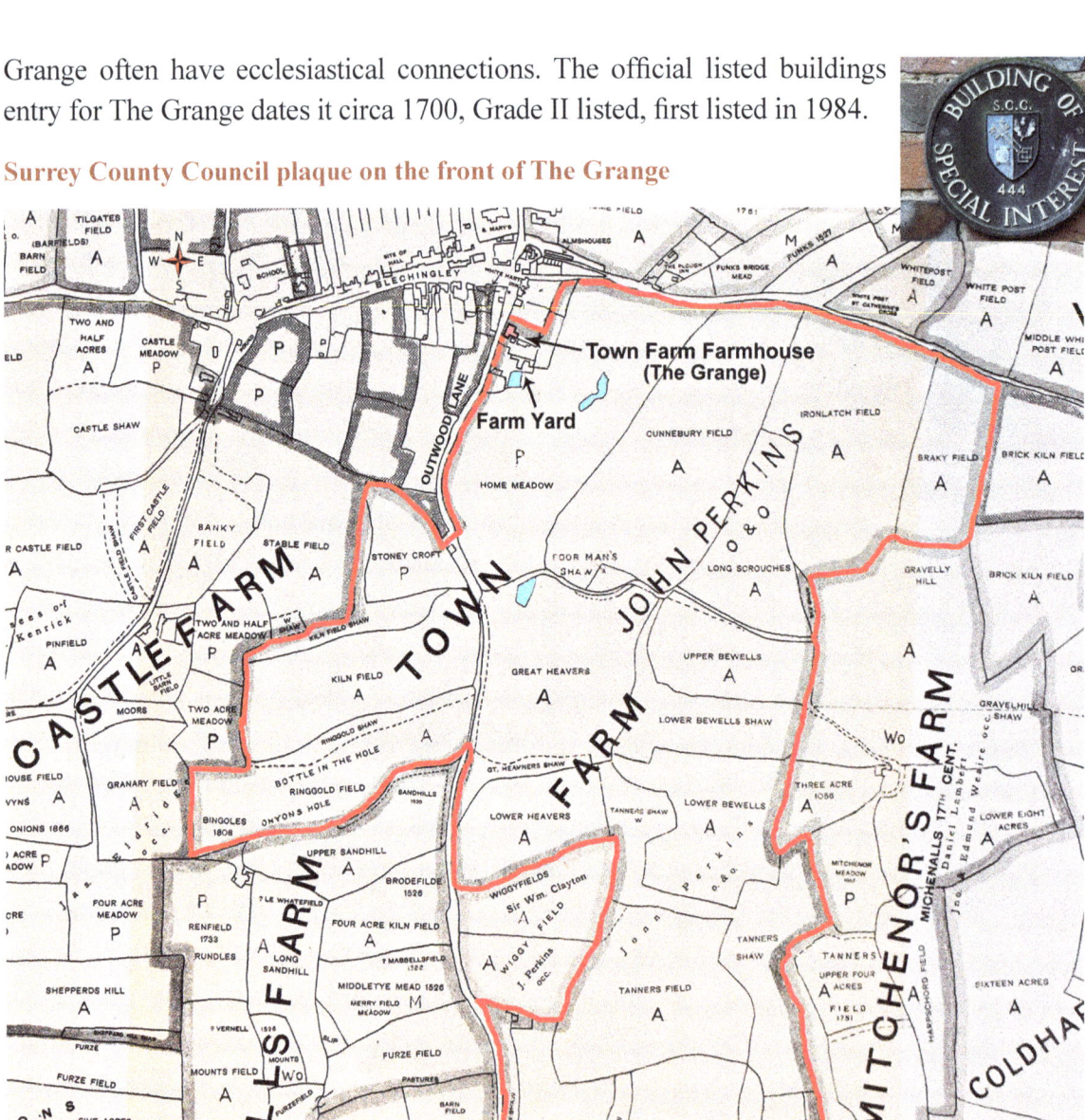

Uvedale Lambert Snr's Bletchingley tithe map – 1841
Copied from Blechingley Parish Council's copy in 1911, with his and this author's annotations, showing The Grange and Town Farm land within the red border. Key: A – arable; P – pasture; O&O – owner & occupier; OCC – occupier; Wo – woodland.

Town Farm covered 206 acres of Blechingley in 1841 and was owned by John Perkins Esq., Lord of the Manor of Blechingley, who was based at nearby Pendell Court. The Perkins family owned Town Farm from 1809 to 1855. Many of the current houses in Outwood Lane were Town Farm fields at this time, as was the White Post housing estate and Blechingley Village Primary School, off Rabies Heath Road. The housing estate and school were built after a government compulsory purchase of Town Farm land around 1950.

The Grange from the southeast – 2020
Illustrating the current layout and other properties with historic connections.

The annotations show: 1) Town Farm stone barn, now two dwellings in Town Mead; 2) Town Farm cowsheds, now part of dwellings in Town Mead; 3) Town Farm black weatherboarded barn, now two dwellings in Town Mead; 4) Former Town Farm farmhouse, built after 1866, now a private dwelling called Town Farm; 5) The Grange driveway, former stable yard; 6) southern single-storey extension, former doctor's waiting room and larder, now part of 3, The Grange; 7) former coach house, now part of 4, The Grange; 8) former stables, now 5, The Grange; 9) rear single-storey extension, former scullery/utility room, now part of 4, The Grange; 10) The Grange main house, farmhouse to Town Farm before 1866; 11) High Bank Cottage in Outwood Lane, formerly The Grange western plot-plantation; 12) Grange Close, with detached houses built in 1987/9, formerly Grange garden land; 13–14) 9 and 7 Outwood Lane, site of two circa sixteenth-century cottages (the Dewdney Cottages), which belonged to the Leslie family, Grange owners from 1867 to 1924.

The Grange, south courtyard – 2019
The tiled canopy roofs on the right probably gave cover to servants walking from scullery to coal house. The scullery door (now bricked up) on to the courtyard was under the smaller canopy nearest the centre of the photo. The black door on the right was one of two coal house doors, now front door to 4 The Grange. The small tiled roof canopy on the left (above the steps) is a modern addition.

The Grange, south courtyard – 1979
© Surrey History Centre.

The main house is now three homes – 1, 2 and 3 The Grange. The single-storey south extension was probably built shortly after 1822 to replace a timber building seen in the 1822 John Hassell watercolour. The larder section of this extension shows external evidence of being a further add-on, perhaps done in the 1860s when the doctor's waiting room was created. The single-storey east extension is probably a Victorian addition and was originally the scullery, where pots and pans were cleaned and clothes laundered. Scullery maids, sometimes called scullions or skivvies, did the most menial work in the house, hence the phrase 'I'm not your skivvy'.

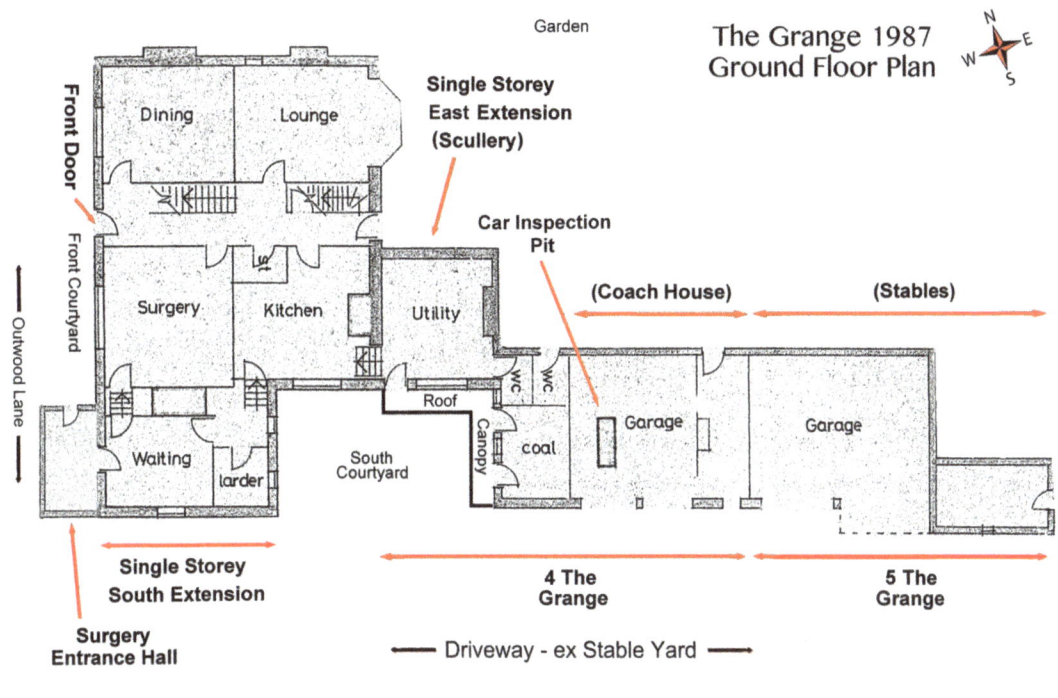

Plan of The Grange – 1987
Before it was split into five units, showing the coach house, stables and scullery/utility at the rear, now cottages 4 and 5 The Grange.

Old plinth of the south-facing wall of The Grange – 2019
View from the south courtyard. A patchwork of materials, including ironstone and pieces of brick, are possibly a remnant of an earlier house. The small stones in the mortar joints are galleting stones, frequently referred to in Surrey as garneting, which were inserted into the wet mortar joints at the time of construction. They can be seen in other areas of the house. It is thought they were used to strengthen the joints, but are also decorative. Folklore has it that they ward off evil spirits.

Galleting in the stonework of The Grange's former scullery – 2020
On the east-facing side of the single-storey rear extension (former scullery), view from the garden. This style could have led to the use of the term garneting or garnets in Surrey. Alec Clifton-Taylor, in *The Pattern of English Building* (1972) described them as looking like little necklaces strung on the wall of a building. The untidy blue and red brickwork between the satellite dish and the window marks the position of a former chimney on the main house.

Nos. 4 and 5 The Grange, part of the former coach house and stables, were described in an 1866 auction catalogue as 'Capital Stabling for Four Horses with Coach House adjoining, and Man's Room over'. The man's room was a type of flat, typically above stables or a coach house, where the coachman or other related staff would have lived. A large walk-in coal house was built on one end (west) of the coach house, and the stables were attached to the other end (east), with the man's room above the coach house. The buildings are constructed in soft red brick in Flemish bond (popular in the UK from around 1700), with extensive modern brickwork added at the time of the 1987/9 redevelopment. They were probably originally Town Farm timber stables, and are shown on the 1841 tithe map as detached from the main house.

The January 1851 *Sussex Agricultural Express* records a fire breaking out in a tiled barn on Town Farm (the stone barn on the west side today). It mentions that the fire spread to the cow sheds but was prevented by firemen from reaching the stables on the north end of the cattle sheds, and the barn and buildings on the east of the yard. On an 1866 auction catalogue plan, and later maps, the stables/coach house are shown as attached to the house, with a slightly different footprint and position compared with earlier maps. The original stables were probably rebuilt (with coach and coal houses added) around 1863/5 by Robert Birkbeck, after the Grange was separated from Town Farm and adapted as a doctor's/gentleman's house. With the advent of the motor car the buildings were eventually used as garages.

View from the south: The Grange, Town Farm and Grange Cottage – c. 1920
L-R: Town Farm, with its new farmhouse, built 1866–70; The Grange, the original farmhouse with its four towering chimneys and coach house and stables attached to the rear (east); Grange Cottage (on the extreme right edge) where the gardener lived. St Mary's Church is in the centre background. *Section of frontispiece photo from volume one of Uvedale Lambert Snr's 1921 book. Photographer Jarvis Kenrick.*

No. 4 The Grange is now a two-bedroom, two-storey cottage, created in 1987/9 when the utility room (ex-scullery), coal house and coach house, were combined. The coach house originally had an inside timber staircase to the first floor (man's room), where Philippa Marshall, resident from 1952 to 1987, had wooden racks and boxes for storing fruit picked from the gardens. She also used the building as an equestrian tack room (storage of saddles, harnesses, etc.). The current entrance hall to No. 4 was part of the coal house, which would have serviced the many fire hearths at The Grange. In the 1970s, hot coal embers in a waste bin started a fire in the coal house, which severely damaged the building. The top section of the coach house was rebuilt in a simpler form, three or four feet lower.

The Grange, coach house – c. 1915
As it looked before the 1970s fire. The coach house is the building with the hayloft ladder on the side.

The Grange, coach house/coal house after the 1970s fire – 1979
Showing the rebuilt roof section, now missing the very top hipped roof section, chimney, dormer window, man's room, hayloft and ladder.
© *Surrey History Centre*.

The Grange, stables/coach house block – 1979
After the 1970s fire and rebuild; the ex-stables is on the right with the Mini in the doorway. Part of the old stable extension can be seen in the extreme right-hand lower corner of the photo.
© *Surrey History Centre*.

No. 5 The Grange, originally the stable block with a door through to the coach house. It probably had two large entrance doors and separate stalls for the horses. Recent damp proofing work in the east and west walls revealed horizontal timber wall plates three feet above floor level, with some English bond

brickwork below. The stable block is now a two-bedroom, two-storey cottage.

The Grange, stables – 1983
With the little extension stable on the far right. *From a section of a photo by local photographer Alan Lyell (the complete photo can be seen on page 105).*

A modern two-storey extension on the east end was built in 1987/9 as a garage with a bathroom above it, and was constructed to match in with the existing brickwork. It was converted to a bedroom in 2015. The extension replaced a small, single-storey, attached brick stable/shed, which had a split stable door and was home to a pony during the Marshall family's residency (1952–87).

Rear of The Grange – 2017
No. 4 The Grange is on the left, and No. 5 to the right. The right-hand section of No. 5 (with the patio and satellite dish) was added in 1987/9, as an extension garage, with bathroom above, to replace a smaller brick stable/shed extension, converted to bedroom/dayroom in 2015.

The Grange 1841 | Farmhouse on Town Farm

In 1841 The Grange was simply known as Town Farm, the farmhouse to Town Farm, owned by John Perkins Esq. The tithe map has plot numbers and a separate list, called the apportionment list, with names of owners and tenants, field names, and details of rents and tithes and so on. The tithe, or 'tenth', system was a church tax. Residential buildings are shown in pink and commercial or farm buildings are in grey.

Tithe map for Blechingley, section – 1841/3
With author's annotations. *Tithe map © The National Archives, Kew, London.*

94) Forge Cottage and the Forge.

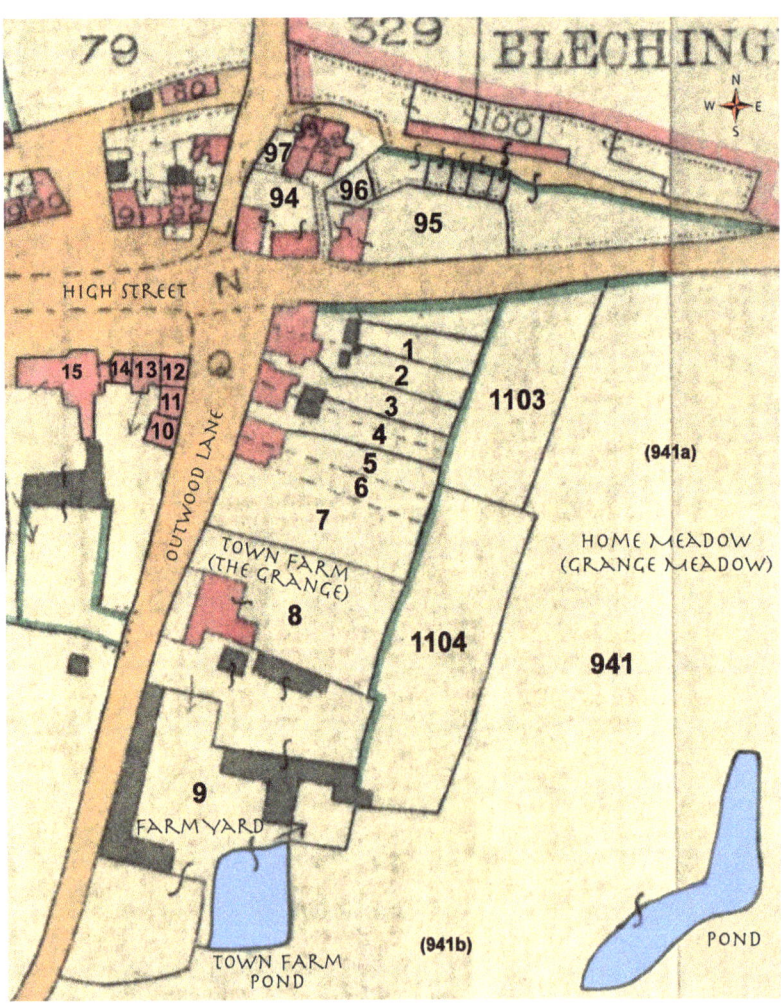

95–96) Land and Forgeside.
97) Cottage and Garden (94 to 97 were owned by the Wren blacksmith/publican family in 1841).
10–14) Kings Cottages, circa sixteenth-century, named after the nineteenth-century owner James King, publican at the White Hart Inn next door. The cottages were demolished in 1899/1900, and replaced with Bank Buildings.
15) White Hart Inn.
1–2) Prince Albert public house and Prince Albert Cottage.
3) Oxstall House.
4) Old Cottage (later Eddolls Butcher).

5–6) Two cottages dating from circa 1500, which I call the Dewdney Cottages, as they were owned by Richard Dewdney in 1841. They were purchased with The Grange in 1867 by Walter Alexander Leslie.

7) Private garden, owned by James Apted. By about 1855 it had been merged with The Grange and remained part of the walled garden until the 1987/9 redevelopment, when it was swallowed up by the newly built Grange Close and two houses – Nos. 1 and 2 Grange Close.

8) Farmhouse and garden, owned by John Perkins Esq., later to be known as The Grange. Showing two Town Farm buildings in grey immediately adjacent to the house, where the coach house, coal house and stables were probably rebuilt in the 1860s.

9) Town Farm yard and farm buildings, owned by John Perkins Esq.

1103) Town Farm orchard, owned by John Perkins Esq. The plot was added to The Grange garden in the 1860s, and the gardener's cottage was built there (now Grange Cottage).

1104) Town Farm orchard, owned by John Perkins Esq., added to The Grange garden in the 1860s.

941) Home Meadow, owned by John Perkins Esq. The Meadow was divided into two in the 1860s. The northern end (941a) was leased with The Grange for a while and was given to the village in 1929 as Grange Meadow Sports Ground, which it still was in 2023. The southern end (941b) stayed with Town Farm and was used for grazing cattle; it is now called Town Meadow and is still used for grazing.

The Grange 1861 | From Farmhouse to Home and Medical Practice

The earliest that the farmhouse was referred to as 'The Grange' was on the 1861 electoral roll, where John Henry Sharp Esq. was listed as leaseholder 'The Grange-on-Town Farm'. Whether he had any involvement in Town Farm is not clear. He was listed with the profession of fund-holder, that is, he was wealthy and living on his own means/investments. In later years he was listed as a businessman and justice of the peace in Sussex. Uvedale Lambert Snr says that The Grange was separated from Town Farm under Edward Birkbeck's ownership in 1866. However, The Grange deeds and records list the owner as Robert Birkbeck, with Edward, his brother, as one of the mortgagees. It seems the separation happened shortly before 1866.

The following is a fictional diary account, interwoven with some actual dates, facts and events to give a possible scenario for the evolution of The Grange. Some newspaper articles of the day mention that Robert Birkbeck was considered to be a gentleman of good character.

THE DIARY OF ROBERT BIRKBECK

15th December 1863. I became acquainted with Surgeon-Major Leslie at the Portland Club in Piccadilly. Mr Leslie is a man with a most confident disposition and has an excellent knowledge of the arts and music. In the course of polite conversation, I discovered that he had recently returned from serving in the 35th Regiment of Foot, in India, and that he was in search of a suitable country house in which to establish his new medical practice, and to accommodate his family. He was anxious to establish his practice before his imminent retirement from the army. It later occurred to me that my recent acquisition of Town Farm in Blechingley, which has a handsome farm house, might be suitable for Mr Leslie. My current tenant, John Sharp Esq., has given notice to vacate, thereby presenting an opportunity to accommodate Mr Leslie. Over the following days we corresponded, to which end we arranged to meet at Blechingley in January.

25th February 1864. I submitted a proposal to Mr Leslie: The Grange will be completely separated from the farm, some farm land is to be added to provide ample pleasure gardens surrounded by a lofty wall and hedges. There will be French style doors onto the pleasure gardens, and a summer house will be erected overlooking the very picturesque meadow of some seven acres, suitable for use as a paddock and recreation, along with fruit and kitchen gardens, and a new cottage for the gardener. Furthermore, a coach house and stabling for four horses will be provided. The doctor's surgery area will be fashioned to Mr Leslie's design, and the house is to be completely decorated and adapted in keeping with the standards of a gentleman. We later reached an agreement on a rental of one hundred and sixty two guineas, and it was agreed that Mr Leslie would take possession of the property after the works were completed to his satisfaction in January of 1865.

27th August 1865. I was pleased to hear from my new tenant at The Grange, Surgeon-Major Leslie, who reports that his practice is growing, and that his family are happily settled in their new home.

20th January 1868. The unforeseen and regrettable events of 1866 in the City, which *The Times* rather sensationally referred to as 'Black Friday', brought the happy arrangement with Mr Leslie to a rather unseemly and abrupt end when I was obliged to sell my Blechingley properties at auction in November 1866, to service some of my liabilities. However, I am happy to report that Mr Leslie was able to complete the purchase of the freehold interest in The Grange in December last year at a most agreeable consideration, through Messrs Turquand & Harding, thereby securing his practice and residency. For my part, in these most vexing of times, I am exceedingly blessed to be in receipt of the most gracious support of my family and friends, to whom I am eternally indebted, and thankful to God.

The Grange, French doors – 2020
At the rear of The Grange, added in the 1860s by Robert Birkbeck. The steps, walls and pillars are original. There was a further set of steps below this point, which were demolished in 1987/9. An 1866 plan shows a summer house further down the garden, which was demolished at some point.

An ornate garden wall was built by Mr Birkbeck at the front (west) of The Grange on Outwood Lane, which can be seen in photos from the early 1900s. The wall extended around the north and south borders. The east border, adjoining the meadow (Grange Meadow), consisted of hedges and fences. The front section of the wall on Outwood Lane was demolished in the 1987/9 redevelopment. In 2023 the wall still ran along the south and east (rear) borders of No. 9 Outwood Lane, then along the east (rear) borders of 7, 5, 3, and 1 (the former Prince Albert public house) Outwood Lane, and around the borders of Grange Cottage. The length of the original wall from The Grange driveway (former stable yard) to Grange Cottage, was about 200 metres, and up to about 12 feet high. See page 93 for a plan showing the wall, and pages 97–98 for early photos.

Grange Cottage, 1 High Street – 2021
Formerly the gardener's cottage. Photo taken from the north side of High Street, showing the old Grange boundary wall.

The Grange, old boundary wall – 2021
On the forecourt of 3 Grange Close (behind the modern lower curved wall). Behind this lofty wall is the garden of 7 Outwood Lane.

The Grange 1866 | The Blechingley Auction and Black Friday

The Grange was caught up in the fallout of the collapse of one of London's 'top drawer' banking institutions, Overend Gurney and Co Ltd, and was put up for auction in 1866, along with many other local properties and lands. This is the story of how it came about.

Thirty-year-old Robert Birkbeck owned Town Farm and Grange in 1866. He had purchased it from Thomas Fowler Wood in 1861, with a mortgage provided by his two brothers, Edward and William, along with Sir John Lubbock (Robert's father-in-law) and Neville Lubbock, who were all bankers. Robert had previously lived in Blechingley, but in 1866 he was living at Nutwood, in Gatton, near Reigate, Surrey. Robert Birkbeck and Henry Edmund Gurney were the joint managing directors of Overend Gurney and Co Ltd. Robert's brother Edward was living in Nutfield, near Blechingley, around 1863, and brother William was a banker living in Norwich. The Gurney family owned extensive property in Nutfield.

Overend Gurney and Co Ltd were the largest bill brokers/wholesale discount banks in the City of London, known as the 'banker's bank'. On Thursday 10 May 1866 at 3.30pm, a note appeared on their doors, announcing that payments were suspended. Large crowds gathered outside their offices in Lombard Street, and the following day there was a run on the banks in London and other parts of the UK. Their debts were said to be around £11 million. In the financial crisis that followed, around 200 companies failed, including banks.

Robert Birkbeck owned other local properties in 1866, but our interest is limited to his ownership of Town Farm with its farmhouse (The Grange) and outbuildings; Home Meadow (now Grange Meadow); the gardener's cottage (now Grange Cottage); and a joined pair of circa sixteenth-century cottages, next to The Grange in Outwood Lane, which I refer to as the Dewdney Cottages. These and other properties were put up for auction in 1866, by order of the liquidators of Overend Gurney and Co Ltd. At the time of the auction, Walter Alexander Leslie (Surgeon-Major Leslie) was tenant at The Grange with its outbuildings, gardens and the meadow at the rear. For more on Outwood Lane and the Dewdney Cottages, see page 126.

Two local auctions were advertised in 1866, one dated 14 November for Blechingley properties of 742 acres, to be sold in 9 lots; the other dated 7 November 1866, for

Nutfield properties, which included farms, buildings, a mansion, houses and cottages, totalling 1,050 acres, to be sold in 29 lots. The auction venue was The Auction Mart, Tokenhouse Yard, near the Bank of England in London. The auctions were advertised in the *Pall Mall Gazette* of 13 October 1866, and the *Brighton Gazette* of 18 October 1866. The auctioneer was Messrs Norton Trist and Co, with instructions from Messrs Turquand & Harding, the liquidators of Overend Gurney and Co Ltd. Robert Birkbeck's Blechingley properties were among those to be auctioned as per the following abbreviated newspaper advertisements [with author comments]:

Lot 1 – CASTLE FARM and buildings –160 acres.

Lot 2 – The Town Farm and Mitchener's Farm, the whole containing 232 acres, 0 roods, 3 perches, in hand [vacant possession]. Offering some charming sites for the erection of a residence. [Mitchener's Farm was adjoining Town Farm. There was no residence/farmhouse on Town Farm, as its farmhouse, The Grange, had been recently separated].

Lot 3 – COLDHARBOUR AND PART OF UNDERHILLS, with buildings, brick yard, and kiln – 213 acres.

Lot 4 – UNDERHILLS FARM – 113 acres.

Lot 5 – LAND near the Red Lion public house – 5 acres.

Lot 6 – A VERY COMFORTABLE RESIDENCE, with Capital Stabling, Coach-House, tastefully-disposed pleasure-grounds, large kitchen and fruit gardens, gardeners cottage and small plantation. The whole containing 1 acre, 0 roods, 26 perches, let to W.A. Leslie as yearly tenant [The Grange, lot 3 on plan].

Lot 7 – TWO FREEHOLD COTTAGES, with gardens, situate fronting the road, adjoining lot 6, let to weekly tenants. [Circa sixteenth-century cottages, the Dewdney Cottages, lot 4 on plan].

Lot 8 – AN ENCLOSURE OF MEADOW LAND situate in the rear of lot 6 [The Grange], having an important frontage to the road, from Redhill to Godstone, containing 6 acres, 2 roods, 24 perches. [The meadow land was called Home Meadow, later to be Grange Meadow].

Lot 9 – FIVE FREEHOLD COTTAGES with gardens, adjoining the White Hart Inn. [Lot 6 on the plan. These were later owned by James King, landlord at the White Hart, and known as King's Cottages, probably sixteenth-century buildings, it's likely that he purchased them via this auction. They were on the corner of Outwood Lane and the High Street; demolished around 1900 and replaced with Bank Buildings].

The Times of 12 May 1866 referring to the day following the closure: 'Altogether, and for many reasons, the occasion and the day will probably long be remembered in the City of London as Black Friday'.

'The assault on the bank of Overend Gurney, in Lombard Street, London' – 1866
Sketch by M. Hobblethwaite. *From the front page of* L'Illustration, *French news periodical, 19 May 1866.*

After protracted investigations and hearings, the directors of Overend Gurney and Co Ltd were tried by jury at the Old Bailey, London, in December 1869, for fraud by way of converting to a limited company while they were insolvent, and for making false statements in the prospectus for the offering of shares in 1865. Those in the dock were: John Henry Gurney; Henry Edmund Gurney; Robert Birkbeck; Henry Ford Barclay; Henry George Gordon; and William Rennie. The jury returned a verdict of not guilty. The Lord Chief Justice, Sir Alexander Cockburn, commented that the directors were guilty of 'grave error', rather than criminal behaviour. So none of the directors went to jail – much like modern failed bankers.

Sir Alexander Cockburn was a somewhat controversial character. He acquitted Lieutenant Henry Hawkey in 1846 of killing James Seton in a pistol duel. Seton was the last British person to be killed in a pistol duel in the United Kingdom. Several prime ministers offered to nominate Alexander for a peerage, and he finally accepted the offer in 1864. However, Queen Victoria refused, noting that 'this peerage has been more than once previously refused upon the ground of the notoriously bad moral character of the Chief Justice'.

Sir Alexander Cockburn, Lord Chief Justice – 1866
© National Portrait Gallery.

Many of the casualties of 'Black Friday' were obliged to sell their private estates, including the Birkbeck and Gurney families. A newspaper article mentions that 'Mr Gurney's Nutfield properties realised £150,800 at auction', which was considered to be a fair price. The Gurney Bank of Norfolk had started a new partnership two weeks before the collapse of Overend and Gurney, so they emerged unscathed and continued in the banking business. The Gurney Bank was one of the founding partners of Barclays Bank in 1896.

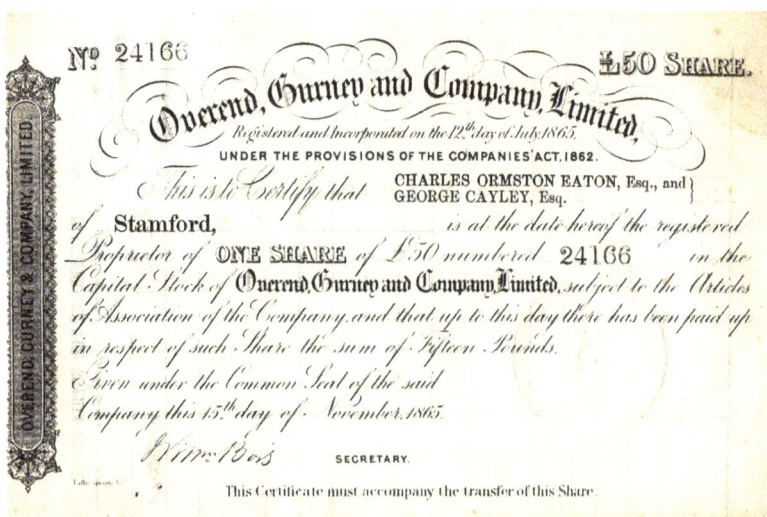

Overend, Gurney and Company Limited share certificate 100,000 of these £50 shares were offered to the public. £15 was paid to purchase one share before the company was formed. The balance of £35 could be called in if the company required it. Unfortunately, shareholders not only lost their £15 investment, but were obliged to pay the balance of £35 after the collapse of the company. £50 was equal to about £5,000 in 2022. *Property of the author.*

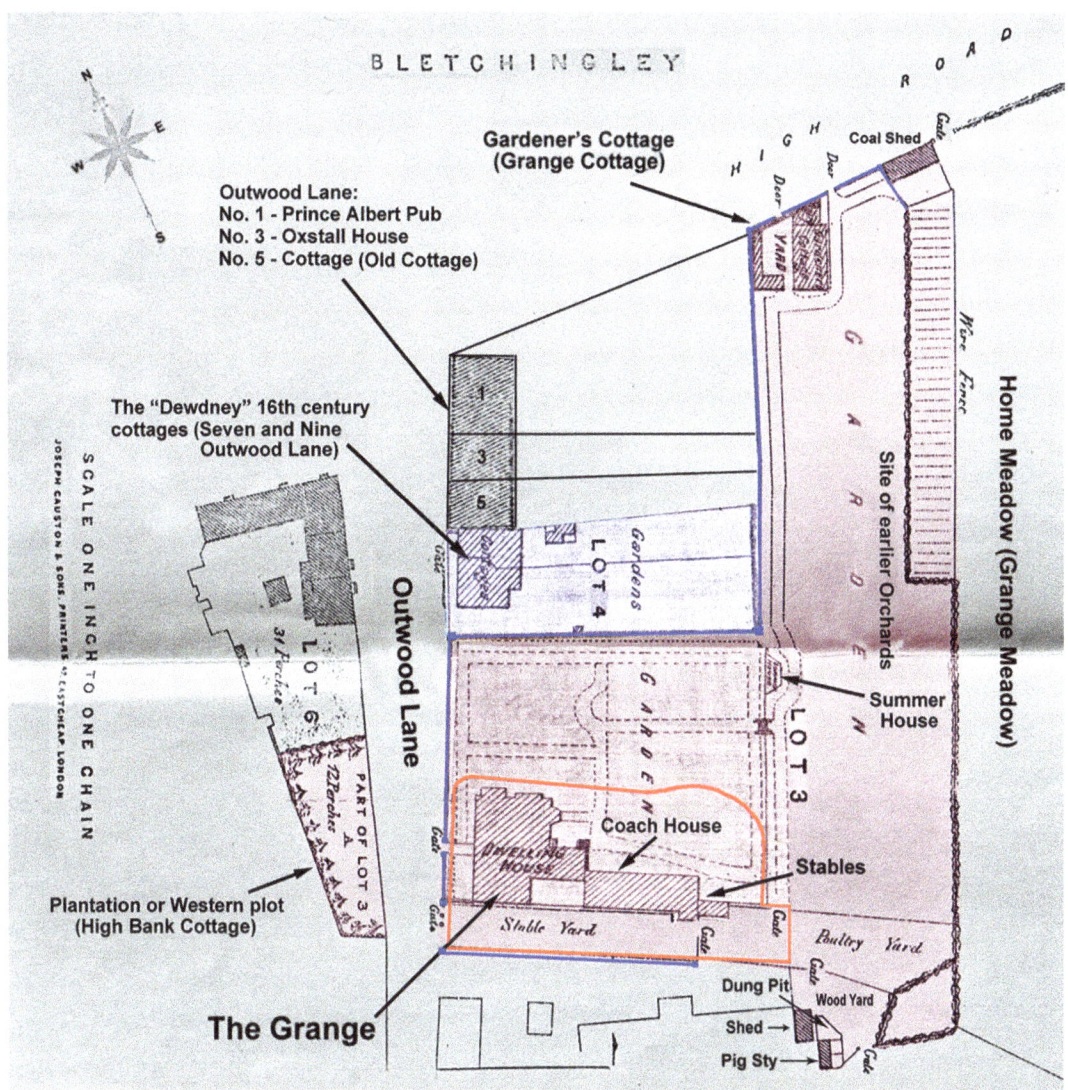

Plan of The Grange – 1866
From the auction catalogue, with author's annotations. Walter Alexander Leslie purchased lots 3 and 4 (in pink and blue). The blue line marks the 1866 boundary walls, the right-hand (east) boundary consisted of hedges and fences. The red line marks the approximate boundary of The Grange site in 2023.

Town Farm itself, along with Mitchener's Farm, (also known as Michenalls/Mitchenors/Mitchenells etc.) was purchased by Henry Thomas Lambert JP in 1866 (the year of his wedding). His descendants still own a large part of the old Town Farm lands, now incorporated into Cuckseys Farm. James Norris purchased Castle Farm and built himself a 19-bedroom mansion on the top of the hill, which he named Castle Hill. It was partially demolished in the 1950s and then extended in about 2010. In 2023, it was called Castle Place and was situated at the end of a private lane at the end of Castle Square. For more on Castle Hill, see page 201.

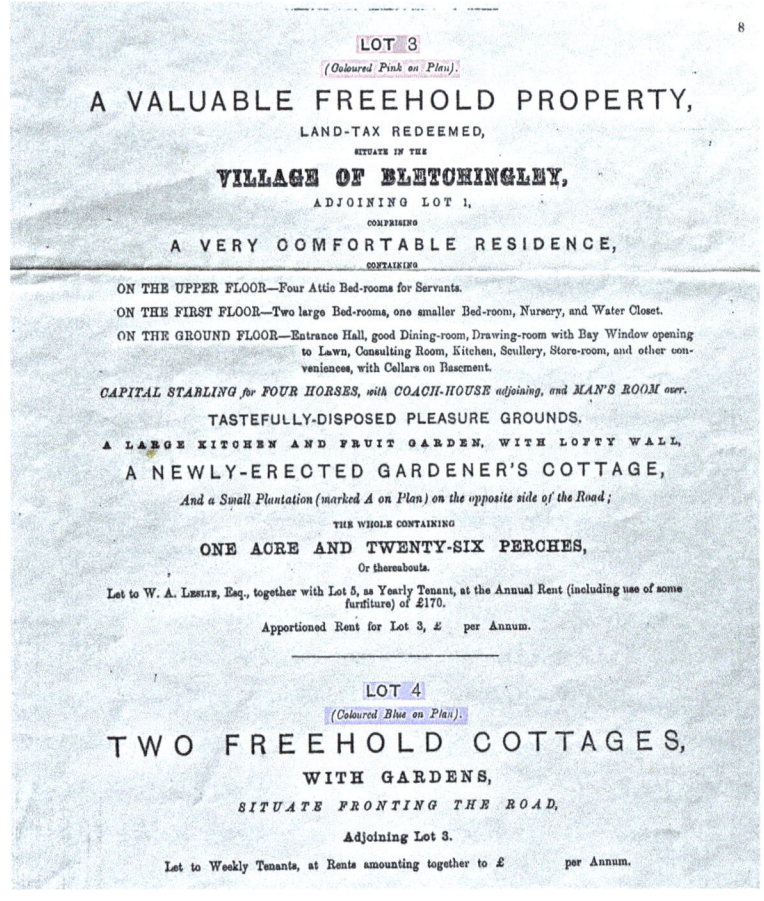

Blechingley auction catalogue page – 1866
W. A. Leslie Esq. (Surgeon-Major Leslie) is listed as a sitting tenant at lots 3 and 5 – The Grange and Home Meadow – paying an annual rent of £170, which included the use of some furniture. He subsequently purchased lots 3 and 4: The Grange site (without the meadow), and the two freehold cottages with gardens (the Dewdney Cottages). The sale was completed for a consideration of £2,470, on 31 December 1867. Home Meadow at the rear of the house (later to be Grange Meadow), was sold separately to the Reverend Charles Fox Chawner, rector at St Mary's Church, Blechingley. This is the only page of the auction catalogue we have. The lot numbers in the catalogue differ from newspaper listings, probably due to lots being sold by private treaty prior to the auction.

After the sale of The Grange to Walter Alexander Leslie in 1867, the layout, outbuildings and land stayed pretty much the same for many years. The Leslie family sold the adjoining Dewdney Cottages in 1906, and retained ownership of the rest of the property until 1924, when Doctor Frederick William Robertson's wife, Hope, purchased it. In 1952, Hope Robertson's son, Doctor Douglas Robertson, separated Grange Cottage (the gardener's cottage) from The Grange and sold it with one-third of an acre of land. For more on the Birkbeck family see page 157.

The Grange | Edward VII to Charles III

The Grange 1906–20 | The New Domesday Book Entry

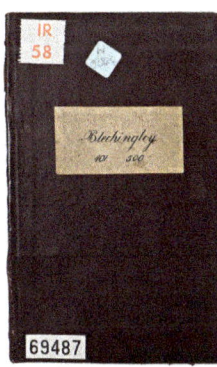

The Inland Revenue carried out a nationwide survey of properties from 1910 to 1915. It was part of the chancellor of the exchequer David Lloyd George's famous 'People's Budget' of 1909, coined the Lloyd George Domesday Survey. He went on to be prime minister from 1916 to 1922.

A surveyor would visit properties and make handwritten notes, often scribbled and abbreviated, in a field note book that was linked to an Ordnance Survey map.

Inland Revenue surveyor's field note book – 1915

The following is the field note book entry for The Grange, 21 January 1915:

Situation: The Grange, house, grounds, cottage and plantations.

Extent: 1 acre, and 26 perches [1.2 acres].

Occupancy: Tenant: Dr FW Robertson. Owner: Miss EM Leslie. Occupiers tenancy term: 7 or 14 or 21 years. Rent: £120. Tithe: 14 shillings (paid by owner). Gross site value: £2150. Rates, taxes, insurance and repairs paid jointly by owner and occupier.

Overview: Detached tiled house near centre of town. House with coal and gas in fair repair. Recent built shed with tiled hall [presumed to be the entrance hall/hut to doctor's surgery on the south end of the front courtyard of the house, now demolished].

Ground Floor: Tiled hall, dining room with panelled oak and inglenook fireplace, drawing room, consulting room leading to surgery, waiting room with matchboard, pantry, kitchen, three steps down to scullery.

First Floor: Landing, three bedrooms, bath dressing room, W.C.

Second Floor: Oak staircase, landing, five bedrooms.

Back: Walled garden with lawns, kitchen garden, fruit gardens, pig sty, basement with cellar, coal shed and 2 log boxes, small open yard, back tiled coal house.

Rear outbuildings: Garage with loft over, second garage and shed [now 4 and 5 The Grange].

Rear outbuildings: Detached tiled cottage, four rooms, washhouse in lean-to, coal store and back paved yard [Now Grange Cottage. Tiled house, tiled cottage, and tiled coal house is presumed to refer to the roof structure of the buildings].

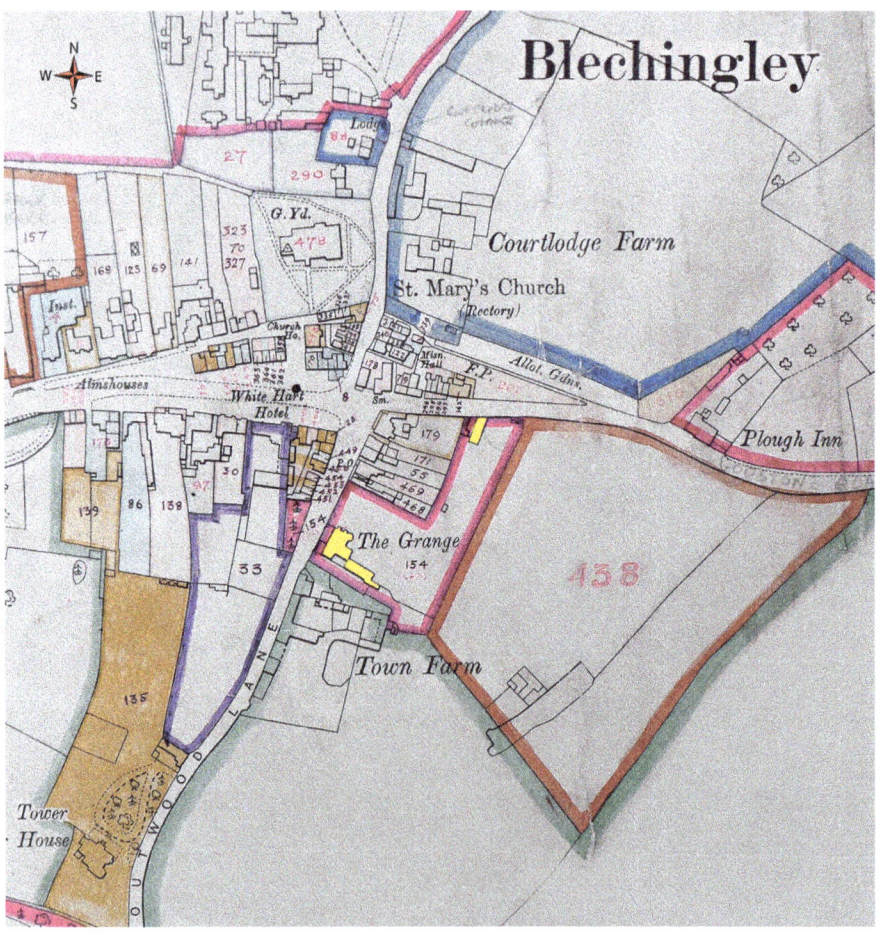

Inland Revenue Survey Map – 1911
The Grange land is within the pink borders near the centre of the map (plots 154). The Grange and Grange Cottage are highlighted in yellow. Grange Meadow (then called Town Meadow) is within the orange border, (plot 438). Town Farm is adjacent, within the green border.
© *National Archives, Kew, London.*

Outwood Lane, looking north – 1906
The Grange is on the right, when Dr. CA Robinson was the tenant. The front surgery entrance building (or hut) is behind the wall to the right of the two children by the pillar. In later years, the hut was the entrance for NHS patients, while private patients would use the main house entrance. The rear chimney, seen on the far right, was missing in 2023. On the far left is The Grange western plot or plantation, a bank with trees and a retaining wall, now High Bank Cottage (2023). The building in the distance, behind the girl with the cart/pram, is Wren's Forge in the High Street; a pair of horses with a cart can just be seen in front of it. To the left of the forge is Forge Cottage. © *The Francis Frith Collection. Colourised by author.*

Outwood Lane, looking south from the High Street – 1911
L-R: Oxstall House (3 Outwood Lane); Eddolls the Butcher (5 Outwood Lane); Post Office (7 Outwood Lane); Mount Pleasant and Blechingley Dairy (9 Outwood Lane). The Grange is behind the dairy shop's milk churn sign and the trees in the centre of the photo. The Victorian Town Farm farmhouse is just to the left of the cart, with attached cowsheds behind. The fields behind the gentleman driving the pony and trap is where the 16 Sackville Cottages were built in 1921. The Grange western plot or plantation, with its tall fir trees, is on the right, behind the pony and trap. Barclays Bank is on far right. © *The Francis Frith Collection. Colourised by author.*

The Grange – c. 1920
When Doctor Frederick William Robertson and family were tenants. On the right is the stable yard. At the front gate, on the road, is the 'carriage step', as I call it, which was still there in 2023. The whole of the ornate, 120-year-old front garden wall was sadly demolished in the 1987/9 redevelopment. *Photo taken by Doctor FW Robertson, three of his photos are in this book. Courtesy of his grandson Doctor Andrew Robertson. Colourised by author.*

The Grange 1971 | A Bird's-Eye View

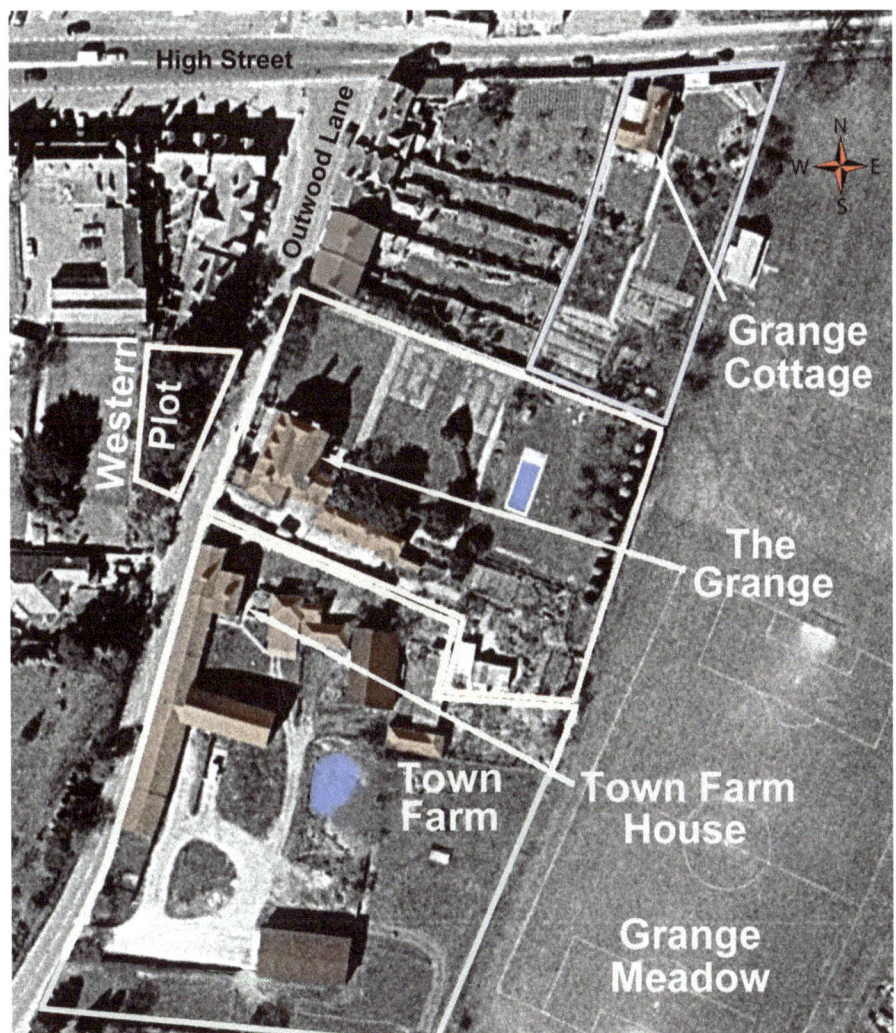

The Grange, aerial photo – 1971
Showing four plots and Grange Meadow on the right: Grange Cottage still had a large garden plot of one-third of an acre. In 1971 it was independently owned, having been separated from The Grange and sold in 1952. Nos. 3 Grange Close and 1a High Street were built in the garden of Grange Cottage in 1988/98. The Grange was owned and occupied by the Marshall family. The garden has a swimming pool to the right. The small western plot, or plantation, a walled earth bank with trees, is now High Bank Cottage (2023). Town Farm was intact but no longer a working farm. Today it is Town Mead, a residential cul-de-sac (2023). *Photo © National Collection of Aerial Photography (NCAP) Historic Environment Scotland, with author's annotations.*

The Grange 1987–2023 | From One Home to Eleven

In 1987 The Grange site was sold by the Marshall family to Raymond Foster Lettings Ltd for £160,000 for redevelopment. The house and its outbuildings were split into five separate dwellings, each with its own entrance. Grange Close was created in the main garden, with five large detached houses, and High Bank Cottage was built on the western plot in Outwood Lane.

Rear of The Grange – 2021
The nearest rear section of 5 The Grange (ex-stables), on the left, with the orange roses, looks old and in character, but it was actually quite skilfully built as an extension to match the rest of the building in 1987/9. It replaced a single-storey attached brick building, with a tiled roof, which had a stable door and was home to a pony during the Marshall family's time here (1952–87). The two roof dormer windows in the centre of the photo were added in 1987/9.

The main house was cleverly split into three dwellings, Nos. 1, 2, and 3. No. 1 occupies the whole front of the house on three floors, with three bedrooms. Nos. 2 and 3 are at the back of the house, each with two bedrooms. No. 3 has two bedrooms and two floors

– the old cellar and a first floor. No. 4, the ex-scullery/coach house/coal house, is a two-bedroom cottage. No. 5, ex-stables, is also a two-bedroom cottage.

High Bank Cottage was built slightly later on the western plot in Outwood Lane, due to initial planning refusals; planning was granted on appeal in 1992. Up to 1987 the western plot had been preserved as a picturesque walled bank with trees. A restrictive covenant concerning rights of light and air had been in place to prevent building near or on the plot and to maintain the outlook and privacy for The Grange owners. Presumably the covenant was discharged at some point as four new houses have been put up behind the cottage (2017/18 - De Clare Court).

The front of The Grange still appears as a grand detached house, with red and blue bricks on a brick plinth and hanging tiles on the upper levels. The Venetian windows on the front of the house, said to be original, are unusual in that the top centre windows are not the usual full semi-circle. Four of the original six chimneys remain, three on the main house and one on the rear single-storey extension (ex-utility/scullery). Some original internal period features remain, but generally the insides have been modernised. No. 2 The Grange has impressive exposed wooden roof timbers in a top-floor bedroom, and some of the fireplaces around The Grange are operational. Nos. 4 and 5 have been heavily altered internally and externally, with some new brickwork, doors, windows and staircases. A few old-looking, exposed wooden beams can be seen in No. 5. There is a small rear garden shared by the residents.

The Grange | Connected Properties and Institutions | Businesses

Blechingley Farm/Town Farm | Town Mead

The farmyard of Town Farm, known as Blechingley Farm in the eighteenth century, is now a private residential road called Town Mead, off Outwood Lane. After the original farmhouse (The Grange) was separated from the farm around 1863–5, a new farmhouse was built on the north-west corner of the farm yard, next to The Grange, now called Town Farm, a private home. Henry Thomas Lambert JP, of Sandhills, buyer of the farm in 1866, probably built the new farmhouse; it first appears on maps around 1870. Mr Lambert's first tenant farmer was James Flint and family, who were still there in 1898. The 1915 Inland Revenue Survey lists the farm as: 'Farm with 184 acres – owner H.C. Lambert – tenant U. Lambert – house with five bedrooms – two cottages – cart shed – coach house – barn – cow stalls – calf box – chaff room and granary'. Local farmer, Michael Uvedale Lambert, lived with his family in the farmhouse on Town Farm in the 1950s. His father, Henry Uvedale, converted some of the adjoining cow sheds to add two extra bedrooms to the house.

Sir Henry Charles Miller Lambert sold a plot of Town Farm land to Godstone Rural District Council (GRDC) in May 1920, to build the 16 Sackville Cottages in Outwood Lane, which were completed around 1921.[2] The cottages were built due to housing shortages. They were named by the housing committee after consulting with Uvedale Lambert Snr. Then around the end of the 1940s, 28 acres of Town Farm land was sold to GRDC under a government compulsory purchase order, to build the White Post

---

2 GRDC was the governing council for Blechingley; it has been Tandridge District Council since 1973.

housing estate and St Catherine's School (now Bletchingley Village Primary School), off Rabies Heath Road. The estate was completed in the 1950s. The loss of this land marked the beginning of the decline of Town Farm.

Under Lambert ownership the land was always farmed by a tenant. The last tenant retired in 1957 and the land was then attached to Cuckseys Farm and farmed by the tenant on that farm, except for Town Farm Meadow (formerly part of Home Meadow), which was farmed separately by Mr Selmes, the local butcher. By 1970 the farmyard buildings were being used for storage and other non-farming purposes.

Blechingley village aerial view from the south, looking north – 2020
1) Nos. 1 and 2 Sackville Cottages; 2) Town Mead, formerly Town Farm farmyard; 3) Stone barn in Town Mead, re-built (and cow sheds) after 1851 fire, now two dwellings; 4) Town Farm, former farmhouse to Town Farm, built 1866–70; 5) High Bank Cottage, Outwood Lane, formerly The Grange western plot; 6) Dew pond in Town Mead; 7) Black weatherboarded barn in Town Mead, probably the oldest farm building, now two dwellings; 8) The Grange and outbuildings, farmhouse to Town Farm before 1866; 9) Nos. 7 and 9 Outwood Lane, site of former Grange-owned properties; 10) Grange Close with five modern detached houses, formerly part of The Grange garden; 11) Grange Cottage, formerly The Grange gardener's cottage; 12) The old cricket pavilion in Grange Meadow.

Town Mead was created in the mid-1980s when Town Farm farmyard and buildings was sold by the Lambert family (Blechingley and Hathersham Estate Co Ltd) to developers. Some existing farm buildings were demolished and two of the barns, one of black weatherboard and one of stone, were converted into four dwellings. Nine new houses were built, and some other farm buildings were repurposed.

The converted farm buildings are not officially designated as historic listed buildings. The black weatherboarded barn may be the oldest remaining farm building, having some ancient-looking internal timber framing, today known as the Black Barn. Peter Grey, writing in 1975, said that the weatherboarded barn had a corrugated metal roof, with parts of an older thatched roof still visible. The aforementioned January 1851 *Sussex Agricultural Express* article reported that the tiled barn and the tiled cow stalls/sheds (west side of the farmyard) were destroyed in the 1851 fire, so the stone barn and cowsheds we see today were rebuilt. The Victorian farmhouse (built after 1866) remained intact and is now a separate private residence called Town Farm, with part of the cow sheds still incorporated. The house has a front entrance in Outwood Lane and a rear entrance in Town Mead. Town Mead was an early name for the farmland now occupied by Sackville Cottages, Sackville being the owner of the land in the early 1500s.

Town Farm and Hevers Pond from the south – c. 1915 The Grange can be seen at the rear of the farm, in the centre, between the two large barns. The spring-fed Hevers Pond is on the right. *From a Quinlan's Photo Series postcard with a postmark of 1917. Postcard produced and sold by Quinlan's Post Office and Library, book seller, stationer, and dealer in fancy goods, 32 High Street, Blechingley. Colourised by author.*

In 2023 there was a farm gate to the grazing meadow (Town Meadow) at the beginning of Town Mead and a permissive footpath to Grange Meadow. The original farm dew pond is still at the end of Town Mead. Despite the name, dew ponds are believed to have been fed by rainwater, as is this one. The pond is home to moorhens and the rare great crested newt has also been seen. The three willow trees by the pond were added at the time of the new development. The pond is maintained by the residents of Town Mead and Surrey County Council.

Town Farm, viewed across Town Meadow – 1983
Formerly Home Meadow. Part of Town Farm is to the left, with The Grange behind and St Mary's Church in the background. Doctor Mark and Philippa Marshall were living at The Grange at this time. *Photo courtesy of local photographer, Alan Lyell. This photo has also been published as a postcard.*

Town Mead dew pond – 2020
Just after the three willow trees had been pruned. The stone barn is on the left (rebuilt after the 1851 fire), and the black weatherboarded barn on the right. In the background, behind the left willow tree, the top of Town Farm (farmhouse built 1866–70) can be seen, and behind the centre tree is the top of The Grange (the original farmhouse).

Town Farm (ex-farmhouse) from Outwood Lane – 2020
L-R: south corner of The Grange and driveway; Town Farm (former farmhouse built 1866–70); former cowsheds (rebuilt after the 1851 fire), in Reigate stone with a slate roof. Some of the Sackville Cottages can be seen on the extreme right in the distance.

Grange Meadow | Bowls | Quoits | Blechingley Amateur Dramatics | Cricket | Hevers Pond | Ivy Mill

In the early 1800s Grange Meadow was part of a larger meadow on Town Farm called Home Meadow. The following are some history snapshots.

1863–8 The north end of Home Meadow was separated from the south end around 1863–5 by Town Farm owner Robert Birkbeck. The south end stayed with the farm and is still used for grazing and is known as Town Meadow (2023). The north end was leased with The Grange to Surgeon-Major Leslie in about 1865. When Robert Birkbeck's properties were put up for sale by auction, after the 1866 financial crash in London, it was listed as 'an enclosure of meadow land in the rear of lot six [The Grange], containing 6 acres, 2 roods, 24 perches [about 7 acres]'. The buyer was the Reverend Charles Fox Chawner, rector at St Mary's Church, who completed the purchase for £800 in May 1868.

1872 The north end of the meadow (now Grange Meadow) was still owned by Reverend Charles Fox Chawner. His tenant was Doctor William Henry Sargant, who was living at Berry House in the High Street. William had a surgery at Camden House, 50 High Street, from about 1829. For what purpose Doctor Sargant used the meadow is not known.

1915 The north end of the meadow was owned by Reverend J Hamton, with tenant Mr Weller of the Plough Inn (the Bletchingley Arms since 2015). It was described as, 'A level meadow of seven acres, being accommodation for fairs and grazing, with a rent of £35, and gross value of £750, including the buildings and structures.' Mr James Weller was residing at the Plough Inn, Blechingley, in 1911, age 22, listed as single, servant, handy-man, and licensed victualler (publican).

1929 Mr Edmund William Blessig of Garston Park (off Ivy Mill Lane, Blechingley), gifted the north end of the meadow to the National Playing Fields Association (NPFA), for use by Blechingley village as a sports ground. Mr Blessig's instructions were that it should be named Grange Meadow Sports Ground. It was leased to the newly formed Bletchingley Sports Association for one shilling (5p) per year, not as a public recreation ground, but for the use of the tennis, cricket and bowling clubs. Provision was later made for quoits, netball and hockey, with changing rooms and equipment provided. Mr Blessig stipulated that no persons under the age of sixteen were to use the facilities and that it should not be used for football. A children's recreation ground had been opened a few weeks earlier at Upper Tilgates Meadow (Stychens Lane), the gift of Mr and Mrs Atkinson Adam. The age restriction and the no-football rule were lifted by Mr Blessig in 1946. Uvedale Lambert Jnr says Mr Blessig purchased the meadow from Doctor Holman at The Grange, however, I have not found any records of Doctor Holman at The Grange, or in Blechingley, apart from one late-1800s newspaper article, which mentions Doctor Holman and family of Blechingley during a flu epidemic. I suspect that both these instances should have read 'Doctor Oldman', Grange resident from 1877 to 1904, who kept poultry and some cows.

The Grange Meadow Sports Ground opening ceremony was on 6 July 1929. Speaking at the event, Mr Blessig said: 'I purchased the meadow many many years ago with the intention of putting it to its present use, but it had taken a long time to complete the project due to many hurdles and heavy costs to make the bowling green and tennis courts.' Mr Blessig had always taken a keen interest in the Blechingley Cricket Club, who had previously used the meadow. Part of the inspiration for the sports ground had originated with Mr Blessig's wife Ella, who had always been anxious to start a much-needed tennis club and to assist in providing facilities in the village for the playing of games. She had been ill for some time but still managed to employ experts regarding the laying out of the ground before her death in 1927; she asked that her wishes be carried out in this respect. Tribute was paid to Mrs Blessig, 'who had been a very public-spirited woman whose charm and sympathy would be remembered most perhaps in all that she had done for the good of the residents in Blechingley'. Miss Nye, Ella's sister, who generously contributed to the cost of the works, said that the meadow project was always very close to her sister's heart. Miss Nye also mentioned Brigadier-General AH Cotes James, chairman of the committee for the construction of the meadow: 'he had been wonderful in pushing the scheme forward and surmounting many difficulties'. The ceremony was concluded with tea and refreshments in a marquee, after which the company proceeded to the bowls green, which Mr Blessig opened by playing several ends with Doctor Robertson [Doctor Frederick William Robertson OBE, of The Grange]. For more on Edwin William Blessig and Garston Park, see page 238.

Doctor Frederick William Robertson was president of the bowling club and meadow grounds committee chairman for a number of years. Some of the labour and funding for the layout of the field and construction of the facilities, which included draining and levelling the field, was provided by local residents. Further funding was received via grants from the Carnegie UK Trust and the NPFA.

Grange Meadow Sports Ground, opening day ceremony – 1929
1) Believed to be Walter Hubert Tobitt (known as Hubert), farmer at Sandhills and Pendell, who was also a cricket enthusiast. 2) Benjamin Ashdown, UK Grand Master of the Oddfellows in 1926, and clerk to Blechingley parish council for 38 years. 3) Edmund William Blessig Esq., farmer based at Garston Park. 4) Brigadier-General Alfred Henry Cotes James, of Waterhouse Farm. 5) Doctor Frederick William Robertson OBE, of The Grange. The lady on the far right edge of the picture may be Frederick's wife, Hope, who was present on the day, 6 July. Others present at the ceremony were: Miss Nye, Mr CE Mott, Mr W Jenkins, Mr and Mrs Kohn-Speyer, Mrs Bell, Mrs Wellesley, Mrs Turton Hart, Mr and Mrs C Clay. Mr and Mrs Hamilton Rowan, Mr and Mrs P Still, Mrs B Ashdown, Mrs WH Tobitt, Mr and Mrs CA Goodwin, Mr and Mrs AF Bristow, Mr and Mrs AE Martin, Mr and Mrs EW Pillinger, Mr and Miss Temple West, Mr J Kent, Mr and Mrs VP Lacroix, Mr and Mrs A Carter, Mr G Cooper, Mr and Mrs L Heath, and Messrs J White, H Bryant and J Gunn.[3]

Bowling at Blechingley – 1929
The gentleman at the rear with the beard looks like Mr Blessig. *Photo taken by Doctor Frederick William Robertson OBE.*

3 Article published in *The Surrey Mirror and County Post*, 12 July 1929. © Mirrorpix/Reach Licensing. Group photo courtesy of Derek Moore. Colourised by author. Some of the information was also obtained from the August 1929 edition of *St Mary's, Blechingley, Parish Magazine*.

In April 1938, at the annual general meeting of the Blechingley Sports Association, it was noted that, 'Mr J White had re-levelled and re-turfed the cricket pitch at a cost of £50, after a very dry summer'. The committee 'expressed their regret at the retirement of Mr Blessig from the office of president and tendered to him grateful thanks for all he had done for sport in the village during a great many years and for giving Grange Meadow to the National Playing Fields Association as a sports ground'.

Grange Meadow Sports Ground commemoration
This bronze plaque was fixed near the pavilion in 1938.

The Plough quoits team
Grange Meadow Quoits Pitch was laid out in 1938. Handwritten annotations on a copy of the original photo (with question marks) are L-R: Jack Hook; Ted Coppard; R Groombridge? Putland; Wren? Ted Bryant?; Alf Mann; Balcombe; Tom Carter; Tom? Jim Parsons; Tom Sivyer; Alf Charman; Tony Wilson. *Photo courtesy of the Blechingley Conservation and Historical Society. Colourised by author.*

In 1963 an extra piece of land was purchased by GRDC from the owners of Town Farm (Roger Lambert, Blechingley and Hathersham Estate Co Ltd) for £125 to extend the south end of the meadow for the football pitch. The green tin-looking building on the west side of the meadow was the original cricket pavilion (over-clad with timber since April 2021). Mr Blessig's instructions were that the pavilion was to remain the property of the cricket club.

Brigadier-General Alfred Henry Cotes James DSO, MVO, JP (1873–1947)
Of Waterhouse Farm, Blechingley. Chairman of the committee for the construction of Grange Meadow Sports Ground. He served in WWI and was the Divisional Warden for Diversion II of the ARP (Air Raid Precautions) in WWII. Division II covered Blechingley, Nutfield, South Nutfield, Horne, Smallfield, Outwood, Godstone and South Godstone. He was a well-known and popular public figure.
Photograph 1918 by Walter Stoneman, © National Portrait Gallery.

Bletchingley Amateur Dramatic Society (BADS) started in 1963. They rehearsed in Clerks Croft's Nursing Home (the old workhouse in Church Lane), while props were stored in a barn at Waterhouse Farm. Later, they had a permanent base in two temporary classrooms, adjacent to Grange Meadow, on the bank behind the current children's playground. St Catherine's School had previously occupied the classrooms, which were built by the Canadian Army during WWII. This is where sets were built and rehearsals took place. Regular performances were staged in the village hall on Thursday, Friday and Saturday evenings. Around August 1984 the classrooms were destroyed in an arson attack and a great deal of equipment was lost, which was when they moved to the vacant Scout hut at Grange Meadow, near the entrance. The hut was formerly used by the Army Cadets.

Before television became available to all, local entertainment was created by institutions, clubs and families. Local drama groups borrowed backstage staff and actors from each other as and when needed, they included: The Victoria League; The Young Conservatives; The Women's (evening) Institute, and St Mary's Players. The groups eventually amalgamated with BADS, which was renamed Bletchingley Players in the 1990s. They sadly closed in September 2019, due to a declining membership. Patron since 2012 was Dame Judi Dench, who lives in nearby Outwood. The old Scout hut at Grange Meadow is now home to the Arts Hub (2023).

The Book of the Month was BADS' first full-length production and tickets for the shows could be purchased from Allan and Betty Bristow at Taylor and Bristow (closed circa 1970) in the High Street, or from society members. Tickets were priced at seven shillings and sixpence (37.5p), five shillings (25p) and three shillings and sixpence (17.5p).

Bletchingley Amateur Dramatic Society, curtain call of *The Book of the Month* –
October 1963
By Basil Thomas. Cast L-R: Jean Risbridger (Hon Secretary, who often produced the plays and lived at Stychens Lane); Geoffrey Cowperthwaite (Hon Treasurer); Kay Winter (née Wilson); Frank Johnson; Doreen Reekie; Michael House; Betty Selmes (of the village butchers family); Stanley Hurrell (committee member). The producer was Mrs Paddy Martin (The Players' business manager, wife of farmer Frank, who lived at Lake Farm). Gerald Risbridger and Frank Martin were listed in later programmes as in charge of lighting and music, with Ingrid Risbridger as properties manager and Barbara Cowperthwaite as make-up. *Photo courtesy of the Bletchingley Players.*

Some of this information has been kindly provided by Marian Buck, née Wilson, former chair of BADS, pictured in the 1964 photo of *My Three Angels* with her mother Mary and brother Michael. Her family moved to Blechingley in 1936, to a house built by her father. Eleven members of Marian's family across three generations have been involved with BADS/Bletchingley Players, from 1963 to 2019. Their roles included chairing the committee, acting, front of house, set design and building. Marian met her future husband, John Buck, at the 1974 AGM and they were married in 1975. Many of the Bletchingley families involved in the productions – such as Selmes, Martin, Bristow and Risbridger – have long family roots in the village.

Productions were reviewed by local newspapers. *My Three Angels*, BADS' third production, was seen by 400 people and received a mediocre review, but with some highlights. Dick Evens, wrote (newspaper unknown):

> The set used was the most ambitious and effective that I have ever seen in an amateur society. Stage manager Warren Trevers, the antique dealer [He had a shop at No 3 Middle Row, High Street], obviously put a lot of thought into the scenery … and money. Michael Wilson was by far the most versatile and comical personality. His sister Marian as the young girl was charming.

Bletchingley Amateur Dramatic Society, curtain call of *My Three Angels* – March 1964
By Sam & Bella Spewack. Cast L-R: Mary Wilson; Anthony Sturge; Peter Benson; Michael Wilson; Frank Johnson; Marian Wilson (now Marian Buck); Frank Ffoulkes; Betty Bristow; Tom Bull; Stanley Hurrell. Produced by Nancy Hoyle. *Photo courtesy of the Bletchingley Players*

Later productions received much more positive reviews, with Paddy Martin and Jean Risbridger often the stars of the show. Paddy won the best actress award at the 1965 Betchworth Festival. A 1965 newspaper article covering the production of *Goodnight Mrs Puffin* mentions: 'Jean Risbridger lifted Blechingley Amateur Dramatic Society's production almost into the professional sphere, she portrayed the character [Amelia

Puffin] magnificently, and was always convincing. She was throughout the nucleus and as such managed to hold the whole cast together.'

Bletchingley Amateur Dramatic Society, publicity stunt for *When We Are Married* **– October 1964**
The initiative of Jean Risbridger. The buildings in the background are 1–3 The Cobbles in the High Street. *Photo courtesy of Bletchingley Players.*

Bletchingley Players Chairman John Tomlin presenting a bouquet to Dame Judi Dench at the AGM – 2016
Front row L-R: Diana Drysdale; Pat Napper (former Blechingley sub-postmistress); Liz Tomlin; Sheila Mighall; Dame Judi Dench; John Tomlin; Jackie Lucas; Pam Wastell; Adele Strange; Nicola Walton; Duncan Hollands. Back row L-R: Ann Weaver; Marian Buck; John Buck; Joanna Scott; David Mills; Cyril Mighall; Jennifer Hyde; Paul Hyde; Peter Shore; Eileen Shore; Dave Wastell; Ron Napper (he ran the post office with his wife Pat). *Photo courtesy of the Bletchingley Players, photographer Doris Parker.*

Marian and John Buck – 2022
In the garden of the house built by Marian's father in 1936. As well as her involvement in amateur dramatics, Marian arranged Roman Catholic masses that were celebrated at St Mary's for over 30 years, and John is a lay reader at St Mary's. Both continue to be active in local ecumenical events. The lamp post on the left is an original gas lamp found abandoned in the village by Marian's father.

Gilbert and Sullivan's *Patience* – 1925
An earlier Blechingley amateur dramatics group. Front row L-R: Miss Kongpine (Kohn-Speyer), Mr Wilson, Miss Taylor, Mr Clutterbuck, Mrs Weeler (Wheeler), Bertie Warren, Miss Barry, Mr Lacrix (La Croix), Miss Robertson (believed to be Ethel Hope 'Peggy' Robertson, the daughter of Doctor FW Robertson OBE of The Grange, who was about 22 years old at the time), Mr Ball (Bell), Ted Risbridger. Second row L-R: Mrs Goodwin, Miss Abbot (Abbott), Mrs Trisgarder, Mrs Clutterbox, Miss Mott, Mrs Goodwin, Miss Smith, Mrs Argkell (Arkell), Mrs Lacrix (La Croix), Mrs Tobbit (Tobitt). Rear row: The seven soldiers are not named. The names are handwritten on the rear of the photo, some are mis-spelt, the correct or probable spellings have been added by the author. *Photo courtesy of Doris Parker*.

More information on BADS/Bletchingley Players can be found on the Bletchingley Players website.

Cricket has been a popular sport in Blechingley for well over 200 years. There is a record of a match between Blechingley and Brighton on the 16 September 1820 at Brighton, the score being Brighton 361, Bletchingley 178. Local land owner and village benefactor, Henry Partridge Esq. formed the Blechingley Hornets cricket team, and presented a new cricket pitch to the village in April 1896, the location of which is unclear. Many cricket legends have played in benefit matches on the pitch at Grange Meadow, organised by Surrey and England cricketer, Maurice JC Allom, who lived in the village from the mid 1930s to the early 1970s. Some of the big matches here were:

1946 Bletchingley CC v PGH Fender's XI: Fender was a famous Surrey captain and Test player.

1949 MJC Allom's XI v PGH Fender's XI: ERT Holmes (Surrey & England) scored 140 in front of a large number of people. The old Surrey and England batsman Andrew Sandham played aged nearly 59. The entire profits went to Bletchingley CC.

1964 Bletchingley CC v Ken Barrington's XI: Bletchingley CC included some famous cricketers, such as the great Peter BH May, Eric Bedser, Donald Carr (England Test captain), ATC Allom (Son of Maurice) and local Stan Southam. Barrington's side included Micky Stewart (Surrey & England), Subba Row, Geoff Arnold and Arthur McIntyre.

1966 Six-a-Side County Tournament including two Surrey teams, Glamorgan and the Black & White Minstrels (including TV celebrity Leslie Crowther). Over 3,000 turned up and there was a Ladies' Challenge Match at the end.

Cricket information kindly supplied by our local cricket expert, Roger Packham, chairman of The Bourne Society, who has published a number of books on the subject.

The great Peter May batting on the pitch at Grange Meadow – 1964
He had retired from first class cricket the year before, seen here displaying the classic style that made him famous. *Photo from Surrey Mirror and County Post, 12 June 1964. Courtesy of Surrey Mirror & County Advertiser/ Mirrorpix/Reach Licensing.*

Grange Meadow Sports Ground today. Among the meadow's many facilities there is a football pitch, a cricket pitch, an indoor rifle range (also used by a slot car racing club), a children's recreation ground and an outside gym. The southern corner of the meadow is home to Bletchingley Bowling Club, with a good-sized pavilion and six rinks. The main sports pavilion has a children's nursery and the parish council rent an office. The old cricket pavilion is currently used for keep-fit classes (2023). The British Legion used to meet in the rifle range building, but these days about ten members meet in a home in the village. The Meadow is also used for village fetes and fairs. Tandridge District Council hold the meadow in trust on behalf of the village and lease it to the trustees of Bletchingley Sports Association. The south part of the old Home Meadow, called Town Meadow today, is still used for grazing and is owned by Blechingley and Hathersham Estate Co Ltd.

Hevers Pond – 2016
Formerly part of Town Farm, is spring fed and was said to have never dried up since 1850 – until the summer 2022 heatwave, when it did dry up completely! Godstone pond also dried up that year. The bridleway by the railings on the right is thought to date from Norman times. The pond was licensed by the owners, Blechingley and Hathersham Estate Co Ltd (Lambert family company), to Blechingley Parish Council in 2010.

Hevers Pond and Ivy Mill. In earlier days there was a stream called the Lay Brook (brook of the meadow), running down from Hevers Pond, through Grange Meadow, to lowlands next to the Plough Inn (now The Bletchingley Arms, 2023). The brook was piped underground around the mid-1800s. It emerges and runs behind the cemetery in Godstone Road, where it eventually joins the Stratton Brook, which is barely a trickle during dry spells, and is joined by other brooks on its meandering way. It then runs south-west under the Godstone Road and Waterhouse Lane, on to what was Ivy Mill, in Ivy Mill Lane, where it runs under the Lane. From there it continues to Leigh Mill Lake, Godstone, after which it becomes the Gibbs Brook, which then joins the River Eden at Crowhurst. The Eden joins the River Medway at Penshurst, Kent, which in turn empties into the River Thames estuary at Sheerness, Kent. The online Medway Catchment Partnership Map shows the route of the Stratton and Gibbs Brooks quite clearly. Ivy Mill, on the parish border, is referred to as Blechingley's mill, but Godstone also lays claim to it.

Ivy Mill House, Ivy Mill and Mill Pond – early 1900s
This flour mill is identified in the 1086 Domesday Book as the mill at Chevington. The dam of the mill pond collapsed during a storm in 1909 and was rebuilt. The flour mill was in use up until the 1920s, when it was destroyed by a fire. The mill pond was drained and filled in the 1950s. Ivy Mill House was rebuilt in 1698 with timber framing and has since had further alterations and additions. Today it is a private dwelling. *From a Hall's Photo Series postcard. Colourised by author.*

IVY MILL, A POEM

> "... tongues in trees, books in the running brooks,
> sermons in stones, and good in everything."—*Shakespeare*.

THE WATERS SPEAK TO ENGLAND.

Here Saxons ground their corn,
  And when the Normans came,
However changed their lot,
  I turned my wheel the same.

Dammed for the use of men
  Some thousand years ago,
My streamlets trickled in,
  And turned my wheel below.

From Hever's pond above,
  Down the Ley-brook I flowed,
Through Funk's Bridge mead to fields,
  Your Saxon forebears mowed.

There in the swampy ground
  Joined in my western brook,
And sluggish down the vale
  Their course my waters took.

To old Isemongers' Farm
  Their floods brought silt and sand
Till by the pray you passed
  To knightly Stangrave's land.

There 'neath the alders' shade
  They scoured a deeper course;
Then, spread in Ivy Pond,
  Stored up their hidden force.

So, fed from every ditch
  That drains good corn-land still,
My waters gathered strength
  And turned our English mill.

* * *

Envoi. Saxon and Norman both
  Seem faded in the past,
But what they made is yours,
  Has lasted and shall last.

Our Island liberty
  A thousand years has grown,
And taught in far-off lands
  Freedom to hold her own.

No German blood and iron
  Shall tyranny renew,
If England stand for truth,
  And to herself be true.

Yours is the task to see
  Her heritage be kept:
Hold fast to-day, or die
  Unhonoured and unwept,

* * *

For you my stream was dammed
  A thousand years ago:
For you to-day it runs
  And turns my wheel below.

U. L.

Ivy Mill, a poem by Alfred Uvedale Miller Lambert – 1918

Mr Lambert commented on his poem in the parish magazine of October 1918, when Ivy Mill was still in operation:

> From a short distance east of Place Farm the valley runs eastwards and much of the water goes to Ivy Mill. The Ley Brook runs along the area behind the cemetery. John Isemonger (means ironmonger) lived in Blechingley in 1375, and his family held land in the parish for many generations. Isemongers Farm was the very early name for Waterhouse Farm. The 'Pray', (a now forgotten Surrey name) was a long plank foot-bridge crossing a stream by the side of a ford.

Stratton Brook
The brooks flowing from Blechingley towards Ivy Mill Lane seem to be generally referred to on modern maps as the Stratton Brook, which takes its name from Stratton Farm/House in Godstone. Viewed here from Waterhouse Lane, Blechingley.

Remains of Ivy Mill and Ivy Mill House – 2020
Permission to rebuild the mill has recently been sought, but at the time of writing had been refused. Leigh Mill, in Godstone, was used for making gunpowder up to 1636, and was owned by the Evelyn family. Folklore has it that Guy Fawkes stored his gunpowder in the cellar of Ivy Mill House before his ill-fated attempt to blow up the Houses of Parliament.

Grange Cottage

Grange Cottage at 1 High Street was originally a four-room cottage, part of The Grange estate from about 1865 to 1952. It was listed in an 1866 auction catalogue as 'newly-erected gardener's cottage'. The earliest map showing the cottage is the 1872 six inch to one mile OS map.

Grange Cottage, view from Grange Meadow – 2021
The left third of the cottage (plain bricks) was added in the 1950s. On the far left is the old green cricket pavilion, which was clad with timber shortly after the photo was taken. A zoom lens makes the church appear close to the cottage, when it is actually 150 metres beyond.

GRANGE COTTAGE HISTORY SNAPSHOTS

1863–5 Built as the gardener's cottage on a Town Farm orchard by owner, Robert Birkbeck.

1866 Walter Alexander Leslie (Surgeon-Major Leslie) was tenant at The Grange and purchased the whole site, with the cottage, in 1867.

1871 Owned by Walter Alexander Leslie. No definite residential listing found for Grange Cottage; it may have been known as Stables Cottage, which appears to be listed on the census as part of The Grange site, with coachman Walter White, age 28, living here.

1876 A 27-year-old man, with an address at Grange Cottage, placed an ad in the *Kent and Sussex Courier*, seeking employment: 'WANTED a situation as Groom and Coachman, single age 27, One or a pair, ride and drive well, country preferred. W.H.E. Grange Cottage, Blechingley, Surrey'.

1878 Walter Alexander Leslie and his wife Elizabeth died, and their daughter Elizabeth Mary Leslie either inherited The Grange site with the cottage, or it was held in trust by her.

1881 No listing for Grange Cottage found, but it may have been called The Lodge, which was listed on the census in close proximity to The Grange and the Prince Albert Public House. Gardener Charles Brown, age 30, was listed, along with his wife Emma and two young children.

1891–1930 In 1891 widower William Wood, age 42, gardener, was living here with his son Albert, age 11. He was probably the gardener for three doctors at The Grange over a period of some 30 years: Charles Edmund Oldman; Charles Allen Robinson; and Doctor Frederick William Robertson OBE, for whom he was still working as gardener in 1920 aged 71; his 35-year-old daughter Jessie was also living in the cottage. Late 1800 maps show a water pump/well in the garden of the cottage.

1915 The Inland Revenue Valuation Office entry describes it as: 'Detached tiled cottage at the rear [of The Grange], with 4 rooms, washhouse in lean-to, coal store and back paved yard'.

1924 Doctor Frederick William Robertson OBE and family were tenants at The Grange to New Zealand-based Elizabeth Mary Leslie. Doctor Robertson's wife, Hope, purchased The Grange with Grange Cottage in 1924.

1950 Advertisement in local *Courier* newspaper dated 1 December: 'GARDENER: Single-handed Gardener Wanted for early December; good cottage available, gas. electric light, h. and c. [hot and cold water] etc. Apply by letter to Mrs Robertson. The Grange. Blechingley [Mrs Bessie Robertson]'.

1952–4 The cottage, with about one-third of an acre of land, was separated from The Grange in 1952, and sold by Grange owner Doctor Douglas Robertson (Hope Robertson's son) to Maurice Alfred Freeth Esq. of The White House, Blechingley, for £2,250. Doctor Robertson had applied for planning permission in 1946 to add what looks like a single-storey rear extension with a bathroom and WC. Further planning permission was granted to the new owner between 1952 and 1954 for vehicular access, extensions to the cottage and a detached garage.

1988–98 The south end of the cottage garden was sold in 1988, and a new detached house was built there by Domus Homes Ltd, which is now 3 Grange Close. In 1998 the centre section of the cottage garden was sold and another detached house, Grange Meadow House, 1a High Street, was built there by Chatsworth Homes Ltd. The land was sold in 1988 and 1998 by Lydia Kathleen Daws, owner of Grange Cottage.

Grange Cottage in its original smaller form – c. 1920 When gardener William Wood was living there. *Section of the frontispiece photo from volume one of Uvedale Lambert Snr's 1921 book, photographer Jarvis Kenrick.*

Grange Meadow event – early 1900s
Showing Grange Cottage in the background on the left. Handwritten annotations on the photo say: PC Carter (Alan Samuel Carter, age 49, police constable, who was living with his wife at Bank Buildings in 1911) and Jane & Maude Balcombe (listed in the village at Fernleigh and Stychens in 1920). The Balcombes were a well-known local family, recorded in the bell ringing hall of fame in the bell tower at St Mary's Church. Some of the Balcombes were publicans in the late 1800s/early 1900s, at the Cottage of Content in the Godstone Road, near The Plough Inn, and at the Three Tuns in the High Street. *Photo courtesy of the Blechingley Conservation and Historical Society.*

What was once a Town Farm orchard is now a residential site with three detached houses: Grange Cottage and Grange Meadow House, with a vehicular entrance gate onto the High Street, and 3 Grange Close, which has its entrance in Grange Close.

Grange Cottage is probably over double its original size, with its side and rear extensions. Of note is the original front chimney stack with three pots of finely crafted moulded bricks. The chimney stack and the original front elevations of the cottage have diamond pattern blue brick detail. Peter Grey, in *Blechingley Explored* (1975), commented on the chimney as 'being quite the most attractive of any in the local villages'.

Grange Cottage, original front chimney stack

Grange Cottage, snow scene – 2021

The Outwood Lane Story | The Dewdney Cottages | Seven and Nine | Post Offices | Postmen | Engineers

In 1867 Robert Birkbeck sold The Grange site, along with a pair of circa sixteenth-century cottages adjoining the north border of The Grange with a frontage on Outwood Lane. The buyer of the estate with the cottages was Walter Alexander Leslie (Surgeon-Major Leslie). For simplicity I refer to the cottages as the Dewdney Cottages, as Richard Dewdney owned them in 1841. He had probably purchased them at a bargain price when the larger part of the village was put up for auction in 1835 (lot 27). In 1906 the owner/trustee of The Grange, Miss Elizabeth Mary Leslie, daughter of the late Walter Alexander Leslie, sold the cottages to local dairy farmer, Albert Denny. Albert demolished them and built two houses on the site, 7 and 9 Outwood Lane. No. 7 was the new village post office building, and No. 9 was the Mount Pleasant and Bletchingley Dairy. Today, No. 7 is a private home called Coneybeares, No. 9 is also a private home. Albert, who was known as the guv'nor, is covered in detail, along with his family on page 250.

Outwood Lane, north end, c. 1740 – artist's impression by Don Coe
Looking south from the High Street. L-R: Single sixteenth-century house at 1 Outwood Lane, which from at least the mid-1800s was the Prince Albert public house; single seventeenth-century house, later split into two; Oxstall House and Old Cottage; single circa sixteenth-

century house, later split into two; the Dewdney Cottages, demolished in 1906, and replaced with 7 and 9 Outwood Lane; The Grange; Kings Cottages were a group of five joined cottages on the corner of Outwood Lane and the High Street, probably built in the sixteenth or the seventeenth century, named in the 1800s after James King, a publican at the adjoining White Hart Inn for some 40 years. James had probably purchased them when they were put up for sale in the 1866 Blechingley auction (Lot 6/9). They were demolished and replaced with Bank Buildings in 1899–1900. James retired to Melrose Cottage in the High Street, where he died in 1896. *Line and wash sketch by Don Coe Hon. FSAI, commissioned by the author from early records and photos.* © David John McCleave.

Outwood Lane, looking south from the High Street – 2021
These buildings are now all private homes: 1 Outwood Lane, the former Prince Albert public house, originally a single circa sixteenth-century hall house; in 1881 the left side was the Prince Albert public house and the right side was Prince Albert Cottage; the Prince Albert first appears in records in 1849, it closed in 2013; 3 Outwood Lane, Oxstall House, is from the mid to late eighteenth century, with some remnants inside of a seventeenth-century house, it was originally part of Old Cottage next door; 5 Outwood Lane, Old Cottage, a seventeenth-century building which was the Coffee House around 1900, and then Eddolls Butcher up to the 1930s; 7 Outwood Lane, now Coneybeares, was the village post office from about 1906 to 1913; 9 Outwood Lane, The Mount Pleasant and Bletchingley Dairy from about 1906, later leased to master dairyman John A Tobitt by Albert Denny; A is The Grange, the original Town Farm farmhouse; B is Town Farm, the second Town Farm farmhouse; C is Bank Buildings, where Barclays Bank and the post office were located from 1900.

Dewdney Cottages, 7–9 Outwood Lane – early 1900s
Where builders and carpenters Thomas English and the Hollands family lived. Perhaps the three ladies are standing in protest at the imminent demolition of this ancient building. *Photo courtesy of Derek Moore.*

The address of properties at the top (north) of Outwood Lane was listed in the late 1800s as The Square, while The Grange was sometimes listed as in The Square. From around the 1870s to 1901, builder Thomas English (1841–1921) was listed at The Square in the Dewdney Cottages. Carpenter William Hollands lived in one of the Dewdney cottages in 1841, and his son James Hollands, also a carpenter, lived there in the late 1800s, a neighbour to Thomas English. The Hollands family are recorded in Blechingley in the 1700s, and the English family from the early 1800s. Both families are related by marriage to the Coppards, whose Blechingley roots go back to around 1710.

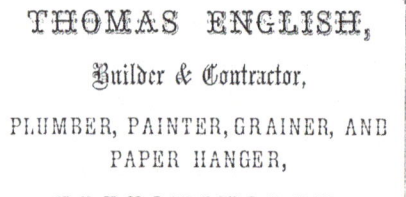

Thomas English's business card
Courtesy of Derek Moore.

Thomas English married Ellen Hollands (1840–1912), daughter of carpenter William Hollands, in 1866 at St Mary's, Blechingley. After leaving the Dewdney Cottages, circa 1906, Thomas built his dream retirement home in 1907, Glenroy at Barfields, Blechingley. The house had an outside toilet and no bathroom. English Brothers Builders were listed at Glenroy in 1938. The address of Glenroy is now Castle Street.

The Dewdney Cottages would originally have been one house, likely a hall house (a house with an open fire in the centre of the main room), when built in the 1500s or earlier. In 1841, Sarah Rance, schoolmistress, was a tenant in one of the cottages and carpenter William Hollands occupied the other. An 1868 abstract of title for the sale of Town Farm Meadow (now Grange Meadow), notes that Town Farm owners and tenants had right of access to a well in Sarah's garden.

A gathering around the baker's cart in Outwood Lane (The Square) looking south from the High Street – 1900/06
Left side of road: Oxstall House; Coffee House (Old Cottage); the Dewdney Cottages (demolished 1906), showing Thomas English's sign and yard/stables with a collection of chimney pots over the entrance, giving it a castle look; The Grange is hidden by the trees, its long front garden wall can be seen, starting immediately to the right of the Dewdney Cottages; Town Farm farmhouse and cowsheds; distant fields are now occupied by Sackville Cottages. **Right side of road**: Bank Buildings (built 1900); four Victorian Cottages –Bank Cottages. *Postcard courtesy of the East Surrey Museum. Colourised by the author.*

Richard Dewdney was a local miller, and from around 1797 to 1847 he leased Ivy Mill in Ivy Mill Lane from Sir William Clayton Baronet. He was churchwarden at St

Mary's, Blechingley, at various times between 1826 and 1846. He is listed as a witness on the aforementioned 1868 abstract of title, where he speaks of the owner of Town Farm in the early 1800s, JGW Perkins Esq., and his wife Mary: 'they were always considered by myself and known and accepted and received by their friends and in the society in which they moved as man and wife.' Richard had retired by 1851 and was living in Dorking, Surrey. He died in 1857, at 86, and was buried in Blechingley.

Oxstall House is an interesting building. Parts of an earlier seventeenth-century house, over which it was built, can be seen inside. It is said to have had a connection with oxen, which were used for ploughing and pulling heavy loads, and were kept in an ox stall (stable).

Title deeds for 7 and 9 Outwood Lane mention the conveyance of the Dewdney Cottages to Albert Denny, dated 30 June 1906. The parties on the deeds are: Elizabeth Mary Leslie (vendor and Grange owner) and Albert Denny–Alicia Blakesley (purchasers). Mortgagee Alicia Blakesley and her sisters were also mortgagees to The Grange from around 1885 to 1924. Alicia was born in 1861, in Ware, Hertfordshire. Her father, Joseph Blakesley, was the Vicar of Ware and later Dean of Lincoln. Her mother Margaret was from Bungay, Suffolk. Alicia was a successful artist and exhibited at the Royal Society of British Artists and the Royal Academy of Arts in London. In 1901 she was living in a large house at 15 Stanley Crescent, Kensington, London, with her two unmarried sisters, all living on their own means. Alicia died a spinster in 1939, age 78, in Berkshire.

Outwood Lane, an original colour construction plan for 7 and 9 – c. 1906
The new post office and house adjoining (left) and dairy store (right). Some original outbuildings (cart shed, stables, etc.) are still at the rear of No. 7, and the owners still have the old post office sorting table and some of the sorting shelves (2023). *Plan courtesy of Derrick & David Smith.*

Restrictive covenants were placed on Nos. 7 and 9 stating that they 'should not be used for any purpose (such as a gasworks, asylum, public house etc.) which may be or grow to be a nuisance or grievance to the vendor her heirs or assigns or tenants or which may tend to depreciate or lessen the value of the adjoining property of the vendor, known as The Grange, or any part thereof as residential property'. A June 1907 covenant mentions that No. 9 should be built 'four and three quarter inches' from The Grange garden north wall, with no windows overlooking The Grange garden.

Post office staff at 7 Outwood Lane – c. 1912
This photo may have been taken to mark the retirement of sub-postmistress Catherine Ann Legg and the end of some 100 years of the Legg family running the village post office. The gate to The Mount Pleasant and Bletchingley Dairy yard can be seen on the right; the two doorways with the brick arches are bricked up today, and the bay window has been converted to an entrance porch to 7 Outwood Lane, Coneybeares (2023). L-R: 1) unknown lady; 2) telegraph messenger, name unknown, messengers had flat hats and bicycles without front carrying racks; 3) postman Charles Albert Phillips; 4) telegraph superintendent Daniel Quinlan; 5) postman Edward (Teddy) Benjamin Davis; 6) postman William (Gaffer Bill) Lord; 7) probably postman Gilbert William Risbridger; 8) telegraph messenger, name unknown; 9) unknown lady; 10) probably sub-postmistress Catherine Ann Legg. Four persons were identified by Derek Moore. *From a postcard courtesy of the East Surrey Museum. Colourised by author. The postal uniform colours were added with the kind assistance of The Postal Museum, London.*

Blechingley postal staff listed in the 1911 census were: postmen Gilbert William Risbridger (age 19), Edward Benjamin Davis (age 30), Charles Albert Philips (age

37), William Lord (age 41); telegraph messengers George Arthur King and John L Smith (both aged 14); telegraph postal clerk Nancy Osbourne (age 22); post office assistant Kate Amelia Veale (age 38); post office clerk Agnes Irene Denny (age 18, Albert Denny's daughter); sub-postmistress Catherine Ann Legg (age 53) and her housekeeper Clara Morse (age 43). Shortly after 1912 Georgiana Grace Quinlan and her husband Daniel took over the post office at a new location in the High Street.

THE VILLAGE POST OFFICE 1832–2023

We started with the connections between The Grange, the Dewdney Cottages and Albert Denny's new post office and dairy store buildings. Here we will digress a little further into the history of the village post office, which has been at seven locations since 1832. The story goes something like this …

High Street looking west – c. 1880
Legg grocers and drapers is behind the telegraph pole on the far left at 2 The Cobbles, the centre of the three joined gable-ended buildings. The post office is adjoining on the right at 3 The Cobbles. The large house to the right of The Cobbles is Glenfield House (with six first-floor windows), with Melrose Cottage to its right. *From a Frith's Series postcard, published circa 1902/3 but displaying an earlier photo, as was sometimes done. A cropped view of this photo is at Surrey History Centre, Woking, where it is listed as a circa 1880 photo by Jarvis Kenrick, ref: 7828/2/18/100.*

Post office, enlarged section of High Street looking west – c. 1880
At 3 The Cobbles/27 High Street, with Glenfield House on the right.

In 1832 the post office was at Melrose Cottage, which is immediately to the west of Glenfield House in the High Street. John Legg was probably the postmaster as he was listed as the village postmaster in 1839. Thomas Legg, grocer and draper, was a tenant at The Cobbles in the High Street in 1840. The three joined Cobbles buildings are at 23–27 High Street. Master blacksmith and publican William Henry Wren was listed on his 1852 London church marriage registry entry as Blechingley postmaster. Thomas Legg's brother Frederick was grocer and postmaster in 1855 at The Cobbles. After Frederick's death in 1879, his wife Ann became sub-postmistress. Ann died in 1898 and the reins were handed over to her daughter, Catherine Ann Legg.

Bank Buildings – 1906
On the corner of Outwood Lane and the High Street. The buildings were put up around 1900, probably by Henry Partridge, to replace the old timber-framed Kings Cottages. Barclays Bank opened here in April 1900 and the post office probably opened around the same time (seen to the left of the group of people).
© *The Francis Frith Collection (section of a larger photo).*

Bank Buildings, enlarged section showing post office
With some postal staff outside and some young ladies posing for the camera. The large sign on the post is that of The White Hart Inn (now The Whyte Harte Hotel).
© *The Francis Frith Collection.*

Around 1900 the post office moved 60 yards east along the High Street to the newly built Bank Buildings, next door to the Whyte Harte Hotel. It was there for about 6 years. In 1906, local farmer, landowner and respected village benefactor, Henry Partridge Esq. of Castle Hill, left the area and most of his property was put up for auction, including the 'Post Office and the Bank Building'. The post office then moved to Albert Denny's brand-new building, just around the corner at 7 Outwood Lane.

Post office when it was at Bank Buildings – early 1900s
© The Francis Frith Collection (section of a larger photo).

Catherine Ann Legg continued as sub-postmistress at 7 Outwood Lane. She died in April 1913, aged 55. The Legg family had lived in the village for some 200 years and were postmasters and postmistresses for almost half of that time. They are recorded in the village over the years with various trades including: clockmakers, watchmakers, jewellers, bell-hangers, grocers and drapers. John Legg looked after the village clock in the church tower in the early 1800s and was paid three guineas a year to wind it.

Bank Buildings under construction – 1899/1900
Courtesy of The Blechingley Conservation and Historical Society.

When the Quinlans took over around 1913, on the north side of the High Street at No. 32, it was known as The Library and Post Office. Their services included the sale of books, stationery and fancy goods. By this time the passing motor trade had become an important business consideration, as Outwood Lane was a bit tucked away. Georgiana Grace Quinlan took on the role of sub-postmistress with the assistance of her husband Daniel. The family had relocated from Brighton where, in 1911, they had five children living at home and Daniel was an assistant telegraph superintendent.

The Quinlans produced one of the largest Blechingley picture postcard series, called the Quinlan's Photo Series, of which there are nine examples in this book. Georgiana died in 1921, at only 41, and Daniel continued to run the post office for a couple of years.

Quinlan's Photo Series postcard – 1917
From a postcard with a postmark of 1917.

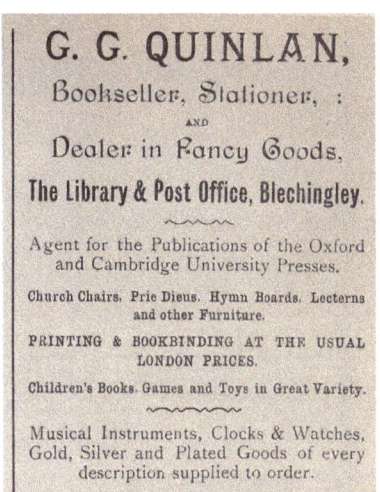

Georgiana Grace Quinlan advertisement and letter from the parish magazine – 1918
For the post office at 32 High Street

Edgar Joseph Stammers was the next postmaster at 32 High Street, from about 1923 until 1925. He was followed by Harry Page Riste for the next 32 years, with his wife Marion Ellen. Harry had previously run a saddlers shop for the Rice Brothers and later their Blechingley Garage. He retired in 1957 and was succeeded for about eight years by Edward Herbert (Bert) and his wife Florence Oborne, who had been publicans at the Tally Ho in Caterham.

From around 1965 to 1984, the post office was located at Norfolk House, 80 High Street (now home to Lawrences Auctioneers, 2023), and was run by Allan and Betty Bristow. It then moved to 46 High Street with proprietor Alan Gayler, who was chairman of the parish council. He died in 1988 and his wife Lesley took over for about a year. Alan's name is commemorated in Gayler Close, built on the site of the demolished Bletchingley Isolation Hospital, off Rabies Heath Road. The bench alongside the post office has a memorial plaque to him (2023).

Much-loved local couple Ron and Pat Napper took over for the next 14 years, with Pat as the official sub-postmistress. Ron had many roles in the village, including treasurer for Bletchingley Players amateur dramatics group and for St Mary's Church, where he was also on the bell ringing team. Ron sadly passed away in 2018; Pat still lives in the village, and the post office is still at 46 High Street in 2024.

POSTMAN STORIES

Edward 'Teddy' Benjamin Davis (1881–1936) was born in nearby Merstham, Surrey. He left school at 14 and worked for a chemist in Redhill, where he got the sack for spilling chemicals on the shop floor. He then got a job in Blechingley as a telegraph delivery boy and went on to become a postman. In 1901 he was lodging with fellow postman William Lord at Barfields, Blechingley. He met his wife-to-be, Charlotte Glasspool, while she was in service at South Park, Blechingley, as under-parlourmaid. They married in 1904 and moved into Ted's home, a flat above Grices Bakery at 96 High Street. The flat proved unsuitable for Charlotte due to the heat from the oven. Through the local cricket club, Ted was acquainted with Henry Partridge of Castle Hill. When Henry heard about their plight he rented them a cottage, the middle of the three Castle Cottages in Castle Street, which were normally tied to employment on his estate. His kindness extended to installing an outside toilet, rather than the earth closet to which they were accustomed. It was one of the first toilets in the smaller houses in the village and was such a novelty that the kids used to run round the back of the cottage to pull

the flush chain. Ted volunteered for service in WWI and served with the Essex Regiment in Ireland. Ted and Charlotte had five children. Margaret Louisa (Peggy) James, born Margaret Louisa Davis in 1904, the eldest child of Edward and Charlotte, recounted this story to Derek Moore while she was visiting Blechingley at age 93. She identified her father, Edward, and three others in the 1912 group photo at the post office in Outwood Lane. Peggy left school at 13 to care for the blind daughter of actor Leslie Faber at Wideways, 100 High Street, Blechingley. The original story was published in the *Blechingley Magazine* in November 1998.

Postman 'Teddy' Davis – c. 1912
From a postcard courtesy of the East Surrey Museum.

William Lord (1870–1951), or Gaffer as he was known to his family, seen here with five good conduct stripes on his jacket. Postmen received one stripe for every five years of unblemished service – they also received a little extra in their pay packet. William worked for forty years, mainly on the Outwood round. Following an accident in 1927, it was conservatively estimated that he had covered over 300,000 miles on his post office bicycle. In later years he progressed to a motorbike and a van. He was renowned for constantly smoking Woodbine cigarettes, which he rolled himself, and was said to be 'a hard worker, steady liver, and a life abstainer'. He was born in Lee, Kent, and in 1896 he married Elizabeth Annie Maynard from Outwood. They had at least one child, William James, born in 1903, who became a bank clerk. Elizabeth died at age 37, in early 1911. *From a story recounted by one of William's relatives, in a letter.*

Postman Bill Lord – c. 1912
From a postcard courtesy of the East Surrey Museum.

Postman Bill Lord with his bicycle – early 1900s

Bletchingley Magazine, *June 1989.*

Postman Gilbert William Risbridger and his engineering family. Gilbert (1891–1955) was the grandson of farm worker William Risbridger (1821–1912). William moved to Blechingley from Betchworth/Dorking, Surrey, and married Mary Huggins at St Mary's in 1853. In 1911, 19-year-old Gilbert was living in Stychens Lane with his father, also William, a gardener and former farm worker, his mother Emma and three brothers. Gilbert was decorated for service in WWI. He married Ethel Gwendoline Fearnley in 1921 and later moved to Redhill where he was head postman.

The Risbridgers. Gilbert's brothers William and John formed the engineering company W & J Risbridger Ltd, still in existence after more than 100 years, under the name Risbridger Ltd. They specialise in the design and manufacture of specialised engineering products, primarily for international aircraft servicing and retail petroleum engineering. An early parish magazine advertisement reads:

> W. & J. Risbridger, Castle Garage, Blechingley, for Motor Repairs and Insurance – Cars, Lorries, Tractors, Motorcycles, Cycles etc., of all makes. – Engineers & Brass Finishers, Tel., Blechingley 58

W. & J. RISBRIDGER,
SCHOOL LANE, BLECHINGLEY.
MANUFACTURING ENGINEERS AND MACHINISTS

W. & J. RISBRIDGER, HIGH STREET
BLECHINGLEY TELEPHONE 243 (LATE GOODWINS)
Enquiries are invited for all classes of
BUILDING, DECORATING AND HEATING, ETC.

Risbridger advertisements – 1935 and post-WWII
School Lane [Stychens Lane], formally Parsonage Lane, was the ancient road to London. During WWII Risbridger's were contracted to supply the government/military. After the war they were also advertising building, decorating and heating services from premises in the High Street.

Risbridger workers in front of the factory during WWII
There were 90 staff working shifts to support the war effort.

William Arthur Risbridger (1894–1969) joined the Royal Navel Air Service, and trained on the HMS Ark Royal, his knowledge from those days led him on to understand pumps, valves and fuel tanks. William worked with his brothers, especially his partner John. William's sons, John, Gerry and Barry all worked in the company, along with a nephew, Patrick. Gerry served his national service in the early 1950s with the Royal Air Force, as a mechanic. He was Chairman until he passed away in 2023.

In 2004 Risbridger Ltd moved their operation from Stychens Lane to a larger factory on the Holmethorpe Industrial Estate in Redhill. The old factory was demolished and replaced with houses. Their equipment is used on many aircraft, past and present, both civil and military. These include Concorde, Airbus and Boeing aircraft, rotary bladed aircraft including the Westland Sea King, Boeing Chinook, utility versions such as the Apache, Lynx or Puma – along with the multi role AW139 search and rescue aircraft. This equipment supports the military sector and includes the Hawker Harrier Jump Jet and Sea Harrier, the Hawk Trainer used by many nations to train pilots and flown by the Royal Air Force Red Arrows, the Tornado, Jaguar and Typhoon fighter jets. Their products are often referred to in the industry as a 'Risbridger' in much the same way that a vacuum cleaner is often referred to as a 'Hoover'.

William Risbridger (1859–1942) and Emma (nèe Burbery, 1861–1947);
William Arthur Risbridger (1894–1969)
Photos courtesy Annie Risbridger Hind

Grices Bakery – 1951
Under the blind on the far left at 96 High Street, where newlyweds Edward and Charlotte Davis lived briefly in 1904. Immediately to the right of it is Clive House, dating from 1690. *Photo by Donald Ashley Birkinshaw, from an original negative.*

Castle Cottages in Castle Street – 2021
At the west end of the village. Postman Edward Davis and his wife Charlotte lived in the centre one, where they had five children. The detached house on the far right is Mead Cottage, where local history expert, Derek Moore, president and former chairman of the Blechingley Conservation and Historical Society, lived with his wife Valerie in the 1990s for about eight years. Derek called it Eyebrow Cottage.

Library and Post Office at 32 High Street – 1930s
Harry Page Riste was proprietor here for 32 years. He was involved in the social affairs of the village; a 1912 newspaper article mentions a series of dances he organised at the village hall, with music supplied by Sargent Gear's band. The yew tree in front of the church was felled in 1948. Uvedale Lambert Jnr in *The Rectors of Blechingley, Surrey*, 1981, wrote, 'The old yew tree in front of the church was finally felled, after a long battle'. *From a Real Photograph Postcard, by Harold Camburn of Tunbridge Wells, for HP Riste. Colourised by author.*

H. P. Riste post office advertisement – 1944

Outwood Lane, looking south – 1912/13
Albert Denny's Dairy Store at No. 9 is advertising teas on the milk churn sign. *From a Vince's Photo Series postcard.*

Eddolls, George, butcher at 5 Outwood Lane – early 1900s
This is presumed to be butcher George Eddolls standing in the doorway, who was listed in 'Outwood Road' from 1911 to 1938. It is now a private home called Old Cottage at 5 Outwood Lane and has a Georgian-style bay window (2023). *Courtesy of The Blechingley Conservation and Historical Society.*

Outwood Lane, looking south from the High Street – 1951
The car in the distance is parked in front of The Grange, where heart specialist Doctor Douglas Robertson lived at the time, and where his brother Dick ran a surgery. *Photo by Donald Ashley Birkinshaw, from an original negative.*

The Grange Farmhouse | Owners and Tenants – 1586–1867

The Hoskins Family | Owners 1586–1767

The name Charles Hoskins is inscribed on the front of The Grange. Hoskins were believed to have lived here for a time, in an earlier version of the house, later, they rented it out. The name of the house in earlier times is not known but my wild guess is Bletchingligh Farm (Blechingley Place was spelt this way in 1622). The family later owned and lived at Barrow Green Court, near Oxted, a large grand house and grounds, built in the 1600s, which more recently has been the home of former Harrods Store owner, Mohamed Al Fayed. The Hoskins lived at Barrow for over 200 years and were wealthy landowners who held the manor of Oxted and Barrow. They were ancestors of the Master family in Oxted, who donated what is now the Master Park recreation ground to Oxted. It seems that many of the Hoskins family had the name of Charles over the years and there is a record of a Charles Hoskins' death in 1768. Uvedale Lambert Snr had access to the Hoskins estate records, which mainly cover Oxted and Barrow, but do mention their Blechingley properties, the last of which they sold around 1768.

Henry Lovell and Family | Tenants circa 1618–25

Uvedale Lambert Snr said that Mr Henry Lovell was indicated as living at The Grange from the early 1600s to 1625 (in an earlier version of the house on the site). He would have been a tenant to the Hoskins. Henry's daughter, Elizabeth, was baptised at St Mary's Church in 1618.

At the parliamentary elections for Blechingley in 1624, Sir Myles Fleetwood and Mr John Hayward were duly elected. However the election result was disputed on the grounds that there were too few voters and that the manor bailiff was not present, as it was claimed was the tradition. A second election was held and won by Sir Myles Fleetwood and Mr Henry Lovell. But objections were lodged and the election was overturned after a petition was made to Parliament. Allegations were made against Mr Lovell of 'ill-affection in religion and bribery'. He was brought before Parliament, where it was held that he had been guilty of contempt in procuring the election. Author Thomas HB Oldfield records that he was accused of giving the men (voters) six pence for drink and they were to give him six pounds if they did not choose him or his friends. It was also noted that: he had not taken communion for 12 months; his mother was a recusant (rebellious Catholic who refused to acknowledge the Protestant Church); his brother was a priest; his daughter was a nun; and that he had 'threatened the town'. He was held in the Tower of London, at the House's pleasure, until he begged in submission, on his knees at the bar of the House.

The scandal also involved the rector of Blechingley, Doctor Nathaniel Harris, who came under censure for aiding and abetting Mr Lovell, and for preaching a sermon in his church in a 'slighting fashion', against those he viewed as corrupt, by quoting from the Bible, 'Now the chief priests, and elders, and all the council, sought false witness against Jesus, to put him to death' (Matthew 26:59). He was admonished and ordered to kneel and beg for pardon at the bar. He was also ordered by Parliament: 'On the following Sunday, in the pulpit of his church, before his sermon, to confess his fault, desire the love of his neighbours, and promise reformation.' Mr Lovell and Doctor Harris acquiesced to their masters and survived the ordeal. Doctor Harris died shortly after, in 1625.

Memorial to Doctor Nathaniel Harris in St Mary's Church
(d. 1625) in Latin, put up by his wife, Mary (d. 1647).

On a side note, a sister of Doctor Nathaniel Harris, Mary, married Nicholas Lambert of Chipstead (1574–1615) and from them (in the female line) Alfred Uvedale Miller Lambert JP is descended in the eighth generation.

The Perkins Family of Pendell, Blechingley | Owners 1808/9–55

John George Wilson Perkins Esq.

Of Pendell Court, Lord of the Manor of Pendell. Portrait miniature by John Cox Dillman Engleheart, after George Engleheart, 1810. *Private UK Collection, image courtesy of Bonhams.*

Mrs Mary Perkins

Née Carter, wife of John George Wilson Perkins.[1] This portrait is from a 1925 painting by Dorothy Kenrick (1887–1983), daughter of Jarvis and Lilian Kenrick, who lived for a time at Pendell House. Dorothy probably copied it from an Engleheart miniature. *Image courtesy of Bonhams.*

---

1 Uvedale Lambert Snr labels this lady in his 1921 book (alongside a portrait of John George Wilson Perkins) as 'Mrs Perkins, née Mille (d. 1798)'. Bonhams Auctioneers, London, comment that 'The miniature portrays an older lady in her 50s, and her costume dates to the 1810s. Mr and Mrs Perkins are recorded in the fee book of London portrait miniature painter, George Engleheart, as having sat for their portraits in 1810.' So the portrait is more likely the wife of John George Wilson Perkins, who was Mary Perkins, née Carter (1750–1831), Margaret Perkins, née Mille (1716–98) was his mother.

John George Wilson Perkins (1747–1827) was an affluent man and a member of the stock exchange. He was the son of John Perkins (1707–77) and resided at Pendell Court, a mile from Blechingley centre, which is now The Hawthorns School (2023). He purchased a lot of land in the area, including Town Farm with the farmhouse (later to be The Grange) in 1808/9. In 1811 he purchased Pendell House, across the road from Pendell Court. John George Wilson Perkins married Mary Carter (1750–1831) and they had twelve children: John, George and Margaret, who died young, then John, William, Charlotte, Thomas, Caroline Seyliard, Margaret, Maria, Clara Matilda Charles and Mary. After the death of John George Wilson Perkins in 1827, his eldest surviving son, John (1774–1846), inherited Pendell and the Lordship of the Manor of Pendell.

National newspapers reported the murder of John Perkins's steward in March 1834:

> Mr. John Richardson, steward to John Perkins, Esq. was murdered on Wednesday evening the 26th ult. [of the previous month], when going home in his gig [type of cart] from Epsom market, on the road near Banstead, in a very lonely spot, at the top of a steep hill leading out of a hollow called Purcells Gap: he was shot in the lungs, and must have died instantly. It is supposed that one of two men seized the horse's head, while the other came up to the side of the gig and demanded the deceased's money. The deceased always travelled with loaded pistols; and it is believed he replied to the demand by firing at one or other of the villains, but missed his aim, and that the ruffian by the side of the chaise instantly fired his pistol, which unhappily took a fatal effect. A reward of 100/., since increased to 200/. by Mr. Perkins, was offered for the discovery of the murderers. Mr. Richardson was a fine-looking man of 45; he has left a pregnant widow and six children.

John Perkins went on to purchase Blechingley Manor for the bargain price of £540 in 1835, via auction at the White Hart Inn, Blechingley. Nineteen years earlier, before the electoral reform act, Blechingley Manor had changed hands for £6,000. From 1835 the manors of Pendell and Blechingley were merged into one and called Blechingley Manor. John was listed on the 1841 tithe map as owner of the 206 acre Town Farm and was, after Sir William Clayton, the largest landowner in the parish, with over 860 acres of land. He died unmarried in 1846, and his estate went to his four surviving sisters.

Sister Maria married John Trotter MP in 1809. Clara Matilda Charles remained single and was Lady of the Manor. She lived for some time at Pendell House with her sister Mary, who had inherited the house and married the Rector of Blechingley, Jarvis Kenrick (1775–1838) in 1804. The grandson of the rector was Jarvis Kenrick IV (1852–1949), an outstanding athlete and skilled photographer, who is credited for taking most of the local photographs in Uvedale Lambert Snr's 1921 book. He inherited Pendell House, where he lived with his family from the late 1800s to about 1916. The Perkins family sold Town Farm (with the farmhouse, The Grange) to Thomas Fowler Wood in 1855. For more on Jarvis Kenrick IV and Pendell House, see page 278.

Pendell Court – 1810
'Pendhill, A Mansion House erected in 1624, in the parish of Blechingley, belonging to John Perkins Esq., by whom this plate is contributed.' Known as Pendhill Court in earlier days.
From a print in The History and Antiquities of the County of Surrey, by Owen Manning & William Bray.

Pendell Court was built in 1624 by George Holman, grocer and citizen of London who died the following year. His son Robert inherited. Robert was a barrister and later one of six members of parliament for Surrey, which included Blechingley (1654). Robert gifted the carved oak Jacobean pulpit at St Mary's Church, which bears his coat of arms and a date of 1630. He also gifted an hourglass to the church, the frame of which remains. He died in 1664, in his 62nd year, and was buried in the chancel of St Mary's. For the next 200 years or so, Pendell Court was owned by the Seyliards, Scullards, Perkins and Mayers families, who were related. The estate varied in size from 300 acres to 600 acres as land and properties were transferred, although Pendell Court itself remained much the same as it had been built.

Pendell Court – 1773
'Pendhill Court near Blechingley in Surrey the seat of George Scullard Esq.' George Scullard, relative to the Perkins, found fishing an agreeable sport, and is seen here fishing from his boat. Records indicate that he probably enlarged the lake and stocked/restocked it with fish. *Artist Paul Sandby, © The British Library Board – Ktop XL, 28 B. Faded colours enhanced by the author.*

Robert Holman and his wife Ann (née Brereton) – 1600s
Original portraits at Pendell Court, photos by kind permission of The Hawthorns School.

George Scullard (1725–76) and Mrs Hester Wade Scullard (d. 1799)
Photos from Uvedale Lamberts Snr's 1921 book

Scullard and Perkins families at Pendell Court
Photo from Uvedale Lambert Snr's 1921 book.

The Perkins family line at Pendell came to an end in 1870 when Lady of the Manor Clara Matilda Charles Perkins died unmarried in May 1870, aged 78. She is remembered for founding the Clara Matilda Almshouse Trust in 1860 and building the now demolished almshouses in Blechingley village centre. The little house adjacent to the front (south) gate of St Mary's Church graveyard was built by the trust in 1973 on the site of one of the original almshouses, and bears a stone inscription to this effect. Clara willed Pendell Court with the Lordship of the Manor to her unmarried niece, Margarette Mayers, whose mother was born Caroline Seyliard Perkins (Clara Matilda Charles' older sister), but Margarette died six months later, aged 52.

It was then passed to Margarette's brother, Lieutenant-Colonel John Perkins Meyers, who died in July 1877 aged 60. John's tombstone at Milton Road Cemetery, Weston-super-Mare, Somerset, states that he was 'the recipient of Pendell Court, near Bletchinley', and that at the time of his death he resided at Holbrook House, Weston-super-Mare. His wife Wilhelminia died in September 1871 and was buried in the same grave. Her inscription mentions that she was the wife of J P Meyers of Pendell Court near Bletchingley. Their two daughters, Clara and Elenor are mentioned on the tombstone, who died in India at 11 and 10 months of age.

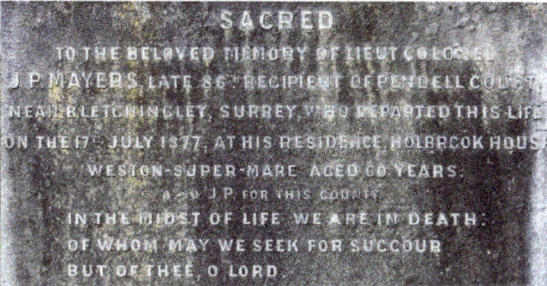

Grave of John Perkins Mayers – 2023
Milton Road Cemetery, Weston-super-Mare. His wife Wilheminia is also in the grave, to the left of the chapel, with the large cross. The inscription mentions Pendell Court

Pendell was then sold to Sir George Macleay KCMG (Knight Commander of the Order of St Michael and St George), who was an explorer of Australia and was, for a time, speaker of the New South Wales legislative council (1843–6). He had been a tenant since about 1870 and, as owner, he extended the house to skilfully match the original, so the whole building now appears as from one generation. He built the new sweeping carriage drive with the lodges at each end. He enlarged the lake and, with his extensive travel experience and love of botany, he and his head gardener, Charles Green, laid out the gardens with great skill. They built extensive glasshouses, which included a fernery, tropical and orchid houses. There were rare and fine trees, shrubs and flower borders, and a walled kitchen garden.

After George's death in 1891, Doctor William Abraham Bell bought the estate from his trustees. William had spent a lot of his time in America, where he was in partnership

with General William Jackson Palmer. They are famed for establishing the Denver & Rio Grande Railway, along with the towns of Colorado Springs and Manitou Springs. William purchased back a lot of the land that had previously been sold, so it now had 700 acres. It is recorded that he met Uvedale Lambert Snr while he was on holiday in France, who told him of the availability of the finest and most important mansion in the parish.

Doctor William Abraham Bell

Pendell Court rear view – circa 1914–20
From a Quinlan's Photo Series postcard, courtesy of the East Surrey Museum.

William's son, William Archibald Juxon Bell, inherited Pendell Court and the Manor in 1921. He leased Pendell Court to the United States Service Club in the 1930s and sold most of the Pendell Court lands, which included farms and houses, mainly to sitting tenants. In 1947 he sold Pendell Court to the Community of St Mary the Virgin, who owned it until 1961. He moved to Berry House in Blechingley High Street and retained the Lordship of the Manor until 1970, when it was passed by will to Uvedale Lambert Jnr.

The Community of St Mary the Virgin are a Church of England group of sisters who, at the time, undertook missionary projects in England and abroad. They were headquartered in Wantage, Oxfordshire, where they are still based. The sisters ran a home for elderly ladies at Wantage, which was relocated to Pendell Court to increase capacity for the sisters at Wantage. It was named St Mary's, Pendell Court, with Sister Juliet as the Superior. They left Pendell in 1960 after 13 years 'because of the impossibility of providing adequate staffing for a house which, for all its gracious beauty, is not an easy one to run'.

Mother General Maribel (1887–1970) served at Wantage for 13 years up until 1953, when she took a sabbatical of about a year at Pendell Court. She was given a quiet studio in a barn to work on some of her famous 15 carved Stations of the Cross. She worked on them over a period of 27 years and the originals are in St Mary Magdalene's Chapel at Wantage. Many of her works of art can be seen in ecclesiastical buildings in the UK and abroad. In the early 1960s, she carved two, three feet tall Epiphany Kings, which were used in a Christmas Nativity at St Paul's Cathedral, London. One of her famous quotations was: 'So often we try to alter circumstances to suit ourselves, instead of letting them alter us, which is what they are meant to do.' A book was published about her life in 1972, *Mother Maribel of Wantage*, by Sister Janet CSMV.

Mother General Maribel
Photo by kind permission of CSMV.

The Community of St Mary the Virgin was founded in 1848 by William John Butler, then the 29-year-old Vicar of Wantage, following the spiritual revival in the Church of England known as the Oxford Movement. It was one of the first Anglican Religious Communities to be founded in England since Henry VIII's dissolution of the monasteries. They work with schools, mission houses and homes for young mothers, young offenders, the elderly, and for the rehabilitation of persons suffering from drug and alcohol addiction. Uvedale Lambert Jnr recalls in his 1981 book, *The Rectors of Blechingley, Surrey*:

> A great help to the spiritual life of the parish were the Wantage Sisters, who ran the old people's home at Pendell Court after the Bells had moved to Berry House. One of them drew 'Descent of the Manor of Bletchingley', in the tower [bell tower at St Mary's Church] and the 'original historical markers', in the church.[2]

Estate agents John D Woods, who were marketing Pendell Court for the sisters in 1960, described it as:

> Jacobean manor in first class order, freehold with vacant possession, on 25 acres. Panelled lounge hall; five reception rooms; 38 bedrooms; nine bathrooms; private chapel (Church of England); two lodges; kitchen garden; paddocks; timbered parkland, and an ornamental lake.

Pendell Court – 2021
View from the south, with the North Downs behind.

---
2 Reproductions of the descent of the manor charts can be seen on pages 297–299.

Pendell Court (The Hawthorns School), front – 2021
An independent day prep school for girls and boys aged 2 to 13 years.

William Judson and Family | Tenants 1849–57

William was born in 1809, in Crayke, County Durham, in the north-east of England. He married Ann Linton in 1832. In 1841 they were living in Crayke, where William was a farmer. Ann died in 1847, aged 36, and by 1849 widower William was living at Town Farm, as a tenant to the Perkins family, then later as tenant to Thomas Fowler Wood. Thomas bought the farm from the Perkins family in 1855 and he also owned nearby Coldharbour Farm. William remained a widower and lived on Town Farm with his seven children, four girls and three boys, along with three servants. In 1851, at age 42, he was farming 210 acres of Town Farm land with nine farm labourers. William suffered great loss in a farmyard fire in early January 1851, as the *Sussex Agricultural Express* records:

> The Blechingley fire engine was quickly brought into play and aided by one from Godstone of inferior power effectually preserved all the ricks in the farm yard as well as the barn and the buildings on the opposite side of the yard and also prevented the fire reaching the stables at the north end of the cattle sheds. The tenant's property destroyed is about 30 quarters of thrashed and unthrashed barley, one waggon, one cart, one landpresser and one scarifier. The proprietor's loss is the whole barn and cattle sheds. There is no moral doubt whatever but that the cause of this destructive fire was the diabolical act of a vile incendiary and it is hoped that a reward will be offered for his discovery.

The farmhouse (The Grange) was still known as Town Farm. After his tenancy, William moved to Isleworth, Middlesex, where he lived with some of his children and had the occupation of bailiff.

John Henry Sharp and Family | Tenants 1859–62

In 1859, John Sharp, aged 29, was residing at The Grange with his 19-year-old wife Elizabeth. His occupation was fund-holder (had investments/lived on his own means), but it is not clear whether he had any involvement in Town Farm. They had the first of their six children in Blechingley, Henry, born in 1860, followed by Basil, in 1862, whose birth was announced in the *Morning Post*, 25 March 1862: 'The birth of a son to J.H. Sharp Esq., of The Grange, Blechingley, Surrey.' John was obviously a man of some standing, as an announcement in the 20 December 1860 edition of the *Brighton Gazette*, in the fashionable chronicles section, stated: 'Mr J.H. Sharp has arrived at 27 Upper Brunswick Place [Brighton], from Blechingley.' John was born in Brixton, Surrey (South London today), the son of a merchant. He was churchwarden at St Mary's, Blechingley, 1860–1.

The family left Blechingley sometime after 1862. In 1864 they were living in Rotherfield, Sussex. They eventually settled in Hove, Sussex, where John served as a justice of the peace. He was chairman of the Brighton and Hove Supply Association Ltd and was a director of the Brighton and Hove Wine Company Ltd. For many years he acted as treasurer, and later as chairman, of the Brighton and Hove Hospital for Women and was actively associated with several other local charities. He died at Hove in 1914, age 82.

The Birkbeck Brothers | Bankers/Owners/Mortgagees 1861–67

Robert Birkbeck owned Town Farm and The Grange from 1861 to 1867, with his two brothers and others as mortgagees. The three Birkbeck brothers – William (1832–97), Robert (1836–1920) and Edward (1838–1908) – were involved in banking, and were from a Quaker family background.[3] They were born in Keswick, Norfolk, and their father and grandfather were bankers. Father Henry was married to Jane Gurney and, after her death, he married Lucy Barclay. The Gurneys and Barclays were also Quakers.

At the time of the 1866 financial crash (Black Friday), the three brothers were residing as follows:

- Robert was listed as a money-dealer, living at Nutwood, Gatton, near Reigate, Surrey, with his wife Mary. It seems he had converted to the Church of England, as he was baptised at St Peter and St Paul church, Nutfield, Surrey, in October 1857, aged 21. In December the same year, he married 22-year-old Mary Harriet Lubbock, who had been baptised in the Church of England as a baby, in 1835.

---

3 The Quakers are a religious group, formally known as the Religious Society of Friends.

- Edward was living in Nutfield, Surrey, at Holmsdale Lodge, with some land; his occupation was banker.
- William was also a banker, based in Norwich.

After the dust of the 1866 London financial crash had settled, Robert and Edward had sold and vacated their properties in Blechingley, Nutfield and Reigate. It would appear that Robert did not return to the banking business. In 1871 he was living in Berkeley Square, London, with his wife Mary, and from this date onwards he was listed as having no occupation/living on his own means. But I think they were doing okay, as they still had a lady's maid, housemaid, cook, butler and footman! Robert died in 1920 with an estate value equivalent to over £5 million in 2022.

Edward was living in London in 1871, listed as a landed proprietor with 206 acres of farmland. He later lived in Norfolk, at Horstead Hall, where he bred Jersey cattle and was a Conservative MP for Norfolk. He served as President of the National Sea Fisheries Protection Association, and as Chairman of the Royal National Lifeboat Institution. He had a close shave with death in 1902 when a ship collided with the German torpedo boat on which he had hitched a ride returning from a yacht race. It sank off Cuxhaven, Germany and the captain and several German crew members drowned. Edward was created Baronet of Horstead Hall, in the parish of Horstead, Norfolk, in 1886. His brother William continued to live at Thorpe Grove, Norfolk, where he was a banker and landowner.

Edward Birkbeck (1838–1908), 1st Baronet of Horstead Hall – 1885
© *National Portrait Gallery.*

The Grange Home and Doctor's Surgery | Owners and Tenants – 1865–1987

Surgeon-Major Leslie and Family | Tenants/Owners 1865–1924 | Elizabeth Mary Leslie's Mission Work and Emigration

The Leslie family lived at The Grange for 13 years, but owned it for almost 60. Surgeon-Major Leslie (Walter Alexander Leslie) served in India in the Madras Army, 35th Regiment of Foot, which later became the Royal Sussex Regiment. He retired from the army in October 1866. He was born in 1820 in Hampshire and his wife Elizabeth was also born in 1820. They were married in Bombay, India, on 19 March 1850 and they had six children. They were said to be lovers of the arts and music. Surgeon-Major Leslie died on 5 May 1878, followed by Elizabeth only two months later. They were both living in Hampstead, London, at the time and were buried in Shirley, Surrey. Walter's parents were Walter Wemyss Leslie (1791–1863), and Elizabeth Danford (1792–1877). Walter Wemyss was a commander in the Royal Navy. Walter Alexander Leslie is listed in the 1873 *Medical Directory* as at Blechingley, with a registration date of 7 March 1866, and in the *Provincial Medical Directory*, 1870, at Blechingley – General Practitioner, Member of The Royal College of Surgeons London, Licentiate Apothecaries Company.

Walter Alexander was a yearly tenant at The Grange from about 1865. His tenancy included the meadow adjoining the bottom of the garden, now known as Grange Meadow. The Grange site and the meadow were put up for auction in 1866 and Mr Leslie purchased The Grange and gardens, with the coach house, stables, gardener's cottage (later called Grange Cottage), two sixteenth-century cottages (the Dewdney

Cottages, later to be 7 and 9 Outwood Lane), and the western plot or plantation (now High Bank Cottage in Outwood Lane). He completed the purchase in 1867 for £2,470 and took out a mortgage for £1,200. The meadow was purchased by Charles Fox Chawner, Rector at St Mary's Church, via the same auction.

From 1875 to 1878 Walter Alexander Leslie was listed on the electoral roll at The Grange, and also from 1876 to 1878 at 9 Thurlow Road, Hampstead, London, where his death was registered in 1878. The Grange electoral roll entries for 1875–78 list him as occupier, but his place of abode was 'East View, St Andrew's, Fife N.B.'.

The Leslie family children were: Kate Leslie (1851–1921); Morice Leslie (1852–1931); Walter Jefferson Leslie (1855–1915); Elizabeth Mary Leslie (1857–1940); William Clarence Colebrook Leslie (1861–1943); and Henry Danford Fitzgerald Leslie (1864–1931).

Residing at The Grange in April 1871 were: Walter Alexander Leslie, age 50, and his wife Elizabeth Leslie, née Morice, age 51. Children: Kate Leslie, age 20; Elizabeth Mary Leslie, age 14; and Morice Leslie, age 18. Staff: John Mcdonald, medical assistant, age 30; Emily Charlwood, housemaid, age 22; and Rose Anna Brown, cook, age 19.

By 1881 the Leslie children were spread out as follows:
- Kate was living with her husband Towers Trevorian Millett in Madras, India
- Morice was working in Hyderabad, India
- Walter was living in Oamaru, New Zealand (where he was a journalist and an artist)
- Elizabeth Mary was living with her aunt, Anna Allardyce Morice, at Matfield Green, Brenchley, Kent
- William was at the Royal Military College, Sandhurst, Berkshire
- Henry was at King's School, Christ Church, Canterbury, Kent.

Elizabeth Mary Leslie was born on 9 February 1857, at Palamcottah, Madras, India, where her father was serving in the British Army. After the death of her parents, The Grange was listed with her as the owner/trustee from 1878 up to 1924. It is not clear why it was in her name. She was only 21 and the fourth-oldest child in the family, but records indicate that her older siblings were abroad at that time. Perhaps she was also the wise and responsible one, and managed The Grange on behalf of the family.

The last will and testament of her father gives the impression he may have had other investments and properties.

Elizabeth Mary Leslie's missionary work and travels took her around the world. In 1883 she took the Gleaners missionary exam in England, and passed with a grade A class.[4] She left England in late 1890 and arrived in China in early 1891. Further training and exams in China included learning to speak and read Chinese. An 1892 article in a missions society journal mentions, 'Miss Leslie took her first language test with a result of 70 marks out of 100', and 'it takes many years to speak Chinese with faculty'.[5] She served as an honorary missionary with the Church of England Zenana Missionary Society (CEZMS). The organisation worked very closely with the Church Missionary Society before amalgamating with them in 1957. Honorary meant she did not receive a salary; in later years she took a salary.[6]

Elizabeth Mary Leslie
Photo from her missionary service portfolio.[7]

Zenana was the name for the quarters of a house in India where women were segregated, and which unrelated men were forbidden to enter. Zenana missionary societies were made up of female missionaries who could reach these women in India, and later China and other regions where women were segregated. The CEZMS became active in Fujian Province, China, in 1884. Elizabeth was based in Foochow City (today Fuzhou), in the south province of Fujian. She ran a girl's boarding school, which was intended to reach upper-class girls, with the assistance of Miss Lee, Miss Kingsmill and Miss Mead. In later years it accommodated up to 75 children who were required to pay the greater part

---

4 Birmingham University, Cadbury Research Library, Special Collections – Church Missionary Society: CMS-OX-1883-03-8-10 (Gleaner entrance exam).
5 Birmingham University: CMS-CRL-IW-1892-05-39 (Language exam).
6 CMS-CEZ-C-AM 1-1 FOLIO 41 (Service records).
7 Birmingham University: CMS-CEZ-C-AM 1-1 FOLIO 41 (Service records).

of the cost of food and clothing – but Elizabeth was sometimes 'obliged to relax the rules a little'. Elizabeth was also involved with Foochow Hospital.[8]

Elizabeth's journal on 7 March 1891 mentions that China was a hard place to work and that understaffing was often a problem resulting in workers getting ill and requiring them to take leave. Some of the resident missionaries had influenza shortly after her arrival in Foochow. She said: 'We are a little amused at having proved the truth of what we have so often heard said, that one of the missionary's first duties is to nurse those who have gone out before.' She mentions 'the horrible empress' of the time, the kind and gentle nature of the local people and that the work was rewarding. The local taxi service consisted of a sedan chair carried by men known as 'coolies'. An extract from Elizabeth's 1892 journal recalls a trip on sedan chairs with some of her colleagues, to visit the home of her Chinese tutor, Mr Ling Senang:

> It was a journey in chairs of more than an hour and a half; these people lived just outside the south gate of the city – too far for us to walk; so at 9.30 our coolies appeared. We are obliged to have three each for long distances and they change about to keep up pace. The morning was wet, so they were dressed in great round hats made of leaves and bamboo. These are so large that they reach quite beyond their shoulders, they are very light too and are piled up one on top of the other on the bamboo rods of the chair when not wanted. Strangely most of the people out in the streets and fields are men, and a number of them stare curiously at us as we are carried along, as if they thought us strange beings, and I am told they often ask the coolies whether we are men or women! When we at last reached the house we were set down at little tables with much ceremony and given cups of tea with a sort of wafer biscuit and pressed very much to eat. Little bowls too were brought in with china spoons, full of some liquid and queer-shaped white objects floating about. Upon attacking these bravely, we found these were made of paste filled with chopped cabbage (I think); they tasted sweet and rather nasty. While we were eating our hosts apologised for the crowd of onlookers gathering next to the open room of the house, they had never seen foreigners and were evidently intensely interested in us.[9]

---

8 Birmingham University: CMS-CRL-IW-1895-05-10-11 (School in Foochow).
9 Birmingham University: CMS-CRL-IW-1892-04-33-36 (Elizabeth's Journal).

Foochow, China, school group
Rear right: Miss Kingsmill, Miss Mead and Elizabeth. From *India's Women and China's Daughters*, published September 1905.[10]

The Kucheng Massacre took place about 50 miles from where Elizabeth was based and some of her CEZMS colleagues were victims. It was carried out against a group of Christian missionaries in 1895 by a Zhaijiao religious group, known in England at the time as the Vegetarians, so called as the followers had taken vows of vegetarianism. They were a rebel anti-government movement who were opposed to western imperialistic influence in the country. Church Missionary Society workers, including the Rev. Robert W Stewart, his wife Louisa and their five children, were staying in two houses adjacent to the village of Huashan, just outside of the walled city of Kucheng (or Gutian) in Fujian province. The missionaries used these houses in the cool hill country during the hot summers. Early on the morning of 1 August 1895 a Vegetarian gang broke in, attacked the group with spears and swords and then

---

10 Birmingham University: CMS-CRL-IW-1905-09 (School group photo).

set the houses on fire. Eleven people died, including Robert and Louisa Stewart, their five-year-old son Herbert and 13-month-old daughter Hilda. Four of the deceased were ladies working for CEZMS. One of the survivors, Miss Flora Codrington (CEZMS) was seriously injured; she eventually recovered in Foochow Hospital but was left with permanent facial scars. She was later accompanied back to England by Elizabeth, who was taking some furlough. Elizabeth returned to China in 1896 and Flora returned in 1897 (dates differ slightly in some reports).[11]

The total number of survivors of the massacre was six, including three of the Stewart children (some accounts differ on the number of survivors). The victims of the massacre were buried at Foochow International Cemetery and their lives were commemorated with a monument in the form of an angel. Some of the Vegetarians were imprisoned or exiled and seven were publicly beheaded.

Scene of the Kucheng Massacre
Upper house the Church Mission Society; lower house the CEZMS. *From the 1895–6 edition of the Church Missionary Society annual publication,* The Story of the Year, *published May/June 1896. Colourised by author*.

---

11 Birmingham University: CMS-CRL-IW-1896-06-14/18/CMS-CRL-IW-1907-06 (Kucheng massacre and Miss Flora Codrington).

The Grange Home and Doctor's Surgery | Owners and Tenants – 1865–1987 | 165

Sketch of the houses at Huashan
Showing some coolies and a sedan chair. *From the 1895–6 edition of the Church Missionary Society annual publication,* The Story of the Year, *published May/June 1896.*

AFTERNOON TEA AT KU-CHENG. (*From Photograph lent by Capt. Star.*)

[The gentleman is the Rev. W. Banister, and then, beginning at our left, looking at the picture, we see Miss Hartford (American Methodist Mission), the late Miss Gordon (C.E.Z.M.S., Tasmania), Miss Weller (C.E.Z.M.S.), Miss Codrington (C.E.Z.M.S.), Miss Nisbet (C.E.Z.M.S., Australia), Mrs. Banister, Tom Banister.]

Photo taken before the Kucheng Massacre
Miss Annie Gordon (second from the left) died in the massacre. Two survivors are in this group: Miss Mabel C Hartford (far left) and Miss Flora Codrington (fifth from the left). *From the 1895–6 edition of the Church Missionary Society annual publication,* The Story of the Year, *published May/June 1896. Colourised by author.*

Dedication of the monument to the martyrs of the Kucheng Massacre
Foochow Cemetery, which was destroyed in the 1950s during the Chinese Cultural Revolution under Mao Zedong. © *Special Collections Yale Divinity School Library*.

Elizabeth's extended travels, culminating with her emigration to New Zealand, began when she sailed back to England in 1896 with her colleague, Miss Flora Codrington, after the Kucheng Massacre. After returning to Foochow later that year, she did a deputation tour of Canada in 1897 (giving talks to promote the missions), after which she returned to Foochow. Then in 1902 she returned to England on sick leave. On 29 October 1903 she sailed from Liverpool, England, on board the SS *Tunisian*, to Quebec, Canada, for another deputation tour. From there she sailed on to New Zealand to continue her deputation work.[12] Her plan was to return to Foochow after New Zealand to continue with her mission work. But perhaps the work, travels and events in China had taken their toll as she resigned on the grounds of ill-health on 17 May 1905.[13]

Elizabeth settled on New Zealand's North Island, in a small village called Apiti, Manawatu, which is about 38 miles from Palmerston North. Her house was named Matfield Cottage, in memory of her auntie Anna Allardyce Morice's house, at Matfield

---

12 Birmingham University: CMS-CRL-IW-1903-12-2 (Leaves Liverpool for Canada Oct 1903).
13 Birmingham University: CMS-CEZ-C-AM 1-1 FOLIO 41 (Deputations and resignation).

Green, Kent, where Elizabeth lived before she left England. She continued to support the Chinese mission work from New Zealand, giving talks and fundraising.

Kate Leslie, Elizabeth's older sister, married Towers Trevorian Millett on 20 February 1878 in Hampstead, London, and they had two children. Towers died of typhoid fever in August 1882, age 29, while serving as assistant police superintendent in Madras (Chennai today), India. Towers' diary mentions that he received a reward of 500 rupees in 1873 for shooting a tiger of nine feet seven inches in length, in Pachipenta, India. Tigers were greatly feared and were said to have killed at least 500 head of cattle in the area each year, along with numerous villagers.[14]

Towers Trevorian Millett (1852–82)
Husband of Kate Millett (née Leslie). *Photo courtesy of Antony Percy Upton Millett (Tony), born in 1942 at Takapuna, Auckland, NZ – son of Edward Tracey Fletcher Millett, who was the son of George Nicholls Millett, who was the son of Towers Trevorian and Kate Millett.*

Kate came back to England after her husband's death, then emigrated to New Zealand in 1901 to join her sons, Martin Leslie Millett (went in 1898) and George Nicholls Millett (in 1900). Kate lived in Wellington and later with Elizabeth in Apiti. Kate died in 1921. Brother Walter Jefferson Leslie and his wife Marya lived in Wellington, about 125 miles south of Apiti. Walter died in 1915 and Marya in 1940.

Elizabeth was mistakenly reported as having died in the April 1937 issue of the missionary society's periodical. They published an apology in August 1937: 'Miss Leslie was in good health for her age and is still a supporter of missions work with her collection boxes, and is well loved and respected in the community.' The article also mentioned that 'she had the great joy of a visit of her brother from England in 1936, whom she had not seen for some 50 years'.[15] The brother was Lt Col William Leslie, the last surviving of her siblings. He died in 1943, at Tunbridge Wells, Kent, England. Elizabeth did not marry and lived in Apiti until her death on 5 December 1940, aged 83.

Rowena Rosa Purnell was Elizabeth's companion at Matfield Cottage in Apiti; whether she was a formally employed companion is not known. She was born in 1888 at Yeovil, Somerset, England. After Elizabeth's death she lived in Palmerston North, New Zealand, where she died in January 1976.

---

14 Tony Millett, *The Western Mail* (Cardiff, Wales), Saturday 14 February 1874.
15 Birmingham University: CMS-CRL-IW-1937-08-3 (Death wrongly reported).

SS *Tunisian*
Elizabeth Leslie made her last missionary voyage from England aboard her in 1903, bound for Canada. The ship made its first sailing in 1900 and accommodated: 240 first-, 220 second- and 1,000 third-class passengers. *From a Peacock Series Postcard 1911, published by The Pictorial Stationery Co. London, with a 1913 postmark.*

Missionary exhibition in a court in Napier, New Zealand
Elizabeth Mary Leslie (centre). *Published in* The Gleaner *1908.*[16] *Colourised by author.*

---

16 Birmingham University: CMS-OX-Gleaner-1909-08-15 (Court in Napier photo).

Leslie family tea party in New Zealand – early 1900s
L-R: 1) Marya Isabella Camilla Leslie, née Ulkjar, wife of 2) Walter Jefferson Leslie (Walter and Marya were married in 1879 in New Zealand); 3) Elizabeth Mary Leslie; 4) Kate Millett, née Leslie; 5) Rowena Rosa Purnell (Elizabeth's companion). *Photo courtesy of Tony Millett. Colourised by author.*

Leslie family, New Zealand – 1906
L-R: 1) Kate Millett, née Leslie, holding grandson Edward Tracey Fletcher Millett (younger son of George and Isabella Robertson Millett), born January 1906; 2) Elizabeth Mary Leslie; 3) Isabella Robertson Millett, née Fletcher (wife of George Nicholls Millett – Kate's son), holding her son, Charles Trevorian Millett, who was born in 1903. *Photo courtesy of Tony Millett. Colourised by author.*

The Grange was sold in 1924 to Hope Robertson, Doctor Frederick William Robertson's wife, for £2,400. The deed of conveyance listed the vendors as Miss Elizabeth Mary Leslie (with her New Zealand address) and brother Henry Danford Fitzgerald Leslie (trustee), with Julian Stroode as solicitor/trustee and Elizabeth Blakesley as mortgagee. The outstanding mortgage of £1,200 was redeemed by Hope.

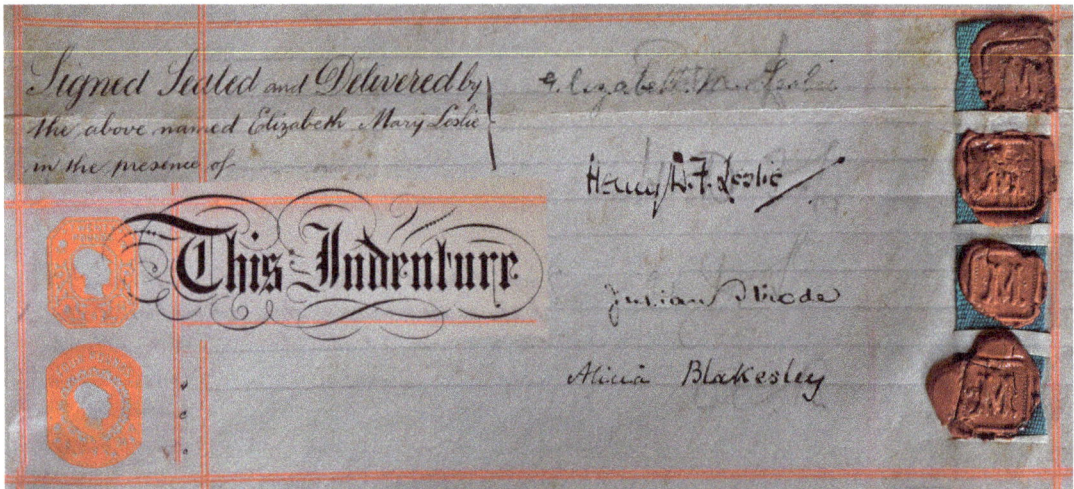

The Grange deed of conveyance – 1924

Elizabeth's obituary was published in the *Manawatu Times*, Palmerston North, New Zealand on 10 December 1940 (*courtesy of Tony Millett*):

> Miss Elizabeth Mary Leslie, a lady greatly beloved and long resident in Apiti, passed away at her home on Thursday evening. About 57 years ago she went from England as a missionary to China, where she laboured for over 10 years until her health failed and she decided to come to New Zealand and make her home with her sister, the late Mrs K. Millett, of Apiti. Miss Leslie resided in Apiti for 35 years, and during all those years until failing health prevented her from travelling, she continued her very active interest in the mission and the Chinese whom she loved. Miss Leslie from her slender income helped to support her substitute in the mission field and for many years she lectured and sold Chinese work and goods to augment this fund. At the funeral service at St Luke's Anglican Church on Saturday afternoon many friends of the deceased lady gathered to pay their last respects.

The service was conducted by the vicar, the Rev. F. E. Fleury, with the assistance of a former vicar, an old friend of Miss Leslie, the Rev. Mayo, of Wellington, who paid tribute to a fine Christian lady, taking as his text the words 'Of such are the Kingdom of Heaven'. He referred to Miss Leslie's outstanding service for the missionary work so dear to her, and also to the sincerity of a character that reached up to the highest ideals in her devotion to her church and in her associations with her friends and neighbours. Much sympathy is extended to Miss Purnell, her friend of many years, who for a long period has made her home with the late Miss Leslie.

Elizabeth Mary Leslie and Edward Tracey Fletcher Millett
Her grand-nephew. In New Zealand. *Photo courtesy of Tony Millett.*

British missionaries were influential in lobbying the UK government to pass laws in 1910 to end the opium trade, which had contributed to the two Opium Wars (1839–42 and 1856–60). The People's Republic of China was founded by Chairman Mao in 1949 and the last Christian missionaries were expelled in the early 1950s. There are various statistics regarding the number of Christians in China today, from about two per cent up to five per cent. There are said to be large numbers of unofficial underground, or house, churches, which are not counted in official statistics. The government tolerates them, but there have been reports of state persecution and imprisonments.

Governments supported the missionaries while also having their own political agendas. But no doubt the missionaries themselves were sincere and risked their lives to spread the Gospel, minister to the poor and sick and provide education. I am reminded of the Apostle Paul's words in the New Testament:

> But what does it matter? The important thing is that in every way, whether from false motives or true, Christ is preached. And because of this I rejoice. (Philippians 1:18).

'The Cake of Kings and Emperors in China'
From the Petit Journal, *published in France, 1898. Wiki commons public domain; original in The National Library of France.*

Doctor Donald William Charles Hood and family were also listed as practising and residing at The Grange during the Leslie family's tenure, from around 1872 to 1879. Donald married Alice Flower of Park Hill, Croydon, on 2 November 1871. They had at least one child while living in Blechingley, a son born on 24 July 1872.

Doctor Charles Edmund Oldman and Family | Tenants 1877–1904 | Godstone Union Workhouse

Doctor Oldman (b. 1847) lived with his family, and practised, at The Grange as tenants to the Leslie family. He was a very popular character in the village, and it seems he also dabbled in farming on a small scale and practised at nearby Godstone Green. He previously lived and practised in Spalding, Lincolnshire. His practice at The Grange was called Oldman and Furber. His partner, Doctor Edward Price Furber, had a practice in nearby Oxted. Doctor Oldman was 'Physician and Medical Officer, Public Vaccinator West District Godstone Union, B.A. M.D.' He was medical officer to the Godstone Union Workhouse, which was located behind St Mary's Church, Blechingley. From 1897 he was also medical officer to the newly opened Blechingley Isolation Hospital. Doctor Oldman was chairman of the committee that formed Blechingley Parish Council in 1894. He was also a member of the nearby Caterham Masonic Lodge.

Residing at The Grange in April 1891 were: Doctor Charles Edmund Oldman, age 43, and his wife Beatrice Oldman, age 42. Daughters: Beatrice Helen Oldman, age 17, and Edith Isabel Oldman, age 6. Ellen Margetta, sister-companion, age 45; Gertrude Hitchcock, boarder, age 40. Staff: Dorcas Pultich, cook, age 32; Edith Huggett, parlourmaid, age 23; Elizabeth Edwards, housemaid, age 25; Kolletta Harris, domestic nurse, age 27; and Ellen Eglington, domestic nurse, age 24. Son Montague Charles Oldman, age 16, was away at boarding school in Godalming, Surrey.

The workhouse was a facility where the poor and destitute would be housed and fed, but were also required to work, including the women and children. It was a place of last resort as conditions were harsh, set up in this way to discourage the admittance of the 'lazy and work-shy'. Men up to about age 70 were sent out to dig in the nearby gravel pits. Charles Dickens used his literature to bring attention to the Victorian social systems. In *Oliver Twist* (1838), he painted a bleak picture of the workhouse and the 1834 Poor Law, the antiquated systems of forced labour and mistreatment. In spite of the conditions some of the workhouse inmates, as they were called, seems to lived to a ripe old age in the early days:

> ***Derby Mercury* 29 January 1768** Tuesday died in the Parish Workhouse at Bletchingley, Surry, Thomas Stevens, in the 104th

Year of his Age, who continued sensible till within an Hour of his Death.

Oxford Journal *10 January 1778* Saturday last died in the Workhouse at Bletchingley in Surry, one Slip, aged 107 Years.

Godstone Union Workhouse – c. 1915–20
Photo taken from the tower of St Mary's Church, looking north towards Whitehill. *From a Quinlan's Photo Series postcard, courtesy of the East Surrey Museum.*

Conditions were said to have improved towards the end of the 1800s, but the following newspaper articles paint a picture of a harsh regime:

> REFUSING TO WORK 12 March 1904, George Smith and John Taylor were each sent to prison for seven days' hard labour for refusing to perform their allotted task of stone-breaking at the Godstone Union Workhouse. *Sussex Express, Surrey Standard & Kent Mail.*
>
> WORKHOUSE INMATES AND THE FROST 27 January 1910, at Oxted Police-court, to-day, ten men, ranging from 24 to 56 years of age, inmates of Godstone Union Workhouse, were charged with

refusing to perform the task of digging. They pleaded that it was too cold to work out doors, and that the ground was too hard to dig owing to the severe frosts. They said they were prepared to work indoors like the other men. The magistrates sentenced each man to ten days' hard labour. *The Globe*.

The first workhouse building was put up in 1754 on the Clerks Croft land (St Mary's Church). It was built to serve Blechingley, then expanded in 1839 to cater for a wider area, and was called the Godstone Union Workhouse or Guardians Institute. The new buildings had a separate school block at the east of the site, to the north of the entrance. Further developments included:

Sussex Agricultural Express 3 September 1853:

> BLETCHINGLEY A GOOD EXAMPLE An additional building has lately been erected in the yard of the Union comprising two cells for refractory paupers, and two commodious rooms for the reception of females of loose character. Several of the 'Frail Sisterhood' having, in the union, greatly demoralized the minds of the female inmates, some, it is even stated, having left to associate with them in their life of profligacy. The building is so constructed as not to allow its occupants to hold communion with any of the other paupers in the adjacent union.

Sussex Agricultural Express 8 May 1869:

> BLETCHINGLEY - THE NEW UNION INFIRMARY On Wednesday the 28th April the guardians of the Godstone Union met at the workhouse to inspect the new infirmary, now nearly completed. Present: G Leveson-Gower Esq (chairman), E Kelsey Esq (vice-chairman), Rev EC Walker, Col. Burdett, CH Masters [sic], G Seal, W Harrison, E Stenning, - Harrison Esqs, The building is arranged for the accommodation of 43 beds, with day rooms on ground floor, with separate entrances and staircases for men and women, lavatories, wc's, and slop sinks, are attached to each ward, and hot and cold water is laid on. In the centre of the building are rooms for the nurse, and a surgery, store rooms and sculleries. The plans have been approved by the Poor Law Board, and the works

have been carried out under the superintendence of Mr Alex R Stenning, architect, Mitre Chambers, 157 Fenchurch-street, EC; Mr J Woodward of Wilson-street, Finsbury, the contractor; Mr R Patton, clerk of the works.

Above two articles from Roger Packham's collection.

Godstone Union Workhouse – c. 1908
Photo titled 'The Workhouse when Miss Gower was Matron'. Perhaps this was Louisa Gower's farewell photo after some 50 years of service. Subjects in photographs up to the early 1900s did not smile as it was considered unseemly. Mark Twain wrote: 'A photograph is a most important document, and there is nothing more damning to go down to posterity than a silly, foolish smile caught and fixed forever.' The subjects also had to keep quite still due to the slow shutter speeds of early cameras. *Photographer Jarvis Kenrick, of the Photographic Survey and Record Society of Surrey © Surrey History Centre. Colourised by author.*

By 1910 the workhouse had been extended and an infirmary and separate infectious diseases block were added to the west. In 1929, the workhouse became the Clerks Croft Mental Deficiency Institution. In 1948, with the introduction of the National Health Service, it became Clerks Croft Hospital for the Elderly. The Hospital closed in 1981 and the site was sold in December 1983 for £1,000,000 to Whelan Homes Ltd, of Purley, Surrey. The buildings were demolished and the site was redeveloped in 1985. The new homes are now called Clerks Croft, off Church Lane. Church Lane was formerly called Workhouse Lane.

In 1855, John Coppard Gower and Mary Gower were workhouse master and mistress. Alfred Keaton Gower was the schoolmaster. In 1861, Louisa Gower, age 22, daughter of John and Mary, was serving as joint matron with her mother. By 1901, at age 61, Matron Louisa was serving alongside workhouse master William Howard Walter, who was 36. Louisa retired around 1908, when Mr Samuel George Sneezum (1872–1929) was appointed as workhouse master. He married Grace Josephine Marner (1886–1964) in 1910, who became matron. Mr Sneezum was churchwarden at St Mary's from 1914 to 1921. In 1911 the workhouse had 302 inmates and 16 officials.

The salary for a nurse at the workhouse in 1867 was £16 per annum, including accommodation and rations. In 1911 the salary for a children's nurse was £25 per annum, with uniform, furnished room, rations (beer included, or one shilling [5p] a week in lieu thereof).

In his role as medical officer for GRDC, Doctor Oldman was obliged to produce an annual report of about 50 pages, covering Blechingley and the surrounding villages. The report details sanitary conditions, rainfall, infectious diseases and so on. His 1894 report gives Blechingley a population of 1,940, with 44 births and 28 deaths. Only one case of infectious disease was listed, a child with diphtheria.

Front page of Doctor Oldman's medical report – 1898
Courtesy of The Wellcome Collection. Attribution 4.0 International (CC BY 4.0).

Doctor Oldman was born on 15 May 1847, in Gainsborough, Lincolnshire, and died on 19 March 1904, age 56, in Blechingley. His obituary in *The Surrey Mirror and County Post*, dated Friday 25 March 1904, mentions that at the time of the funeral, 'all business was suspended in the village, houses had blinds drawn and that many poor people of the district felt they had lost one of their best friends'. His family, colleagues and friends filled St Mary's Church on 23 March 1904 to pay their respects. Among the senders of memorials were: Doctor Charles Allen Robinson (who was his successor at The Grange); Mr Edmund William Blessig of Coldharbour Farm; and the Denny family of Mount Pleasant. He was buried alongside his son, Edward Percy, who had died 24 years earlier, at three months of age. Doctor Oldman's wife, Beatrice, moved to Dorset and later Devon. She died in 1940, age 90.

Memorial plaque in St Mary's Church to Doctor Oldman
Twelve inches by seven inches, between the entrance and the Clayton memorial.

Uvedale Lambert Snr comments that the plaque:

> records the memory of one whose unflagging work and never failing kindliness will be long remembered in very many of the cottage homes of the parish. Dr Oldman was for many years the very able and efficient district medical officer for health.

Doctor Oldman's advertisements in local newspapers in the late 1800s:

> WANTED Donkey Mare, must be quiet and accustomed to children.
> WANTED a light Donkey cart in good repair.
> FOR SALE a Village Cart by Tynell and a four wheel basket Phaeton by Lenny.
> FOR SALE half-bred Alderney Cow, full profit, third calf.
> LOST Lost on Sunday evening, a small white, long haired dog, answering to the name of 'Ruffy'. Last seen near Underhills,

Bletchingley. Anyone returning the same to Doctor Oldman at The Grange, Bletchingley, Surrey, will be rewarded.

Mrs Beatrice Oldman's advertisements in the *Surrey Mirror & Morning Post* in 1891 and 1899:

A LADY wishes to recommend a girl, 16, as UNDER HOUSEMAID or to keep half in nursery, half in house. Apply Mrs Oldman, The Grange, Bletchingley, Surrey.

WANTED good PLAIN COOK; Four in family; all found; must be churchwoman and have good references. Apply Mrs Oldman, The Grange, Bletchingley, Surrey. [All found means it includes accommodation, food, drink and often beer].

Blechingley village centre – 1903
When Doctor Oldman and family were at The Grange; looking rather bare with its wide, open area, the market place in earlier times. © *The Francis Frith Collection.*

Auction at The Grange in May 1904, by order of Doctor Oldman's executors, to sell the contents of the house and gardens. The catalogue included, among many other items:

> Cottage pianoforte, by Collard and Collard, in a rosewood case, walnut davenport, etchings. and engravings, clocks, boots, an invalid wheelchair. Dairy utensils including a capital Du Val cream separator; two capital heifers [cows] in calf; a useful pony, a donkey, two cart harnesses, corn bins, eighty head of poultry, fowl houses, a new 30-egg incubator, two foster-mothers, greenhouse plants, garden tools, a smart greenhouse, rolls of netting, and other useful Items.

It is likely that Doctor Oldman kept his livestock in the meadow at the bottom of his garden (later to be Grange Meadow), as the electoral roll lists him at The Grange with land. He was also involved in the local agricultural society; perhaps he was a doctor and a farmer/smallholder.

Doctor Charles Allen Robinson and Family | Tenants 1904–09

There is little information about Charles' brief residency. He was listed as B.A., M.B., B.C. Camb. 1897: M.R.C.S., L.R.C.P. London 1896 (Camb. & St Bart.); Medical Officer and public vaccinator; Western District and Godstone Union Workhouse; Medical Officer for Health Godstone Rural District Council; Medical Officer to Blechingley Isolation Hospital. He was also a member of the Caterham Masonic Lodge.

Before his time at The Grange, he was based at nearby Limpsfield, Surrey. The practice at The Grange was called Furber, Robinson and Bentley. Charles Allen Robinson (1872–1951) married Mary Beatrice Ormerod (1875–1955) in 1901. They had four children: Valentine Charles (1902–45); Allen Ormerod (1904–87); Michael Hanson (1905–91); and Susan Mary (1911–2007). Allen Ormerod served in the army in WWII, with the rank of major, and was a Japanese prisoner of war in Singapore. Doctor Robinson resigned in 1909 and in 1911 he was based at Leominster, Hertfordshire.

Blechingley High Street looking east – 1905
When Doctor Robinson and family were living at The Grange, tenants to the Leslie family. The cart is said to be the village dustcart driven by Albert Morley, who was listed in the census as a carman, living in nearby Barfields. On the far left is Clive House, built in 1690, on the site of an old burgage tenement. The shop with the blind in the centre is Taylor and Bristow, general merchants and warehousemen, at Norfolk House, 80 High Street. Notice the horse dung on the road, something we don't see in glamorous period drama films! © *The Francis Frith Collection*.

Doctor Frederick William Robertson OBE and Family | Tenants/Owners 1909–52 | Robertson Whisky Business | Blechingley Isolation Hospital

Frederick William Robertson lived and practised at The Grange, with his family, from June 1909. Frederick's father, William, created a large business empire from small beginnings, which Frederick could have probably joined, as two of his brothers did. In later years, working from The Grange, he took on a great many responsibilities and almost died of exhaustion during WWI, due to his workload in Surrey.

William Alexander Robertson (1833–97)
Portrait courtesy of The Robertson Trust.

Doctor Frederick William Robertson OBE (1866–1937)
Photo courtesy of Doctor Andrew Robertson, Frederick's grandson. Colourised by author.

Frederick was born in Glasgow, Scotland, in 1866, one of 14 children. His parents were William Alexander and Agnes Heatley Robertson. William and his partner, John Baxter, founded the company, Robertson and Baxter, one of the principal whisky blenders and merchants in Scotland. Agnes Heatley died in 1886 at only 49, followed by William in 1897, at 64. William left £186,000 (equal to about £20 million in 2022) in trust for his children. William's eldest son James (Jim) had joined the family company in 1882, while younger brother Alexander (Nander) joined shortly after his father's death.

After the Great War (WWI), the whisky business was uncertain and the majority of shareholders, which included Doctor Frederick William Robertson and his siblings (apart from James and Alexander) wanted to sell their shares in Robertson and Baxter. The company was forced to sell off a huge amount of its whisky stock, the shareholders were paid and the company was put into voluntary liquidation. James and Alexander immediately started a new company called, Robertson and Company, and later bought back the Robertson and Baxter brand from the liquidators. Alexander Robertson died in 1940, without any children, followed by James in 1944, at age 80. James' heirs, his three daughters (Janet Elspeth, Agnes Heatley and Ethel Greig [Babs]), took a controlling interest in the company. In 1961, the three sisters formed Edrington Holdings Ltd. and The Robertson Trust. Today, the family business operates as the global company Edrington, one of Scotland's largest private companies and owner of several well-known whisky brands. The Robertson Trust is Scotland's largest independent grant-giving charitable trust, and is funded by the dividend income of its shares in Edrington.

Frederick and his three brothers, David Donaldson, Laurence and Philip, went on to pursue their own careers. David became a barrister in London. He achieved fame by winning a bronze medal for golf in the 1900 Olympics in Paris. He also played rugby for Scotland. Frederick's sister, Agnes Roberta, was a teacher, and sister Helen Hay went to Bushy, Hertfordshire, to study art. It seems that Helen's mother, Agnes, was not very keen as she wrote: 'whatever she might learn there'. Frederick graduated (M.A.) in 1888, then studied medicine in Glasgow and at some point moved down south.

Frederick married Hope Aston (b. 1877) on 14 June 1899, at Balham Ascension Church, South London. Hope was one of eight children born to Fanny Aston née Spinks (1850–1923) and stockbroker Charles James Aston (1847–1903). Before moving to The Grange in 1909, Frederick and Hope were renting a house in Wimbledon.

Residing at The Grange in April 1911 were: Doctor Frederick William Robertson, age 44; his wife Hope Robertson, age 34; son James (Dick) Robin Robertson, age 3. Staff: Florence Cook, cook, age 22; Constance Ida Affleck, domestic nurse, age 25; and Drucie Annie Dale, housemaid, age 17. Son Douglas Aston, age 10, was away at boarding school in Putney; daughter Ethel Hope (Peggy), age 8, was away at boarding school in Hertfordshire; and son Laurence Aston, was born at The Grange shortly after April 1911.

Frederick was 'Physician & Surgeon & Medical Officer & Public Vaccinator Western District Godstone Union, Medical Officer to Godstone Union Workhouse and Godstone Rural District Isolation Hospital and Medical Officer for Health to Godstone Rural District Council'. He was also a member of the Caterham Masonic Lodge. In 1913 the medical practice at The Grange was called Bentley, Robertson and Tylor, Physicians and Surgeons. Doctor Joseph Reginald Bentley had a practice in Limpsfield and Doctor Christopher Tylor had a practice in Oxted. It seems that local doctors worked together in those days.

Like his predecessors, Doctors Oldman and Robinson, Frederick produced an annual health report for the GRDC. In 1925 the district included: Addington, Blechingley, Chelsham, Crowhurst, Farleigh, Godstone, Horne, Limpsfield, Lingfield, Oxted, Tandridge, Tatsfield, Titsey, Warlingham and Woldingham. His 1925 report gives the population of Blechingley as 2,200. The report covers the Blechingley Isolation Hospital, also known as Godstone Isolation Hospital, which catered for the Godstone Rural District, mainly dealing with patients suffering with scarlet fever and diphtheria. In 1925 there were 40 admissions of patients with scarlet fever and 58 with diphtheria, with 3 deaths.

The twelve surviving children of William Alexander Robertson, Savoy Hotel – 1921
Key on next page. *Photo courtesy of Doctor Andrew Robertson, great-grandson of William Alexander Robertson.*

- Children of William Alexander Robertson: 1) James 'Jim' 1864–1945; 5) David Donaldson 1869–1937; 10) Alexander 'Nander' Cockburn 1873–1940; 11) Ethel 'Ethey' 1876–?; 12) Dorothea 'Dorothy' or 'Dolly' 1881–?; 13) Agnes Roberta 'Berta' (Tucker) 1865–1928; 14) Jane 'Jean' or 'Jennie' Heatley 1860–1945; 15) Laurence 1871–1945; 16) Frederick 'Fred' William OBE 1866–1937; 18) Grace 'Gracie' Bertram (Baynes) 1877–1970; 20) Winifred 'Winnie' Alys 1879–1955; 21) Philip 'Phee' 1875–1940. William had 14 children; missing are: Helen 'Ellie' or 'Nell' Hay and Frank Heatley (Alexander's twin) who died at birth in 1873.
- Related: 2) Violet, Philip's wife; 3) Hope, Frederick's wife; 4) Gladys, Alexander's wife; 6) William Bile Tucker, Alberta's husband; 7) Elsie, David's wife; 8) Madge, Laurence's wife; 17) Charles Baynes, Grace's husband; 22) Evelyn, Philip's daughter?
- Children of James Robertson, founders of Edrington and The Robertson Trust: 9) Agnes Heatley Robertson (b. 1897); 19) Janet Elspeth Robertson (b. 1896);' 23) Ethel Grieg Robertson 'Babs' (b. 1904).

Blechingley Isolation Hospital, which Frederick oversaw, was located at what is now Nightingale Way, off Rabies Heath Road, and had up to 40 beds. It opened in 1897, with nurse-in-charge Mrs Field. There were two single-storey buildings, plus an annexe, nurses' home and a porter's lodge. The nurses' home was also the administration centre and was built to house sick soldiers during WWI. In March 1901 the diphtheria ward burnt down after a fire believed to have been caused by a stove; the only two patients in the ward were safely evacuated. In October 1940 the nurses' home was severely damaged by an incendiary bomb.

Blechingley Isolation Hospital
From a Quinlan's Photo Series postcard, circa 1914–20. Colourised by author.

Excerpts from Doctor Robertson's GRDC annual reports:

> 1911 30% of children were unvaccinated due to conscientious objectors. Attention has already been called, in previous reports, to the steady increase in the numbers of unvaccinated children in the district. I can do no more than repeat the warning.
>
> 1915 I suggest that the school entrance age be raised from age five to seven years, on the grounds that the oldest child reaches five years old, goes to school, gets measles, brings it home and infects the baby who gets broncho-pneumonia and dies. This is an all-too-common sequence of events. Raise the school age to seven years, and the incidence of measles on the poorer classes would decline, and the mortality would surely decline with it.
>
> 1915 The disinfection facilities were under great pressure due to the amount of bedding and clothing from the troops, clothing mostly infected with parasites. Disinfection in connection with the refugees

and billets in the villages increased the strain on the Sanitary Department. For most of the summer of 1915 we had three large military camps, in Warlingham, Woldingham and Tandridge, and extensive billeting in many of the villages in the district. The fact that we only admitted 17 cases of infectious diseases from the camps to the hospital speaks well for the health of the troops. I have no doubt that the constant vigilance of your sanitary department in helping with the sanitary side of these camps and inspecting billets was largely contributory to this satisfactory state of affairs. There must have been quite 8000 soldiers at one time. [Billeting was a system where householders were required or expected to accommodate soldiers, for which they received a payment of 2s 6d a day for board and lodging].

1925 The rooms of infected houses were fumigated with Sulphur Dioxide Gas or sprayed with Formalin; the bedding and clothes are taken back to the isolation hospital for disinfecting in a 'Thresh's Steam Disinfector'. The same precautions are taken upon the receipt of all notifications of phthisis [tuberculosis] or cancer.

The reports open and close with:

To the Chairman and Councillors of the Rural District of Godstone. Mr Chairman, Ladies and Gentlemen. I have the honour to present to you my annual report – I have the honour to be, Gentlemen, your faithful servant. F.W. Robertson. M.A. Glasgow. M.D. & B.S. London. M.R.C.S. & L.R.C.P. The Grange, Bletchingley.

	No. of Businesses	No. of Hands Employed.			
		Men.	Women.	Young Persons.	Total.
...kers	21	56	10	8	74
...acksmiths, Wheelwrights and Coachbuilders	19	48		5	53
...ickmakers	6	48		2	50
...ilders and Decorators	30	98		2	100
...otmakers and Repairers	5	10			10
...essmakers and Milliners	7		9	11	20
...gineers and Cycle Makers	7	10		1	11
...y Proprietors	6	21			21
...undries (Steam and Domestic)	7	18	139	30	187
...llers	3	9			9
...inters	2	4		3	7
...ddlers	8	11		2	13
...ailors	4	11		1	12
TOTALS	125	344	158	65	567

Godstone Rural District, list of trades – 1911
From Doctor FW Robertson's report. Fly Proprietors dealt in, or hired out, horse drawn carts etc. *Image courtesy of The Wellcome Library.*

War memorial – c. 1921
Photograph taken by Doctor Frederick William Robertson. It was dedicated in 1921. It lists 56 Blechingley men who gave their lives in WWI and WWII. *Photo from Uvedale Lambert Snr's 1921 book.*

In 1898 the isolation hospital was advertising for a caretaker, 'man and wife, without encumbrance, joint salary with accommodation 30 shillings per week [£1.50]'. Mr George Edward Mariner was caretaker in 1901. Mr George Allen was caretaker from 1917 and he lived in the porter's lodge at the hospital for over 25 years. He drove the hospital 'fever van', which was used to collect sick patients, for fumigating infected houses and for transporting infected bedding and clothing back to the hospital to be disinfected. His wife, Mabel Fanny, was required to accompany him as a chaperone when transporting female patients, and to assist in the laundry and with nursing. The van sometimes made round trips of 24 miles to some of the outlying villages in the Godstone Rural District.

George Allen in the Fever Van – early 1900s
Photo courtesy of Derek Moore.

George Allen had a busy life. As well as his caretaker and driving duties, he was the boiler stoker and looked after the gardens where most of the hospital's vegetables were grown. He was succeeded in 1944 by Mr Arthur Lowings. By 1974 it was called Blechingley Hospital with 35 beds for geriatric patients. After a few years of rumours, the hospital finally closed in 1984. It was later demolished, and new houses were built on the site in the early 1990s. The porter's lodge is the only remaining building and is now a residence on the corner of Gayler Close and Night-ingale Way, off Rabies Heath Road.

Blechingley Isolation Hospital porter's lodge – 1914–20
At the entrance, with the porter standing by his gate.
A Quinlan's Photo Series postcard, courtesy of the East Surrey Museum.

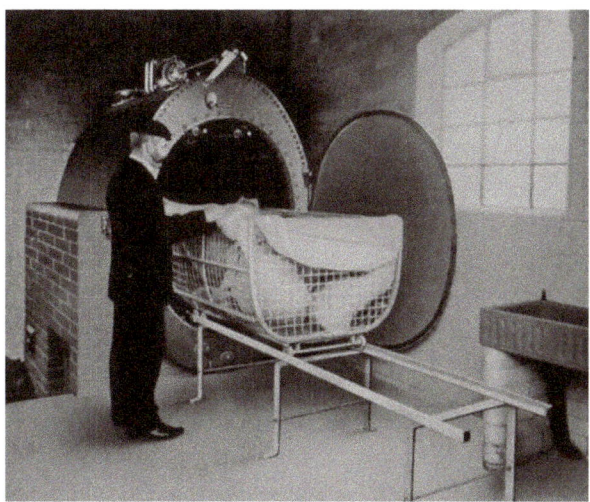

Thresh's Steam Disinfector – 1909
Photo from the Thresh's price list at The Wellcome Library.

Blechingley Isolation Hospital nurses' home
Photo courtesy of Derek Moore.

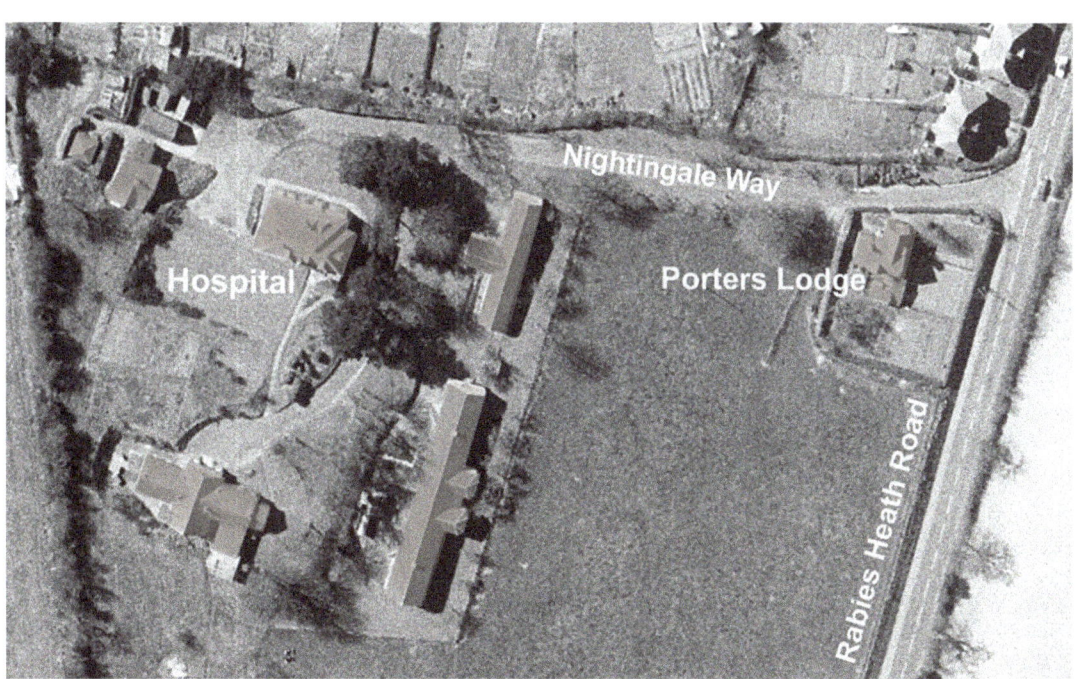

Blechingley Isolation Hospital aerial view – 1971
Formerly Blechingley Isolation Hospital. The entrance drive was named Nightingale Way when the new housing development was built on the site in the 1990s. © *NCAP*.

Blechingley Isolation Hospital, the old porter's lodge – 2021
The only remaining part of Blechingley Isolation Hospital. Now a private home called The Lodge, on the corner of Nightingale Way and Gayler Close – named after Alan Gayler, village sub-postmaster and chairman of the parish council in the 1980s.

An article in the *Blechingley Magazine*, published in 1995, recalls a story of a gentleman who moved to the village when Doctor Frederick William Robertson was practising:

> We found that Dr Robertson was universally liked and admired for his patient care. Being a Scot myself, my wife and I were quickly invited to have tea with him. His first action was to put his hand into the side pocket of his jacket, draw out a handful of loose cigarettes, and say 'Hae (i.e. have) a cigarette laddie'. He went on to tell me how much more primitive life had been in our village when he arrived here, his car had been one of the few in the neighbourhood. He described to me the philosophy which guided his practice; he charged the owners of large houses, with their knowledge and consent, Harley Street fees, in order to keep his charges to the poor low.

Excerpt from the 1937 obituary of Doctor Frederick William Robertson OBE:

> For 28 years Dr. Robertson was the greatly loved physician and friend of the inhabitants of Bletchingley. Since his retirement from practice in 1930, Dr. Robertson had taken a particularly keen interest in the game of bowls, and it was while he was playing at the Beckenham Cypher indoor rink on Monday evening that he collapsed with a heart attack.[17] Formerly Godstone's Medical Officer of Health, Dr. Robertson, the son of a Glasgow distiller, was born Christmas eve 1866. He was educated at Glasgow University and St Bartholomew's Hospital, and held the degrees of M.A. Glasgow. M.D. London. M.B. with honours in surgery, midwifery, forensic medicine, and B.S. He was a member of the Royal College of Surgeons, and Licentiate of the Royal College of Physicians. He was House Surgeon at Bart's, and at the Carshalton Children's Hospital, and Casualty Officer of the East London Hospital. He came to Bletchingley in June 1909 and very quickly won the hearts of the people. For a good many years, up to 1928, he was Medical Officer of Health (then a part-time appointment) to the Godstone Rural District Council, and was also Medical Officer to the District Hospital for Infectious Diseases at Bletchingley and the Bletchingley Guardians Institution. He retired from practice in 1930, and was succeeded by one of his sons, Dr. D. A. Robertson; lately, another son, Dr. J. R. Robertson, has joined his brother in the practice.
>
> **Bletchingley Interests** – Dr. Robertson took the keenest possible interest in local activities, and in one capacity or another was actively associated with most of them. He was school manager for a period, a governor of the Bletchingley Grammar School Trust, President of the Bletchingley Bowling Club, Chairman of Grange Meadow Grounds Committee, and for 26 years a brother of the Bletchingley 'Major Barclay' Odd Fellows. He was the first Hon Treasurer (to 1933) and then Chairman of the General and Tuberculosis Care Committee for the Division, and took a share in the formation of the Godstone

---

17 Frederick died the following day; a memorial service was held at St Mary's, Blechingley, and he was cremated at West Norwood.

Division the St John's Ambulance Brigade and was lecturer of the instructional classes. He was well known in East Surrey as a bowls player, and besides the Bletchingley Club, for which he played frequently, he was member of the Wiggie (Redhill) Club, and also the Beckenham Indoor Club. At the annual dinner of the Godstone Bowling Club on Wednesday, the company stood in silence in memory of Dr. Robertson.

An Appreciation – Doctor Robertson was the keenest bowler I have ever played with, or played against, during the whole of my bowling career. His zeal and interest in every point of the game created the right atmosphere, and to me it was a pleasure to have him in a rink game, either for or against, because he inspired me to play my very best, and yet with all this, he was charitable, and would rather give away an advantage than take one. He will be sadly missed at the Cyphers Indoor Bowling Club, and at Redhill, where he had endeared himself to all the members. Erected on the Pavilion at the Redhill Club is a Weathervane, recently given by the Doctor. The indicator represents a bowler, delivering a bowl. When we are on the green we shall often look at this, to get the direction of the wind, and the memory of the 'Doc' (as we used to call him) will come before us, and these words:

For when the one Great Scorer comes to write against your name, He marks not that you won or lost, but how you played the game.[18]

Frederick and Hope Robertson had five children: Douglas Aston, born in 1900; Ethel Hope 'Peggy', born in 1902; Phyllis Grace, born 18 June 1906, baptised 14 July 1906, she died later that year; James Robin 'Dick', born in 1907; and Laurence Aston, born in 1911.

Ethel Hope married Frank Bagnall in July 1933, at St Mary's Church, Blechingley, and they lived in Putney. Hope was tragically killed during a German bombing raid in London in 1941, and her husband was severely injured. *See photo of Ethel Hope on 184.*

---

18 Obituary published in *The Surrey Mirror and County Post*, Friday 12 February 1937. © Mirrorpix/Reach Licensing.

Redhill Bowling Club, newly built in 1931
The weathervane on the right is presumed to have been the one gifted by Dr F W Robertson OBE, and was put up on the new pavilion at a later date. The pavilion was destroyed by a fire in 1981 and rebuilt. At the time of writing the weathervane was in the possession of Redhill Bowling Club, pending restoration. *Photos courtesy of Redhill Bowling Club.*

Memorial to Doctor Frederick William Robertson OBE and his daughter Ethel Hope Bagnall, St Mary's Church – 1942
The staircase mentioned goes up to the oak pulpit given by Robert Holman in the seventeenth century.

Laurence Aston married Helen Mary Jackling in 1941, and they lived in Bridge Blean, Kent, and later at Petworth, Sussex. According to a newspaper article regarding a serious motor accident in which he was involved in 1934, he owned a 1927 Bentley, 14 feet in length, which could do 90 mph. He died of tuberculosis around 1946, aged only 35. His two brothers, Douglas and Dick, followed in their father's footsteps, and went into the medical profession …

DOCTOR DOUGLAS ASTON ROBERTSON

In 1921 Doctor Douglas Aston Robertson embarked on a seven-year apprenticeship with his uncle, Tatham Batters Aston, a stockbroker. At some point he must have had a change of heart, as he went on to became a heart specialist and was a pioneer in the development of the electrocardiograph. He married Bessie Kathleen Wells on 3 December 1927 at St Peter's Church, Limpsfield, Surrey. Bessie was the only daughter of Mr and Mrs R Sidney Wells of Lunchwood Cottage, Limpsfield. Douglas and Bessie had three children: Jill, Mac and John.

Douglas co-developed a portable electrocardiograph machine in the early 1930s with Mr LH Bedford. It was known as the Cossor Robertson Electrocardiograph, and was built using an AC Cossor Ltd cathode ray oscilloscope (British Patent No. 442513). Cossor developed and manufactured radar systems, radios and television sets. The machine was powered from the mains or via two internal 300 volt batteries. A camera with 25 feet of unperforated 35 mm film or recording paper could be attached to the machine to produce a permanent record. The machine was installed in Stalingrad Hospital around 1945. Douglas published a number of papers on the electrocardiograph and the Council of the British Institution of Electrical Engineers awarded him the Ayrton premium. Willem Einthoven is credited with actually inventing the electrocardiograph and he received the Nobel Prize in Physiology or Medicine in 1924 for his 'discovery of the mechanism of the electrocardiogram'.

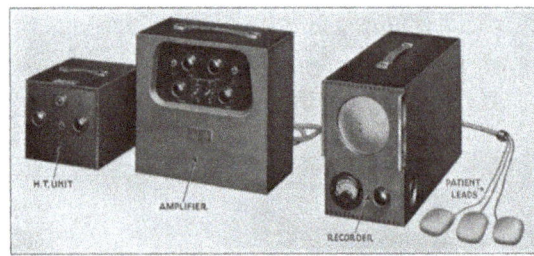

Cossor Robertson Portable Electrocardiograph
Image from Douglas Robertson (1934) 'A New Electrocardiograph Employing the Cathode Ray Oscillograph as the Recording Device', *Proceedings of the Royal Society of Medicine*, 27(12):1541–54. © SAGE Publishing, CA, USA.

Also from the previously quoted 1995 *Blechingley Magazine* article:

> Douglas was a clever scientist, and more interested in research than in the work of a village doctor. He made an electrocardiograph machine in an attic room at the Grange, which he tried out on me. As a heart specialist, he had consulting rooms in Harley Street, London, and he drove himself to and from there in a large American car.

Douglas was associated with many medical institutions, including: The Queen Victoria Hospital, East Grinstead, Surrey, as consulting physician and cardiologist; the National Heart Hospital, London, senior clinical assistant; East Surrey Hospital, Redhill, Surrey, and 86 Brook Street, Mayfair, London W1. It is difficult to track where Douglas lived after his marriage. In the early 1930s he was living at The Green, Godstone, and then at The Grange up until about 1952, but his work was generally outside the area. After he left The Grange, he lived in Forest Row, Sussex. He died in 1974.

DOCTOR JAMES 'DICK' ROBIN ROBERTSON.

There was romance at The Grange when Dick met his wife-to-be, Betty Marion, while she was nurse to his brother Douglas' children at The Grange, after they had their tonsils out. Dick opened a medical practice at Ridge Green Farm, Nutfield, in 1938, where he lived with his wife and three children. He also continued to practise at The Grange and Godstone. In about 1954, Ridge Green was sold, and Dick and his family moved to Quarryhanger, Springbottom Lane, Blechingley.

Local lady Marian Buck recalls:

> late arrivals for surgery visits at The Grange had to wait and sit on a bench in an unheated wooden porch, once inside there were proper chairs. I remember there was a glass display cabinet full of gruesome surgical instruments, much to the delight of us children! In later years my dad commented to the doctor that it would be nice to have some pictures on the wall to look at instead.

Lieutenant-Colonel Dick Robertson
Photos courtesy of Doctor Andrew Robertson.

Dick and Betty Robertson's wedding

Dick served in WWII as a medical officer with the Seventh Armoured Brigade (Desert Rats) in North Africa, then later in Italy and Greece. On his retirement he moved to a house he had bought on the Isle of Seil, off the north-west coast of Scotland. He died in 1970.

DOCTOR ANDREW ROBERTSON

Dick's son, Doctor Andrew Robertson, was born at Ridge Green in 1938 and went on to practise as a GP in Lingfield, Surrey (about seven miles from Blechingley), and was also an anaesthetist at The Queen Victoria Hospital, East Grinstead. He mentioned that 'for some historical reason the Lingfield Practice were doctors to the Bletchingley Hospital [formerly Blechingley Isolation Hospital], and Clerks Croft Hospital [formerly Godstone Union Workhouse], until their closure [in the 1980s]. I was therefore the last of the Robertsons to practice in Blechingley'.

Andrew retired in 2003, having practised at Lingfield alongside Doctor Fiona Glover, wife of Doctor Michael Glover, who practised for about thirty years at Blechingley's current local surgery, The Pond Tail, Godstone Green (the old police station). Michael and Fiona Glover retired on the same day in November 2019 and live in Blechingley.

The Robertson family were tenants at The Grange from 1909 until 1924, when Mrs Hope Robertson (Frederick's wife) purchased The Grange from New Zealand-based Miss Elizabeth Mary Leslie and trustees. The purchase price for The Grange, gardens, gardener's cottage (Grange Cottage), stables, coach house and yards, plus the western plot in Outwood Lane, was £2,400. Frederick's 1937 probate value was £40,000, about two million pounds in 2022, which went to Douglas and Dick Robertson, who were then listed as joint owners of The Grange. Douglas bought Dick's share for £1,400 in 1938 and became the sole owner.

Doctor Andrew and Rosemary Robertson – 1964
They were married at St Mary's Blechingley on 11 July, pictured here in Church Walk. *Photo courtesy Doctor Andrew Robertson.*

Doctor Frederick William Robertson OBE and his wife Hope – 1921
Photos courtesy of Doctor Andrew Robertson. Black & white photos colourised by the author.

Douglas sold The Grange to Philippa Marshall in 1952. He also sold Grange Cottage separately in the same year to Mr MA Freeth of Blechingley. Philippa's husband, Doctor Mark Marshall, remained in partnership with Doctor Dick Robertson at The Grange until the 1960s. So the Robertson family practised at The Grange for over 50 years.

Mrs Hope Robertson was advertising for staff in *The Surrey Mirror and County Post* in 1924: 'WANTED House Parlourmaid in no basement house; good wages and outings; comfortable situation; buses pass near door. Apply Mrs Robertson, The Grange, Bletchingley, Surrey.'

Doctor Douglas Robertson was advertising for staff in 1947: 'WANTED live in cook in Heart Specialists house. Apply to the secretary, The Grange, Bletchingley, Surrey.'

Commemorative rose garden at rear of The Grange – late 1930s
Dedicated to Mrs Hope Robertson (1877–1932) and Doctor Frederick William Robertson OBE (1866–1937). *Photo courtesy of Doctor Andrew Robertson.*

THE DIARY, LETTERS AND MISCELLANEOUS WRITINGS OF AGNES HEATLEY ROBERTSON

In the late 1800s Frederick William Robertson chose a career in medicine over joining the family whisky business. Some 125 years and four generations later there is still a doctor in the Robertson family. Perhaps Frederick was influenced by his mother Agnes to pursue his own career path. Agnes almost died during the birth of her first child in 1860, and over the next 22 years gave birth to 13 more children, one of whom died at birth (Frank Heatley in 1873). She made sure her children received a good education; the boys all went to St Andrews. In later life, when the universities in Glasgow opened to women, she was one of the first to enrol. She was a devout Presbyterian and her faith is reflected in her diary, letters and writings, which were published as a book for private circulation in 1895, by Glasgow University Press.[19]

The following are some extracts:

> January 1858: [before her marriage the following year] I'd rather be a mountain torrent than a stagnant pool, but, best of all, a clear rippling stream, spreading life around.
>
> April 1880: You were quite right about deeds making the gentleman. … We must never forget that the most perfect gentleman that ever walked this earth had no where to lay His head.
>
> June 1880: Fred would scarcely go up to Glasgow. 'No use–no lessons'. He was lifted out of bed, dressed, carried downstairs, fed with breakfast, his cap put on his head, and lifted into the carriage. Of course there is a little hyperbole in this, but Miss Hay and Bertha almost did as much.
>
> June 1880: I think, my man, that it is time you were at Sandhills, home among your kith and kin [family], when you are beginning to forget their names. Well, Baby's name is Winifred Alys, in common parlance Winnie, and a blithe wee lass she is, and the very image of

---

19 Presbyterianism is a Christian protestant denomination/system, with roots in the Church of Scotland and the Reformation.

her eldest brother, especially when asleep. The weather is beautiful, and you know how bonnie Sandhills looks in fine weather. Punch, your little pup, is a beauty, long, flaxen hair, tipped with black, soft and silky. Jess still keeps scrubby. Vic is a splendid animal. You heard that poor Nellie and her puppy died. The horse we have got is a very good one, as big as Laddie, but rather lanky, though a capital goer. We have a small pony of Mr. W.'s, and a two-wheeled phaeton. The pony shies little, and requires plenty of whip. Fred and David have not been fishing yet, as they haven't time, being still at school. Geely-Gally put up the new swing yesterday at the end of the house, near the wee wood. It has a bar, so nothing will be the fashion for a while but swinging and gymnastics.

December 1882: I have felt somehow, today, my inability to do all that is required of me; I feel that, as it were, 'I have trodden the wine-press alone, and of the people there is none with me'. Neither can there be in many things and, bless me! how is my head fitted to plan and scheme for all this so great a people: and yet it is possible and practicable, I know 'I can do all things through Christ who strengtheneth me'. So goodbye old year! You and I have had many a gloomy day, but oh, how many bright ones! We have stumbled oft and wandered oft, but the hand that has led me and mine, has been my father's hand; so lead me, my husband, and all my children, Jeanie, Ellie, Jim, Berta, Fred, David, Laurence, Nander, Phee, Ethel, Grace, Winnie, Dolley, all, everyone, to our father's house at last.

January 1883: [speaking of her son James, who had just joined the family whisky business] God grant him grace to walk uprightly, truly, and honestly before God and man. We walked back again to the golf house; it was a fine after-noon, and we watched the sun sinking like a golden goblet into the sea. The fresh air was like fresh life to me. O the blessed country air! Why are men, women, and poor little bairnies [children] condemned to stifle in close cities? Is it not that the other half of the population may be fed and clothed, and live in ease? Will these not be accounted their brothers' keepers?

June 1884: Fred went out on his bicycle Wednesday. Dear independent Fred, too self-contained and independent, he does not seem to feel that he is part of the human world and must join in the fight and race.

January 1886: God be in their dear hearts, that like Jesus they may die to sin and live again. Nander, I think, is much improved – quieter, gentler, and more thoughtful. Dear laddie! the first night he played the violin I saw a vision of another wee boy, not so sturdy, not so ruddy, lying on a couch listening to Nander with a glowing face. A silly vision! If Franky had lived he would have been a weakly boy, but now he is strong in his Father's house. Yet this vision is sweet, but the reality is soul inspiring.

Agnes Heatley Robertson 1837–86

Bletchingly, village scene – c. 1909
From around the time Doctor Frederick William Robertson and family lived here. They moved into The Grange in June 1909. The caption says looking east, but it is actually looking west. On the far right is Camden House, which was the other medical practice in the village, run by Doctor Alfred Pratt. The vehicle in the background is a horse-drawn hearse. *From a Frith & Co Ltd postcard, with a postmark of 14 July 1909.*

Doctor FW Robertson's work in WWI Soldiers' Hospitals | Red Gables | Castle Relief

Excerpt from the 1937 obituary of Doctor Frederick William Robertson OBE:

> During the war he held the rank of Lt.-Colonel in the R.A.M.C. [Royal Army Medical Corps] and worked extremely hard, adding to his private practice, itself a big one, that of the membership of the medical staff of several military hospitals and soldiers' homes in East Surrey. He must have done the work of three normal men during these four years, he was awarded the OBE (Order of the British Empire – Military) for his services and as a result was very ill for a number of years afterwards, and it was only his Scots stamina that enabled him to pull through.[20]

Red Gables Hospital was one of the WWI military hospitals which Frederick was involved with. Located in the north of Blechingley, near Hextalls Lane, it was run by Doctor Francis Charles Abbott, who was commandant and surgeon-in-charge. The private hospital was opened on 5 November 1914 and operated as a convalescence home until February 1919. It dealt with nearly 700 of the more serious bone fractures and medical cases of men who suffered from shell or gunshot fire. At the start of WWI over 5,000 private buildings in the UK were offered to the War Office free of charge, for use as convalescence homes.

Red Gables was built for Doctor and Mrs Pauline Abbott in the early 1900s, next to their home at The Hermitage, with a connecting drive between the two. The house is now Red Gables Court, The Conduit, off Hextalls Lane, about one and a half miles from the village centre and split into four private homes. According to www.bombsight.org, a German bomb exploded near the Hermitage and Red Gables in 1940–1, which may explain why one end of the house is missing today. A German bomber aircraft also crashed on White Hill during the war. A unit of the Royal Corps of Signals were stationed at Red Gables and the Hermitage for a time during WWII. The Hermitage is still there today, believed to be on the site of a medieval house. In

---

20 Obituary published in *The Surrey Mirror and County Post*, Friday 12 February 1937. © Mirrorpix/Reach Licensing.

the 1990s the crossroads at the top of the hill, at War Coppice Road and Hextalls Lane, was still remembered by locals as having the somewhat politically incorrect name of 'Cripples Corner'.

Red Gables. group photo at – 1915
1) Doctor Francis Charles Abbott; 2) Doctor Frederick William Robertson. **Front row on the ground**: Rifleman Connelly, Sgt. Millgate, Pte. Kewley, Sgt. Thornton, Sgt. Mortimer. **First row sitting**: L/Cpl. Clark, Cpl. Stallard, Driver Greenaway, Pte. Thierrin, Sister Hardwicke, Mrs Way (Matron), Mrs Pauline Abbott, Miss Dixon (Secretary), Sister Newton, Pte. Fox, Driver Gunneen, Pte. Ridgeway. **Second row**: Pte. Harris, Pte. Flack, Nurse Atkins, Gunner James, Bombardier Russell, Sgt. Gathercole, Nurse Jephson, Pte. Barnard, Dr. Baker, Dr. Curtis, Dr. Abbott, Dr. Robertson, L/Cpl Jeffries, Pte. Wells, Nurse Ford, Driver Sach, Sister Hodgson, Strapper Tyler. **Back Row**: Trumpeter Parker, Pte. Athersmith, Pte. Mott, Sgt. Sharp, Cpl. Woolmer, Cpl. Davidson, Pte. Pauffley, Pte. Meek, Pte. Fox, Pte. Thompson, Pte. Grosvenor, Pte. Bostock, Pte. Ainsworth, Pte. Orbell, L/Cpl Exon, Pte. Hallson, Driver Piggott, L/Cpl Imerson, Pte. Davies, Bombardier Partridge.[21] *Photo from a postcard photographed by Robinson and Son, Redhill, courtesy of Steve Clifford, Canada, of* Doing our Bit – Military and Family History Research.

---

21 The list of names was published in the *Surrey Mirror* on 15 October 1915. © Mirrorpix/Reach Licensing. Edited by Steve Clifford, Canada, *Doing our Bit – Military and Family History Research.*

Red Gables soldiers' hospital – c. 1915
The two ladies on the hill are identified on the rear of this postcard as Matron Mrs Way (Doctor Abbott's sister) and secretary Miss Dixon. *From an un-posted Frith & Co Ltd postcard. Colourised by author.*

The Hermitage
From a Frith & Co postcard with a postmark of 1915, courtesy of the East Surrey Museum.

Red Gables, wounded soldiers on the terrace during WWI
Photo courtesy of Steve Clifford, Canada, Doing our Bit – Military and Family History Research. Colourised by author.

Horace Albert Jenner (1875–1938), of Blechingley, signed up as a reservist in 1916, and was on active duty in 1918 with the RAMC (Royal Army Medical Corps). 1918 electoral and military records show him living with his wife Margaret and family at Red Gables Cottage/Red Gables Lodge. His granddaughter, Jean Osborne, recalls that the family may have been residing here before 1918, with Horace working for Doctor Abbott, but electoral registers were not published for the years 1916–17. His work in 1918 included orderly work in the hospital, chimney sweeping, attending to lighting machinery, gardening and superintending 30 acres of gardens and grounds. In fact his workload was so large that he attended an appeals tribunal with Doctor Abbott at Oxted, where a request was made to be exempted from military service or that his grade be lowered. Unfortunately the application was refused (*The Westerham Herald*, 18 May 1918).

Horace and Margaret's grandaughter, Margaret Jean Osborne (known as Jean, born 1938 in Bletchingley) was still living in the village in 2024. A total of seven of Jean's Blechingley relatives served in WWI (including Horace), two of whom were killed in action in France: James Osborne on 26 October 1917; soon followed by his brother John, on 30 November 1917.

Margaret (1878–1964) and Horace Albert Jenner (1875–1938)
Photo courtesy of Jean Osborne.

Red Gables, nurses and sisters
Photo courtesy of Steve Clifford, Canada, Doing our Bit – Military and Family History Research. Colourised by author.

Bletchingley Castle Relief Hospital was based in the 19-bedroom mansion house, built as Castle Hill, and the nearby six-bedroom Dower House, on the 326 acre Castle Hill Estate, a ten-minute walk from The Grange. The mansion house was known during WWI as Bletchingley Castle, a fitting name for a military hospital. Over 1,000 soldiers convalesced there during WWI. From 1906, Castle Hill was the country home of Mr Augustus Philip Brandt and his wife Jean.

Article in *The Gentlewoman* magazine, 19 December 1914:

Away from the wards, in that part of the house set aside for the use of the convalescents, everything possible is done for the entertainment of our gallant fighting men. While Sister Morgan, of the London Hospital, has undertaken the duties of Matron-in-Charge, and superintends the nursing staff, the house is under the supervision of Mrs Brandt, and she is assisted in her efforts to make the soldier guests happy by the energies of her two little daughters, Jean and Gwendoline, who are tireless in their anxiety to be of every possible assistance. Latterly owing to the serious nature of some of the wounded, Mr Brandt has had electrical medical apparatus installed with a special staff for its application, with excellent results. Brightly decorated smoking rooms have been stocked with games of every imaginable kind and on certain days the neighbouring residents visit Bletchingley Castle and arrange various forms of amusement, while Mr and Mrs Brandt provide weekly cinematograph entertainments. For those of the patients who are sufficiently recovered, outdoor sports have been provided in the beautiful grounds which surround the house. The more advanced convalescents enjoy the sport of rabbiting in the grounds of the Castle by means of ferrets and nets which have been supplied for the purpose.

A happy idea of furthering the allied cause in a particularly effective way is carried into practice by allowing the patients, so far as is possible, to mingle with the villagers and folks of the neighbouring towns, so that the stirring tales the wounded have to relate may have due effect upon the youths of the countryside who are wanted to fill the ranks. As a final gift from Mr. and Mrs. Brandt, each soldier upon leaving the hospital is provided with a complete set of warm underclothing, a pair of boots, pipe, pouch, muffler and mittens, for service upon his return to the Front.

Castle Hill mansion, front
Or Bletchingley Castle as it was known during WWI, its name borrowed from the ancient Blechingley Castle, which was destroyed in the 1200s. *From an early 1900s Adamstone Series Postcard. Colourised by author.*

Castle Hill/ Bletchingley Castle, west end The covered terrace was later replaced with an orangery. *From a 1914–20 Quinlan's Photo Series postcard, courtesy of The East Surrey Museum.*

Bletchingley Castle Relief Hospital, group of wounded soldiers – 1914
'Some of the wounded British soldiers and one of the nurses in the grounds at Bletchingley Castle.' The photo was taken on the terrace of The Dower House. On the right is a photo of The Dower House terrace taken in 2021, looking about the same 107 years later. *Photo from The Gentlewoman, 19 December 1914, © British Library Board. Colourised by author.*

Castle Relief Hospital, group of wounded soldiers – 1914
'A group taken at Bletchingley Castle showing some wounded Belgians who recently arrived, and two of the nurses.' On the terrace of The Dower House. *Photo from* The Gentlewoman, *19 December 1914,* © *British Library Board.*

Some authors have incorrectly stated that the hospital was based solely in the Dower House. In 1914 *The Gentlewoman* published a photo of the mansion house with the caption, 'A view of Bletchingley Castle the country residence of Mr. and Mrs. A. P. Brandt, which they have converted into a Relief Hospital.'

James Norris (b. 1826), a partner in wine brokers Norris and Gilbey, built the Castle Hill mansion house. He bought Castle Farm after it was put up for auction on 14 November 1866 by order of the liquidators of the bank, Overend Gurney and Co Ltd, after the 1866 financial crash in London, coined by *The Times* as 'Black Friday'. In the auction listing it was described as a farm of 166 acres with various buildings and cottages 'offering some highly attractive sites for the erection of a mansion'. The farm was being auctioned along with eight other local lots of farms and houses, including The Grange and its farm, Town Farm, all owned at the time by Robert and/or Edward Birkbeck.

Castle Hill mansion house/Bletchingley Castle rear
From a Frith & Co Ltd postcard with a postmark of 1906. Colourised by author.

So, as per the auctioneer's recommendation, James proceeded to build his 19-bedroom mansion house on the west end of the grounds of the ancient Blechingley Castle, and named it Castle Hill. He obtained permission to divert a footpath and he excavated the castle moat before building on the site, where it was said he found many interesting artefacts. The mansion house, along with the east and west lodges, stables, coach house, cottages and so on, were completed around 1868. By 1882 James had retired from the wine business and owned 1,300 acres of land in the area, 550 of which he had purchased from the Clayton family in 1875. He died in 1894 and was buried alongside his wife Susanna Louisa (1825–87) in Blechingley.

Henry Partridge bought the Castle Hill estate in 1895. He was a banker with large business interests in South Africa. He was later said to be one of the most influential farmers in the county of Surrey.

The Dower House, on the steep hill leading down to Castle Hill Farm, was built by Henry Partridge in 1896 as a convalescent home in memory of his 15-year-old-daughter, Ellen Dorothy, who died of acute rheumatism, in summer 1895 in Wales. The home was formally opened and dedicated by the Bishop of Southwark in July 1897, who described it as 'in every way the perfect home'. It catered primarily for those suffering from acute rheumatism, but other local cases were also admitted. A newspaper article says it was intended 'for patients of better classes in poor circumstances'. It could accommodate 18 patients, free of charge, and had all home comforts, including a piano, a small library, a matron (Miss Stewart) and trained nurses. Another article said it had 'the most delightful absence of rules and regulations'.

Tragedy struck the Partridge family again in 1898, when the second of Henry's three daughters, Mary Coralie, wife of Reginald Whistler Ord, died at Dover, age 26. Henry also had three sons: Noel Henry, Graham and Llewellyn.

The Dower House – 1914–20
The house looked pretty much the same in 2022, but was missing the central roof tower and the flag poles. Mrs AP (Jean) Brandt ran the Castle Relief Hospital. *From a poor copy of a 1914–20 Quinlan's Photo Series postcard. Colourised by author.*

In 1906 Henry sold up in Blechingley to relocate, and it seems that the convalescent home was closed. The house was listed for sale by auction in 1906 as The Dower House, along with the Castle Hill mansion and estate. The Dower House has had a few different names: in 1897 it was simply The Convalescent Home; in 1906 The

Dower House; in 1935 Hill Cottage; it was Hill House up to 2007, when the name was changed back to The Dower House. Henry's other local properties were also auctioned, including 22 cottages, the bank and post office (Bank Buildings) and Berry House.

Henry went to live in Grosmont, Hereford (1911), with his wife Laura, daughter-in-law Mary Cicely Partridge (wife of Llewellyn Partridge), four grandchildren and six servants. Laura died in 1922, age 79, in Wadhurst, Sussex, followed by Henry in 1925, age 78, in Southborough, Kent, but they were both buried at Blechingley, alongside their daughters, Ellen 'Dollie' and Mary.

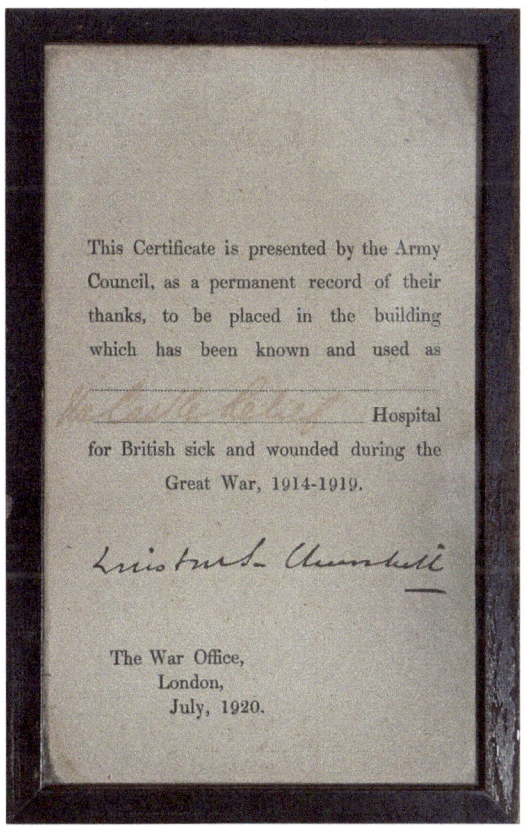

Certificate from the War Office signed by Winston Churchill – 1920
For Castle Relief Hospital. Churchill was Secretary of State for War and Air 1919–21. *Courtesy of The Dower House owners, 2022.*

Frank Smith, age 18 – 1916
He convalesced at The Dower House, October–November 1917, after being wounded in the Somme trenches. He was invalided out of the army, so did not return to France. He married, had a family and lived to 82. *Courtesy of The Dower House owners, 2022.*

When The Dower House was put up for sale with the Castle Hill estate in June 1906, it was listed as having: six bedrooms – three reception rooms – bathroom – electric light and gas – good water and perfect sanitation. The Castle Hill mansion and The Dower House had telephones. The site had its own electricity generator, which was located in a building at the end of Castle Square, known by locals as The Engine Shed, and now a private home called Odstock (2023). There was also a private phone line from the mansion to the stables, so that horses and carriages could be conveniently ordered. Castle Hill would play a role in the next world war when Canadian soldiers were billeted there and at various places around Blechingley. Army trucks were parked up under the cover of trees around Castle Hill, out of the sight of enemy aircraft.

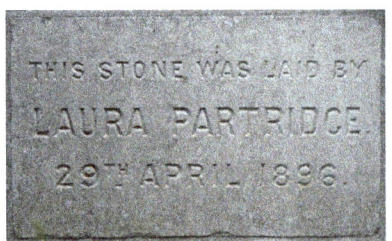

The Dower House foundation stone – 1896

A CONVALESCENT'S POEM OF APPRECIATION OF THE BLECHINGLEY CASTLE RELIEF HOSPITAL

By Corporal WH Cockings of the 2nd Battalion of the Grenadier Guards. 30 July 1915. Published in the parish magazine, November 1992

There's beautiful village named Blechingley
I have stayed there for over four months
And you'll find in summer the scenery
Is a great place better than France

The village you will find is in Surrey
Which is noted for its beautiful views
Right amongst its hills and its valleys
Where artists can paint at their ease

Then again, the air is most bracing
For people who may not feel well
The White Hills with their beautiful facings
Smile down on a beautiful dell

There is also a very fine castle
Stands high in its beautiful grounds
Where many of our brave soldiers
Find comfort while healing their wounds

It's to the owner of this beautiful castle
And also the matron and nurse
That we soldiers are most truly thankful
For the attention we received from the first

To our soldiers who come convalescent
There are amusements and all sorts of games
Such as billiards, croquet and cricket
And other such things for the lame

Such a thing as your eyes being affected
By the way, there is one just arrived
But thanks to the energy of the matron
He is able to learn the Braille code

But these are not all our pleasures
For we have a vast number of friends
If we choose to take, for our leisure
A pleasant afternoon in the grounds

Then again, there're others who invite us
To tea, which we greatly enjoy
And then there's games of all descriptions
And the winners receive a fine prize

Oft times we go out in the motor
The routes we entrust to the Fleet
For a better experienced chauffeur
You could hardly wish to meet

Amongst those who invite us to these parties
Also motoring through Sussex and Kent
Our thanks are due in the first place
To our hosts, Mr and Mrs Brandt

And the others we find are the Blessigs
The Temperleys and Lamberts as well
And others who think of our welfare
Are the Harrissons, who in Antwerp did dwell

But although we go out to these parties
Our home is a haven of rest
For we find that our cook and our housemaid
Have at least had an afternoon's rest

In our pleasures we ought not to forget them
For we own they are two of the best
Great praise is given for the cooking
And to the maid for cleaning the house

And as months and years roll past us
We shall always look back with pride
On this beautiful village of Blechingley
And the home where we used to abide

So here's health to our host and our hostess
And to their children as well:
Good luck, and the best of our wishes
May God bless you and protect you as well.

Norris and Partridge family memorials, Blechingley Cemetery
(left) to James and Susanna Louisa Norris, Blechingley; (right) to Henry and Laura Partridge and their daughters, Ellen 'Dollie' and Mary, Blechingley.

Augustus Philip Brandt bought the Castle Hill estate by private treaty in 1906, after it was listed for sale by auction by the order of Henry Partridge. In the following year Augustus' brother Henry Bernard bought the mansion Capenor, half a mile to the west, in Nutfield, with lands adjoining Castle Hill. Augustus and Henry were also neighbours at their second homes, at Queen's Gate and Queen's Gate Gardens, in Kensington, London.

The 1906 auction listing for the Castle Hill estate described it as follows: Total of 326 acres, including the main mansion house (Castle Hill) – the six-bedroom Dower House – two homesteads – ten cottages and more. The mansion included east and west lodges – harness room – stables for 13 horses – coach houses for six carriages – coachman's rooms – groom's quarters – bothy – motor-house – tennis lawn for three courts – croquet lawn, and among other things, six brick-built dog kennels with iron-fenced runs.

Augustus was chairman of William Brandt's Sons & Co Ltd, merchant bankers, and was of German-Russian origin. Augustus kept an open house at Castle Hill for every member of the family so it was frequently animated by the visits of cousins from

Germany, Russia and America. Russian relatives who had escaped the Revolution came to live with them, some for several years. Augustus' wife Jean lavishly entertained family and friends at Castle Hill most weekends. She is remembered by one of her descendants as a larger than life character and 'a benevolent tyrant with a huge open purse (her husband's)'.[22]

Augustus Philip Brandt (1871–1952)
Oil on canvas, 1927, Philip Alexius de László, M.V.O., P.R.B.A. De László painted many royal and famous people, including the Queen Mother (mother of Queen Elizabeth II) and Princess Elizabeth before she became Queen. *Used by kind permission of and © de Laszlo Foundation/Archive Trust.*

Jean Champion Brandt, née Garmany, was born on 26 August 1867 to a prominent family in Savannah, Georgia, USA. In 1887 she secretly married Heyward Hall McAllister. When their union was discovered her father-in-law publicly denounced the match, arguing that his son could not support her and had no prospect of employment. In reality, Ward McAllister had hoped that Heyward would marry someone with considerable wealth to alleviate his own financial troubles. The marriage was never consummated and the young couple divorced in 1892. Jean's mother took her to Europe and North Africa to avoid the publicity and the weight of the scandal. While walking in Egypt, Jean met and fell in love with the young banker, Augustus Philip Brandt. Hearing the news that Augustus had proposed to her, his family were alarmed and sent out his youngest brother, Rudi, to appraise her. He later sent a telegram home with the following report: 'If Gussie doesn't marry her, I will.' Augustus and Jean were married in May 1898. They had two daughters, Jean (b. 1900) and Gwendolen 'Gwen' (b. 1904), and

22 Some of this text was copied directly from the de Laszlo Foundation website.

they settled in the family home, Castle Hill. They welcomed and supported for a time their nephew Bill Brandt (1904–83), whose fame as an acclaimed British photographer came later. He recorded some of the daily life and social gatherings at Castle Hill and Capenor. Jean died in 1950, followed by Augustus in 1952. They were buried in Blechingley.[23]

Jean Champion Brandt, née Garmany (1867–1950)
Oil on canvas, 1928, Philip Alexius de László, M.V.O., P.R.B.A. *Used by kind permission of and © de Laszlo Foundation/Archive Trust.*

Edwin Mullins, British art critic, journalist, author, television script writer and presenter, grandson of Augustus and Jean Brandt, was born in 1933 to Gwendolen Mullins, née Brandt. He often visited and stayed at Castle Hill in his younger days. In 1983 he published a novel, Sirens, some of which is loosely based on life at Castle Hill during WWII: Castle Hill is referred to as Castlewood; some of the events are based on real life; some actual characters are renamed. Around 1973 he also made a film documentary with the BBC about his relative, photographer Bill Brandt. Edwin recalls:

> The Castle Hill part [of *Sirens*] I wrote very much with my favourite cousin Elizabeth Money in mind. I spent a lot of my childhood and youth there while my grandparents were alive, often playing with my cousins in the ruins of Simon de Montfort's castle. I knew the former stables well because my grandfather had his workshop there. He was a fine carpenter and furniture-maker in his retirement years. I'd watch him at work. I still have some furniture my grandfather made.
>
> My recollection of Castle Hill in the 2nd World War was that the front garden was an army camp. The soldiers used to play games with me as a child and give me their chocolate ration.[24] I recall that

---

23 Some of this text was copied directly from the de Laszlo Foundation website.
24 Canadian armed forces were billeted in the grounds of Castle Hill and various other locations in Blechingley during WWII.

the estate was crawling with servants and gardeners. The last time I was there was for my grandfather's funeral in 1952, when I was in army uniform during national service.

'Cocktails in a Surrey Garden', photo by Bill Brandt – 1930s
Hermann William Brandt (1904–83) is famous for his British social documentaries, photo journalism, surreal landscapes and nudes. He was said to have made poetry with his camera, 'a historian capturing a world that has disappeared for ever'. He was born in Germany to parents of Russian descent and settled in London in 1931. If you would like to own a genuine copy of this photograph, or others, they can be purchased for £2,000 each from the Bill Brandt Archive. His earlier original prints command considerably more. © *Bill Brandt Archive.*

Edwin Mullins has identified this photo as taken at Castle Hill. He comments:

> This is in the back garden [of Castle Hill] overlooking the Weald, with my grandfather, Augustus, left, talking to one of the Russian cousins, Tamara Ashmore, née Vasilevna Schutt, who had been rescued from Bolshevik Russia, by her brother, Cornelius Schutt, and a handsome British naval lieutenant, Leslie Haliburton Ashmore. Cornelius had travelled the length of Russia to find his sister, she was rescued aboard a naval frigate in Soviet Yalta, in the Black Sea. Leslie married Tamara and they had two sons, Edward and Peter, who both became admirals in the British Navy, and were knighted. I knew them both well. The middle of the three ladies in the photo is very likely Mama Jean [Jean Brandt, wife

of Augustus. The other couple nearest the camera could be Augustus' brother, Henry Bernard Brandt, with his wife Alida].

The butler led the staff at Castle Hill. Under his supervision came: the footman; hall boy; parlourmaid; valet; lady's maid; four housemaids upstairs; cook; undercook; and two scullery maids in the kitchen. There were also about 16 staff working in the grounds, all under the head gardener. The east lodge was where the bootboy, the odd-job man and his family, and the man in charge of the electricity generation engine house lived.

The engine house was just across the road, where there was also a kitchen garden. Laundry Cottage (still there today), in Castle Square, was where several of the four laundry maids lived. The long-serving coachman, and later chauffeur, lived with his wife beside the stables. The footman lived in a flat above the stables.

'Parlourmaid and Under Parlourmaid Ready to Serve Dinner', photo by Bill Brandt – 1939
One of Brandt's most famous photos. Head-parlourmaid Dorothy Alice Pratt, on the left, lived and worked at Capenor in Nutfield and later at Blechingley House, in Blechingley High Street. Speaking of Dorothy in *Master Photographers*, a 1983 BBC TV documentary, Bill said, 'she had such terrific character, it was one of those pictures that, again, I didn't really take, anyone could have taken it, this woman had such character, she always looked good, anybody could have taken this picture, anybody.' © *Bill Brandt Archive*.

Twenty-one of Bill's photos were featured in a photo documentary, 'The Perfect Parlourmaid', published in *Picture Post* on 29 July 1939. Twenty of the photographs featured Dorothy, with an accompanying un-credited commentary/narrative. The feature is introduced with, 'A typical present-day example of the perfect Victorian servant is Pratt, head-parlourmaid at a big country house in Surrey.' The big country house (mansion) was Capenor (today called Robert Denholm House), in Nutfield, the home of Henry Bernard Brandt. Bill Brandt was the nephew of Henry Bernard and Augustus Philip Brandt.

Five Bill Brandt photos featuring Head Parlourmaid Dorothy Alice Pratt – pp. 219–221

The Perfect Parlourmaid. The following photos are extras that did not make it into the five-page *Picture Post* article, but are very similar. The following are extracts:

> She [Dorothy Pratt] enjoys the complete confidence of 'the family', and through her, it is possible and proper for 'the family' to express their wishes to those 'below-stairs'. Tall and upright as any guardsman, Pratt in her Edwardian uniform of starched white frills and smooth black silk is equally impressive. She has the bearing of a guardsman and the discretion of a diplomat. Nothing escapes her dark and inscrutable eyes. Everything about her is impeccably correct. Grown-ups are frightened to misbehave in front of her. Small boys adore her because she calls them 'sir'.
>
> Her day begins at 6.30am when the housemaid brings an early cup of tea to her attic room. She directs the other maids like a general in charge of an army. Under-servants must not speak to upper-servants unless they are spoken to, and servants must not talk to each other in the 'front', of the house. But she is free to give an encouraging word to a good housemaid.
>
> She is in charge of the dining room, she does the carving, directs the service, and waits at table. The care of the pantry with all its contents

of plate, china and glass is exclusively hers. She is valet to the gentlemen of the household and holds the keys to the silver safe and wine cellar. She takes telephone messages and answers the front door-bell. Her appearance at the front door is formidable, yet as cordial, as a butler's. The parlourmaid herself is an example of punctuality, and visitors tend to arrive punctually when they know that it is she who is going to receive them. She must put guests at their ease, lead them inside, introduce them.

Every Wednesday Pratt takes her 'half day'. She leaves at noon and makes straight to London, whence she visits friends at Putney. She does a little shopping, sees a film, and is back again by 10.30.

She presides at servants' lunch, sits at the head of the table and carves the joint for the rest of the staff. The Cook's allocated duty is to serve the vegetables and help the pudding. Etiquette is strict. Under-servants must not talk among themselves at the table.

Proud of her profession and jealous of its traditions, she possesses that Victorian spirit of loyalty to the 'family', and has made their interests hers. She is present in the dining-room throughout the meal. She hears every word that is spoken, yet she does not hear it. She is the essence of discretion and tact, the stately parlourmaid of England.

These previously unpublished photos are supplied by and are © Bill Brandt Archive.

Dorothy Alice Pratt was born in early 1895, daughter of labourer Thomas William and Elizabeth Pratt. In 1901 Thomas and Elizabeth had ten children living at home, three boys and seven girls (including Dorothy), at Uxbridge Street, Burton upon Trent, Staffordshire, a small mid-terrace house. Dorothy went into service upon leaving school, and at 16 was under-housemaid for the Pierreponts, an American banking family, at a large house called Higham Grange in Nuneaton.

At the time of her 'moment of fame', in the summer of 1939, Dorothy had served as head-parlourmaid at Capenor for 19 years. She had learnt her craft at Higham Grange where, under a butler, she was taught the strict etiquette which rules 'below stairs

in good service'. In many stately homes the butler had now been replaced by the head-parlourmaid, who ran the house along with the cook and were considered 'upstairs staff'. There were said to be over 1.3 million persons employed in domestic service in England and Wales in 1939.

Dorothy Alice Pratt's childhood home
Uxbridge Street, Burton upon Trent, Staffordshire (first house on the left).

Capenor, as built for Hudson Taylor Esq. – 1887
Since the mid-1970s it has been severed from the Castle Hill lands by the M23 motorway. It is now Robert Denholm House, Bletchingley Road, Nutfield, used as serviced offices and for events (2023). *Image from an article in* The Building News, *13 April 1888. Photo lithographed and printed by James Ackerman, 6 Queen Square WC.*

Capenor was requisitioned by the Canadian Air Force during WWII, and at some point Henry Brandt relocated (with Dorothy) to Blechingley House, in Blechingley High Street, where he remained until his death. Dorothy died a spinster on 8 September 1951, aged 56, at East Surrey Hospital, Redhill, Surrey. Her address at the time was Blechingley House. She was buried in her home town, Burton upon Trent. Her estate of £474 4s 5d went to her older widowed sister, Agnes Ann Richardson.

Bletchingley House –2000
The home of Henry Brandt and Dorothy Pratt after they left Capenor. Built by Richard Drew around 1895, who lived here with his family. This photo was taken as part of the Bletchingley Millennium Project when all of the houses in the village were photographed. *Photo courtesy of Blechingley Conservation and Historical Society.*

Henry Bernard Brandt worked with his brother Augustus in the family banking business. They both bred cattle and regularly won prizes in agricultural shows. Henry's world-famous, prize-winning Capenor herd was founded in 1934 and was put up for auction in 1949 at Castle Hill Farm. Henry died in 1958, at 84, and was buried close to his brother Augustus in Blechingley Cemetery. His wife Alida died in 1963 and was also buried in Blechingley.

Messrs Norris, Partridge and Brandt were all involved in the village, and were benefactors and supporters of various causes, some examples of which are:

James Norris was on the board of the Godstone District Guardians (the workhouse), Blechingley School, and other public bodies in the district. He was also vice president of the local agricultural society, and churchwarden at St Mary's from 1874 to 1894. For the 1887 celebrations of Queen Victoria's golden jubilee, there was not enough space in the village to accommodate all the invited guests, so the celebrations were spread out across a number of buildings, which included James' coach house at Castle Hill. On the day of his funeral in 1894, universal respect was shown, places of business were closed and blinds were drawn.

As mentioned, Henry Partridge built the free-of-charge convalescent home for those suffering with acute rheumatism, he supported the Blechingley Hornets cricket team, and presented a new cricket pitch to the village in April 1896. He was president of the Redhill Agricultural Society, and was also church warden at St Mary's from 1900 to 1904.

Augustus and Henry Brandt, among other things, hosted community flower shows from their homes.

Dorothy Alice Pratt and Henry Bernard Brandt, Capenor nursery – 1939
Photo by Bill Brandt © Bill Brandt Archive.

Felix McCredy, a well-known architect, was the next owner of Castle Hill circa 1954. It is not clear how much of the Castle Hill estate he purchased, but the connected cottages and outbuildings were gradually sold off by him or the previous owners. About two-thirds of the mansion was demolished (the west end and part of the centre).

It is rumoured that the house was suffering from dry rot and/or it was too expensive to maintain. The remnant of the mansion was renamed Castle Place.

Felix built himself a large house on a 33-acre site, about 180 metres to the west of the old mansion house, which he named Castle Hill House. Maps of the time indicate that he built his new home on the site of farm/commercial buildings. His aim was to design a house that was full of sunshine and light, with big windows and views towards the South Downs and long views of the formal gardens. The house covers an area of about 5,000 square feet, with a separate summer house, La Solitude, and incorporates the old Castle Hill mansion west lodge. The new house is still there today, with its main entrance at the original Castle Hill west gate in Castle Street (the A25). Castle Hill House and site was put up for sale in 2017 after the death of Felix's wife, Rachel.

Front of Castle Place, formerly Castle Hill/Bletchingley Castle – 2020
The left (east) side, with seven front windows and a door (the door is a recent addition), and five roof windows, was part of the original building, and was the servants' quarters. The right (west) side was skilfully extended around 2010, with the new gable end in the style of the original. The building is probably half the size of the original mansion. Castle Place is split into six private dwellings, and the old stables, coach house, adjoining cottages and the east and west lodges are also private homes.

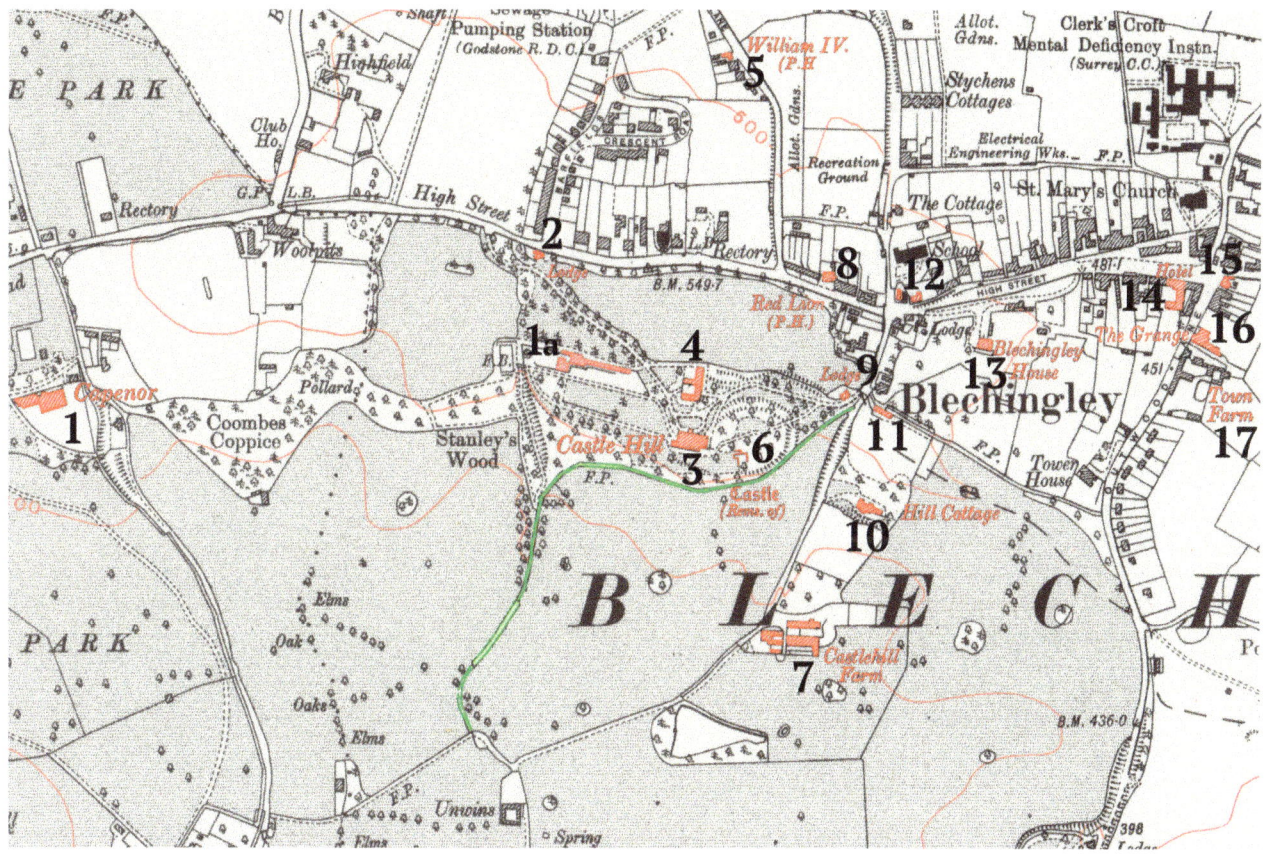

Map of Castle Hill and surroundings – 1934
(Today's names/status in brackets) 1) Capenor in Nutfield (Robert Denholm House); 1a) Farm or commercial buildings (Castle Hill House); 2) Castle Hill Mansion West Lodge; 3) Castle Hill mansion house (Castle Place); 4) Castle Hill stables, coach house, and cottages (Stables House, The Old Coach House, Garden Cottage, Cherry Tree Cottage); 5) William IV public house (demolished 2020); 6) The ancient Blechingley Castle (remains); 7) Castle Hill Farm; 8) The Red Lion public house; 9) Castle Hill Mansion East Lodge (The Moat House); 10) Hill Cottage (The Dower House); 11) The Engine House (Odstock); 12) Congressional Chapel and The Manse (chapel demolished); 13) Blechingley House; 14) White Hart Hotel (Whyte Harte Hotel); 15) The Prince Albert public house (permanently closed in 2013); 16) The Grange; 17) Town Farm (Town Mead). The public footpath is in green. *OS Map of Surrey XXVII.SW Bletchingley-Nutfield, 1934, with author's annotations. Reproduced under a Creative Commons Attribution-NonCommercial-ShareAlike 4.0 International (CC-BY-NC-SA) licence with the permission of the National Library of Scotland.*

Entrance gate to the former stables at Castle Hill – 2021
The left gate pillar bears an insignia with the initials of James Norris and his wife Susanna Louisa (inset bottom left of photo). The right pillar bears an eroded date, which looks like 1868.

Castle Hill, west gate in Castle Street – 2021
The West Lodge is just inside the gate to the left. This is now the main entrance to Castle Hill House and estate, built in the 1950s by Felix McCredy. The insignias on the gate pillars have been removed.

Castle Hill Farm, known in earlier days as Underhills, as it is at the foot of steep hills, is today farmed by the Tobitt family, who have been farmers in the village for about 125 years. When I visited the farm in the summer of 2021, George Tobitt, age 79 (officially retired), was driving a tractor pulling a trailer loaded with hay bales. His father Walter Hubert, known as Hubert, farmed the adjoining Sandhills Farm and Pendell Farm in the north of the village, and served on the parish council. Sandhills and Castle Hill farms are now farmed by George's daughter and son-in-law. Both farms are owned by the National Trust (2023).

Disused cow sheds at Castle Hill Farm – 2021
One of two large cow sheds on this old dairy farm, this one had a capacity of 26 cows. Presumed to be built by Henry Partridge in 1900, along with the farmhouse; they replaced some nineteenth-century buildings.

Castle Hill Farmhouse – 2021

Doctor Mark and Mrs Philippa Marshall and Family | Owners 1952–87 | Gay Kindersley | The Mid Surrey Farmers Draghounds

Doctor Basil Yasil Marshall (known as Mark) ran his practice at The Grange up to 1987. He started practising in a partnership with Doctor Dick Robertson, which continued up to the 1960s. Mark (1918–2002) was born in Limerick, Ireland, of Russian Jewish descent, and was an ex-surgeon-lieutenant naval doctor. He met his wife-to-be, Philippa Margaret Belmont (1924–2022), in Australia in the 1940s, while she was serving in the Voluntary Aid Detachment (VAD) at a naval hospital in Sydney. They married in 1947 at Portsmouth, Hampshire. Before Mark and Philippa moved to The Grange around 1952, they lived for a while at Barmore in Little Common Lane and at Pound Hill Cottage, Outwood Lane, Blechingley. They had four children: David, Sara, Amanda and Patrick.

Doctor Kevin Kelly, speaking at a Blechingley Conservation and Historical Society meeting in May 1998, said other doctors who practised at The Grange around this time were: Doctor Chapman; Doctor Sheila Frost; Doctor Enid Taylor; and Doctor Gillian Hoare – presumably working with Doctor Marshall.

Philippa was an equestrian; she kept horses at The Grange in stables converted from pigsties, at the end of the large garden. She helped run the local pony club and was a supporter of the Old Surrey and Burstow Hounds. She was secretary and later Master of the Mid Surrey Farmers Draghounds (MSFD). This sport is similar to fox hunting, but foxes are not hunted. The riders and hounds follow a pre-laid, or 'dragged', scent over natural fences in the countryside. The MSFD is one of the oldest and most highly successful drag packs in the country. Philippa was known as 'the Dragon', but was said to have had great organisational skills and was the driving force behind the MSFD for many years (1970–2000). Philippa's cousin is the famous British champion amateur jump jockey and horse trainer Gay Kindersley, the son of the Honourable Philip Kindersley, Philippa's uncle, who was married to Oonagh Guinness.

Philippa Margaret Marshall
Photo courtesy of David Marshall.

Sara Macdonald, née Marshall, Philippa and Mark's daughter, recounts:

> My pony was kept in a brick stable attached to the end of the garage block [at the end of what is now No. 5 The Grange, former stables]. The garden had an apple orchard, vegetable and fruit garden, a grass tennis court which became a paddock, and in later years, an open air swimming pool was built there. We inherited Doctor Robertson's secretary at The Grange, a Miss Steer, she was an older woman who sat in the hallway and was hard to forget, being extremely strict and forbidding. The top floor of the house had four rooms, with a kitchen, where my brother David and I lived with a nanny. Eventually it was rented out as a flat, with access via the rear staircase [the top floor was originally the servants' accommodation].

Mid Surrey Farmers Draghounds (MSFD) meet at Wiremill – c. 1950
Philippa Marshall is standing in the centre and the gentleman in the white coat is Frank Ashby (dragman-countryman). L-R mounted: Christopher Soames MP (later Lord Soames); the Honourable Philip Kindersley (Master); Miss Pauline Jones; Gay Kindersley (whip); Ian Patullo (whip). *Photo courtesy of the Mid Surrey Farmers Draghounds. Colourised by author.*

Mark Marshall was great friends with Gay Kindersley, who called him Marko. Mark was best man at Gay's second marriage in 1976. Oliver Reed was previously in a relationship with the bride, Philippa Harper, and attended the wedding reception.

Gay Kindersley's wedding reception at The Punchbowl – 1976
Oakwood Hill, Dorking, Surrey. L-R: Jill Copstick; Doctor Mark Marshall (best man); Oonagh Guinness; Oliver Reed; Gay Kindersley. *Photo by kind permission of Jeremy Greenwood of Quiller Publishing Ltd. Colourised by author.*

Peter Webb, chairman of the MSFD, recalls a drag meeting organised by Philippa Marshall in the late 1950s at what is now the Edenbridge and Oxted Show Ground, Surrey:

> Well known trainer, Ryan Price, who trained at Findon, near Worthing, Sussex, and Gay Kindersley, dared each other to jump a river on their horses. They both charged the river at full speed, but the horses thought better of it, and halted abruptly at the bank-side. To the amusement of the spectators, Ryan and Gay ended up in the river, with their flat caps bobbing off down the stream.

Mid Surrey Farmers Draghounds (MSFD) meet at Warlingford – 1955
L-R: Ian Patullo (whip); the Honourable Philip Kindersley (master); Gay Kindersley (whip). *Photo by kind permission of Jeremy Greenwood of Quiller Publishing Ltd.*

Gay stayed at The Grange for a while in 1955, recovering from a broken back sustained in a riding accident. He was friends with Queen Elizabeth, Queen Elizabeth's mother and various celebrities. His daughter is novelist Tania Kindersley. Gay died in 2011, aged 80.

Ginni Beard, photographer for the MSFD, recalled:

> Mark Marshall was a lovely man and acted as the medic for all sorts of events so they could go ahead in the days before people had to have an ambulance present. He was almost worn to a cinder when there were a lot of Pony Club events on; he would never let people down, even if he was not well himself.

Chris French, a local farmer whose family have lived and farmed at Brewerstreet Farm, Blechingley, since the early 1920s, was great friends with the Marshall family. He recalled the days he went shooting with Mark Marshall on the Lambert family's land and said, 'he was quite a character and great fun to be around'.

Derrick Coppard, who was born in Blechingley in 1938 and still lives there with his wife Ann, recalled that his mother Majorie assisted the Marshalls in looking after their children. She was referred to by the Marshalls as 'Mrs Coppery'. Derrick recalls cutting his finger badly around 1960, after which he went and knocked on the front door of The

Grange, Doctor Marshall took him in and proceeded to put stitches in the wound, without anaesthesia.

George Maddison, Coral Pritchard-Gordon and Doctor Mark Marshall
R-L: Marshall was a tall man; Pritchard-Gordon became a well-known figure in the Newmarket racing world; Maddison was nicknamed Cherry as he was very ruddy cheeked, a well-known show judge and dealer in horses, in whose livery yard Philip and Gay Kindersley's horses were kept. *Photo courtesy of Ginni Beard.*

Watercolour of the rear of The Grange – 1982
Commissioned by Philippa Marshall. *Courtesy of David Marshall.*

Doctor Marshall was a yoga enthusiast and recommended it to people suffering from nervous tension. He started his day doing headstands. Philippa said,

> it takes some getting used to seeing your husband standing on his head first thing in the morning, but agreed he was fitter, less tense and better tempered for it (*Daily Mirror*, 18 May 1970).

Mark Marshall's name appears on planning permissions in 1987 (as Doctor B Marshall) to convert The Grange and its outbuildings into four units, and to build four detached houses in the garden to create Grange Close. The planning was later altered to split The Grange into five units. The Grange Close plans were amended to add a fifth detached house (No. 3 Grange Close), which was built on the end of Grange Cottage garden, owned by Lydia Kathleen Daws. After planning permission was granted, the Marshalls sold to Raymond Foster Lettings Ltd, a developer, for £160,000. The Marshalls moved to a cottage in Ashdown Forest, Sussex, and the medical practice was moved to the Pond Tail Surgery, Godstone Green (the old police station building).

Doctor Mark and Mrs Philippa Marshall
Photos courtesy of Ginni Beard.

Blechingley village looking east – c. 1965 When the Marshall family lived at The Grange. L-R: The Studio, 3 Middle Row; King Charles Cottage Teas; Blechingley Garage, with four pumps at the front, now The Village Stores. On the far right, in the distance, is the Prince Albert public house, which closed in 2013 and was still unoccupied at the time of writing, pending planning permission to convert it to one or two homes (2023). *Photo © The Francis Frith Collection.*

After 120 years of serving Blechingley, The Grange medical practice ended

Alfred Uvedale Miller Lambert in 1921:

> The Town farmhouse, however, recovered status [in 1866] by being lotted separately [sold separately from Town Farm] and was purchased by Surgeon-Major Leslie, whose family still own it. So from that date the old 'capital messuage' of the Sackvilles, Gavells and Hoskins has been The Grange, and has had a doctor for its tenant continuously.

David John McCleave in 2021:

> The Grange having lost her lands and status, having capitulated to modern plans and schemes, overshadowed as she is now by unremarkable modern homes, still stands with dignity, as a legacy to Blechingley, with no doubt many more stories hidden within her walls.

Other Blechingley Medical Practices

There were other doctors practising in the village. One was based at Camden House, 50 High Street, adjacent to the war memorial, started by William Sargent in 1829. He and his son-in-law, Doctor Alfred Pratt, practised there for about 90 years. Scotsman Doctor William Brodie practised there from around 1919 to 1931, followed by Doctor Gwynne Parry from 1931 to 1950. The last doctors at Camden House were Douglas White and Bill Cleverly. Doctor White was in partnership for a time with Doctor Dick Robertson of The Grange. The practice closed in 1983. The people in the following two accidents were attended to by Doctor Alfred Pratt:

> BLECHINGLEY – 26 August 1893 – Serious Accident – On Thursday morning a serious accident happened near Mr. Grice's shop [baker] in High-street. Mr. E. W. Blessig's coachman (Dickens), was out breaking a colt in, the groom (Alfred Day), and one of the farm hands (H. Boren), was leading, when the colt started kicking and became unmanageable, ran up the back near the Congregational Chapel, and struggling across the road, knocked a tricycle into atoms which was standing by the side of road. Day was seriously injured and was taken home and attended by Dr. Pratt. The other two men escaped without much damage except a severe shaking.
>
> BLECHINGLEY – 30 September 1893 – Serious carriage accident took place at Blechingley on Friday afternoon, the Three Miss Drews, daughters of Mr R. C. Drew, of Blechingley House, were driving in their pony cart to the Agricultural Show at Tandridge Park, and had only just got a few yards from their own gate, when, opposite Dr. Pratt's house, the pony suddenly became unmanageable, kicked violently and completely shattered the shafts and threw out the ladies. Two of them were uninjured, but one unhappily remained unconscious for several hours in Dr. Pratt's house to which she was carried. She is now suffering from concussion of the brain and is going as well can be expected. The accident has excited a profound feeling of sympathy in the village.

Tragedies in the Drew family. Architect, Richard William Drew, the designer of Blechingley House, and a land owner, had five daughters and two sons. Daughter Kathleen Harvey Drew died about six months after the carriage accident at age 21. Richard died in tragic circumstances at age 70 in 1903 while he was on vacation with two of his daughters at Little Wittenham Rectory, alongside the River Thames, where his brother-in-law was the rector. He was found drowned in the river at Day's Lock, with an inquest concluding that it was most likely that he fell down a steep bank, which was more slippery than usual due to recent flooding. The jury returned an open verdict of death by drowning. Richard's wife, Anne Bletchley Drew, died in 1899, aged 59.

High Street showing Camden House – 2022
L-R: Berry House; Camden House, said to have been built for Doctor William Sargent in the early 1800s, it remained a doctor's surgery up until 1983; the brick-faced Clerk's House was, for several hundred years, the home of the parish clerk and is now owned by a charity connected to the church. Archbishop Desmond Tutu lived here when he was curate at St Mary's, 1965–67. The house is from circa sixteenth century, updated and altered in Georgian times with a new front. It is possible that the first-floor window was bricked up to save on 'window tax', before the system was repealed in 1851; the village war memorial is in front of the Clerk's House; the old Selmes Butchers Shop; the side of Longhurst store and post office; behind the telegraph pole, enclosed by railings, is the old village water pump.

Doctor Francis Charles Abbott was advertising in 1938: 'Private home for the treatment of nervous disorders at Red Gables and the Hermitage, [Hextalls Lane,] Blechingley'. Both properties he owned. He converted Red Gables to a military hospital during WWI.

Other doctors listed in Blechingley in the early 1800s were the surgeon Robert Allen, who was later in partnership with Doctor Crook. *Pigot's Directory* 1839 has a listing for Allen and Crook surgeons. Robert Allen lived in Glenfield House in the High Street in the early 1800s with a surgery next door at Melrose Cottage. The Uvedale Lamberts mention Surgeon Robert Webb as residing at The Grange in 1816, however I have not found any records to confirm if he was practising from there. Edward Boulger, surgeon and medical officer to the Godstone Union Workhouse, was listed in the village with his family from 1850 until his death in 1870. His address was given as 'freehold house and land in the High Street'. There may well have been other doctors and practices in the village over the years, but here endeth this author's research on the subject.

Remains of the village public water pump
Originally located a few feet away. It is shown on the 1835 Blechingley auction plan as the 'Town Well' (alias Parish Pump). Uvedale Lambert Snr says it was the chief water supply up to 1887. Doctor Frederick William Robertson's 1911 medical report notes that about a dozen houses in the village were still using wells.

Local people and their Homes (with some Grange connections)

Edmund William Blessig Esq. | Garston Park

The donor of Grange Meadow to the village in 1929 and born in West Derby in 1857, Edmund was the last surviving grandchild of PJ Blessig I, who left Strasbourg in 1787 for St Petersburg. After a short period at Clifton College (1869–70), he had a private tutor. He was subject to asthma in early life and spent many winters abroad in the Canary Isles, Madeira and Tangier. During 1880–3 he learnt farming with William Ashcroft at Layham's Farm, near Hayes in Kent, and he also attended an agricultural course at Ashridge Park, Hertfordshire. From 1884 to 1916 he rented Coldharbour Farm (250 acres), Blechingley, from the Horniman family, tea merchants of London. In 1909 he purchased Pound Farm (126 acres) near Coldharbour, from Mr G Sadler. In December 1911 he bought the adjoining country house, Garston Park, with 37 acres, from Mr Stanley Carr Boulter. He added to that part of Chevington Farm (51 acres) in 1921 and in 1926 the Upper Garston Fields, purchased from Sir B Greenwell. By 1929 he owned 240 acres of land around his Garston Park home located in Ivy Mill Lane, Blechingley.

Edmund William Blessig, age 66
Colourised by author.

In January 1912 he married Ella Mary Nye, elder daughter of Edwin Nye of South Nutfield. The wedding was at St Saviour's Church, Knightsbridge, London. On the occasion of his marriage, he paid for the rehanging and recasting of five bells at St Mary's Church, Blechingley. The eight existing bells dated from 1780. The sixth bell bears an inscription to him: 'To the Glory of God | The Treble, 3rd, 4th, 5th, and 6th Bells | were recast A.D. 1912 | as the gift of E.W. Blessig | of Garston Park Blechingley'. Uvedale Lambert Snr said: 'It is pleasing to record that the first peal rung on the recast bells was to celebrate the return of Mr Blessig and his bride from their wedding tour.'

Two more bells were added to the church at a later date, so there is a total of ten today. Edmund was active in the church and village affairs and often made donations to such causes as the church clock maintenance and new furniture for the library. He supported numerous charitable organisations and was a substantial benefactor of the London School of Tropical Medicine. Garston Park gardens were open to the public on designated days to support charities. During some 60 years in Blechingley, he hunted with the Surrey Staghounds, the Old Surrey and Burstow Foxhounds, the Crowhurst Otter Hounds, and the Worcester Park and Buckland Beagles.

His wife Ella was born in 1871 and died in 1927 at Garston Park. Edmund died 23 years later at Garston Park, aged 92, and was buried in Godstone. He was the last bearer of the Blessig name in England at the time. Edmund's probate value was £178,328.

Photos and some of Mr Blessig's story from The History of the Blessig family of Strasbourg, St Petersburg and Liverpool, 1954, *by Hugh Myddleton Heyder. Courtesy of Charles Williams.*

Edmund William Blessig at Garston Park, age 89

GARSTON PARK

Garston takes its name from the Garston family. William De Garston owned land in Blechingley in 1229. Garston Manor was once owned by Tandridge Priory, who held court here. When Henry VIII seized all monastic properties at the time of the Reformation, he passed the Manor of Garston to William Rede. Over the years it has been called Gasson, Garson, Garston Manor and Garston House. The following are a few of the later prominent owners: 1681, Sir William and Lady Haward; 1713, Sir Joseph Jekyll, an MP and Lord of the Manor of Reigate and after whom Jekyll Island off the coast of Georgia, USA, was named; in 1753 it was owned by Henrietta Maria, wife of Sir Kenrick Clayton. Henrietta left it by will in 1774, to her son, Sir Robert Clayton, and thereafter it was let out by the Clayton family.

1839–60 Garston House with 24 acres was advertised to let in the May 1839 edition of the *Morning Herald*, London. From about 1839, Marmaduke Robert Langdale Esq., was tenant at Garston, where he died in 1860.

1860 Garston House was advertised in the *London Times* and the property description was similar to the 1839 advertisement:

> Garston House Bletchingley to rent or lease for 10 years. Eight bedrooms (including servants rooms) – dining room – drawing room – library etc. – Four stall stable – double coach house – carthorse stable and convenience for cows, poultry etc. Gardener's cottage and greenhouse with productive gardens and orchard. Ornamental grounds with park-like meadow, and handsome woodland. The house is amply supplied with spring water on a site of about 25 acres.

Stanley Carr Boulter JP

1900 or thereabouts, Garston was sold by Sir William Clayton to widower, and father of seven, Mr Stanley Carr Boulter JP (b. 1852). He was a businessman and barrister, and founder member of The Law Debenture Corporation Ltd. He entirely remodelled and doubled the size of the house, which dated from about 1757. Remnants of an earlier building or buildings can be seen in the cellar. He added the clock tower to the stables, salvaged from the demolished church of St Peter-Le-Poer in Old Broad Street, London, in 1907. The clock tower bears the inscription: 'John Ainsworth Thwaites, Clerkenwell, 1791'.

Stanley Carr Boulter and family in Brighton
The lady who has Stanley's hand upon her shoulder, is presumed to be Edith Elizabeth Hannah, Stanley's first wife, who died in 1896.

Rear of Garston Park House – early 1900s
As extended/rebuilt by Stanley Carr Boulter. *From a Frith & Co Ltd postcard, with a postmark of 1906. From the Roger Packham postcard collection. Colourised by author.*

In April 1902 Stanley Carr Boulter married Helen D'Oyly Carte, widow and heir to the estate of impresario and hotelier, Richard D'Oyly Carte. Helen, who continued to use the name of Helen D'Oyly Carte in public life, had risen from humble beginnings to become a key person with Richard in the theatre world. Richard, who died in 1901, is famed for producing comic operas in a partnership with Gilbert and Sullivan, under the D'Oyly Carte Opera Company. His empire included: the Savoy Hotel and Theatre; The Royal English Opera House (the Palace Theatre today); The Berkeley and Claridge's hotels; and D'Oyly Carte Island. The island is on the River Thames in Weybridge, Surrey, where he built a 13-bedroom mansion – and kept a crocodile. Helen and Stanley lived in London and at their country home at Garston. Some of the building materials for the house and gardens at Garston were said to have come from the Savoy Hotel.

D'Oyly Carte Island, Eyot House and D'Oyly's Cafe, River Thames, Weybridge, Surrey
The house was built by Richard D'Oyly Carte; it has 13 bedrooms, five bathrooms and a grand ballroom. Gilbert and Sullivan presented concerts here for Richard and his guests. Helen and Richard lived here up until 1901, probably alternating between the Savoy Hotel. Today (2023) the house is a private residence; the owners, Andy and Sheila Hill, are in the process of renovating this once neglected grade II listed mansion. They run a covered/open air cafe, bar and creperie at the east end of the island, called D'Oyly's (and the author highly recommends a visit). Access to the island is by footbridge or boat.

Helen Boulter (Helen D'Oyly Carte) was born Susan Helen Couper Black in 1852. She came from a strict Presbyterian home, the daughter of a lawyer. She was well educated, could speak Latin and Greek and won honours at London University for mathematics, mechanics, logic and moral philosophy. She then embarked upon a teaching career. She later took lessons in elocution, dancing and singing and, for a brief period, performed roles on stage under the name of Helen Lenoir. She was said to have performed in the chorus of a Richard D'Oyly Carte production around 1877, after which she secured an office position with his London agency. This was when her real talent blossomed and she became his secretary and then his right-hand person. One of her notable successes

was tracking down 'pirates', making numerous trips to America to manage and produce operas, which helped protect D'Oyly copyright there. She was at Richard's side when he built the Savoy Theatre and Hotel and the Royal English Opera House. Richard's first wife, Blanche, died in 1885 and in 1888 he married Helen.

Helen D'Oyly Carte
Published in Illustrated Sporting and Dramatic News *10 May 1913. Image licensed by and © Illustrated London News Ltd/Mary Evans.*

Boulter family photo in front of the tennis lawn at Garston Park – 1911
By this time Helen's health was in decline. She is pictured here with her husband Stanley holding her arm. The others in the photo are probably Stanley's children (he had four daughters and three sons), but they have not been definitively identified. Garston Park was sold that year and Helen died at the Savoy Court on 5 May 1913. Stanley Carr Boulter died at Claridge's Hotel on 5 January 1917. *Colourised by author.*
The three photos showing Stanley Carr Boulter courtesy of Alex Askaroff, his great-great-grandson.

Frank Despez, playwright, librettist, essayist and poet, was friends with, and produced work for, Richard and Helen. Up to 1913 he was the editor of *The Era*, a weekly theatrical publication, in which he wrote a long and heart-felt obituary to Helen on 10 May 1913, part of which read:

> Well do I remember the slight figure, the large dreamy depthful eyes of the little lady in a fur-lined cloak who came to D'Oyly Carte's agency offices at Craig's Court to get work of some kind. I happened to be with Carte when she called, and in my youthful innocence, took no particular notice of her. But D'Oyly Carte with his Napoleonic estimate of individuals, was more discerning. 'That's a clever little girl, Despez,' he said to me, 'a very clever little girl. I shall make something of her.' And he did: he made her his consultant, his co-worker, and his wife.
>
> Her generosity was as great as it was secret. No genuine tale of distress in the [theatrical] profession ever reached her ears without her relieving it; and the tact and sympathy with which she accommodated the gift doubled its value. She had 'A tear of pity, and a hand Open as day for melting charity'.

The *Clifton Society* newspaper, 15 May 1913:

> It was impossible to meet her without being deeply impressed both by the quiet charm of her manner and by the brilliant decisiveness of her intellect. She had a short way with wind-bags; a sharp sentence, a quick retort, and the man who endeavoured to impress with loud-sounding words wilted away to nothing. Mrs. Carte was beloved by those who worked under her.

Helen Lenoir at her desk in the Savoy Theatre – 1884
King George V conferred the Order of Mercy upon her in 1912 for her philanthropic work. Some have described Helen as the real founder of the Gilbert and Sullivan era. *Etching by Walter Richard Sickert, The Acting Manager. © William Morris Gallery, London Borough of Waltham Forest.*

Garston Park gardens– early 1900s
With its newly created gardens. *Photo courtesy of Garston Park residents.*

December 1911, Edmund William Blessig purchased Garston Park and in the following year he built the new west wing servants' quarters on to the main house, and the lodge at the main entrance gate. He died in 1950.

1950 – 'The man who refused a £52,000 Mansion' was the headline carried by newspapers after Edmund's death in June that year. The man being Edmund's nephew, Sir Philip Manson-Bahr, 68-year-old specialist in tropical diseases, of Pootings, near Edenbridge, Kent. Garston was left to him with the condition that he must reside in the house, but Sir Philip declined on the grounds that the estate would be too expensive for him to run, costing many thousands of pounds a year. Under the terms of the will the estate then passed to Edmund's 12 nephews and nieces, who instructed Harrods of London to sell Garston Park by auction. The catalogue presented the estate as:

> Residential and agricultural estate of 36 acres, along with the adjacent Chevington Farm of 186 acres. Garston Park house, partially central

heated, with nine bedrooms – four bathrooms – three staff bedrooms and one staff bathroom. Garage for four large cars [ex-coach house] – saddle room and boiler room, with a three bed flat – The Clock Tower Range [ex-stables], used for various purposes – chauffeur's cottage – The Lodge – formal pleasure gardens – parkland with a lily pond – paddock – woodland and various other outbuildings.

Lounge hall, Garston Park House – 1950
From the 1950 auction catalogue. *Courtesy of Garston Park residents. Colourised by author.*

Servants' quarters:

> Domestic offices very well shut off and conveniently arranged in the West Wing, comprising of the kitchen – scullery – pantry – staff sitting room – tiled larder – tiled dairy – brushing room – store room – tradesman's covered entrance with knife and boot hole – WC – furnace chamber with a boiler – wood store – gun store – strong room in the cellar with a steel door, and inner grill with silver safe – wine and beer cellar – back staircase to three staff bedrooms, bathroom with separate WC and housemaid's pantry.

Gardens:

> Crazy-paved long walk – croquet lawn or tennis lawn and a garden chalet – superb rhododendron walk – rock garden with water laid on – kitchen garden with a soft fruit cage – fruit storage room, and a small orchard.

1950–2023 The buyer of Garston Park at the 1950 auction was Mr EG Blake of Farnham, Surrey, and some time after this the properties were separated. Garston Park House was split into three homes, then at a later date, No. 3 was further divided into two homes. Today, Garston Park is a beautiful, private, gated, residential site of nine homes. It is surrounded by meadows with grazing horses, on an elevated site, with spectacular views of the surrounding countryside. Although the estate is private, there is a public footpath through the park. In 2023 the nine homes were: 1–4 Garston Park House; The Clock House (former stables/garages); The Coach House; Rosebay Cottage; Hilltop Cottage (former home farm/piggery); and Eden Brook (former lodge).

Front of Garston Park House – early 1900s
As extended/rebuilt by Stanley Carr Boulter, before the west wing was added by Edmund William Blessig in 1912. *From a C Brooker, Godstone, postcard, with a postmark of 1906. From the Roger Packham postcard collection.*

Front of Garston Park House – 2021
Showing the 1912-built west wing servants' quarters on the left (with the unpainted bricks). The black rainwater head, under the eaves on the far left, bears a date of 1912.

Top of the Clock House at Garston Park – 2021
Former stables, showing the old clock tower. It is now a private home and garden. The garden walls topped with somewhat faded green tiles are remnants of the Italian-style gardens built by the famous gardeners Gertrude Jekyll and William Robinson. They were said to have been employed by Helen D'Oyly Carte. Gertrude Jekyll was distantly related to the former 1713 owner of Garston, Sir Joseph Jekyll.

Local people and their Homes (with some Grange connections) | 249

Former Garston Park lodge – 2021
Built in 1912 and now called Eden Brook. It has a Horsham stone-tiled roof, matching that of Garston Park House.

Princess Patricia's Canadian Light Infantry at Garston Park – 1940–41
Where they were billeted during WWII, July 1940– September 1941. *Photo courtesy of Garston Park residents.*

Garston Park aerial view – 2021

The Denny Family | Brick Kiln Farm | Mount Pleasant Dairy Farm | Kennels Dairy Farm

Albert Denny (b. 1865) was the proud owner of Nos. 7 and 9 Outwood Lane in 1906–7 – the Blechingley Post Office building and the Mount Pleasant and Bletchingley Dairy store. In 1906 he purchased the paired circa sixteenth-century cottages, 'the Dewdney Cottages', next door to The Grange, from Elizabeth Mary Leslie, owner/trustee of The Grange. He promptly demolished the cottages and embarked on building 7 and 9, which he probably completed in 1907. Albert was a dairy farmer and a well-known character in the village. His name often pops up in the local parish magazine, when he donated dairy products to local events. Some of Albert's descendants still live in Blechingley and have kindly supplied the photos for this section.

Albert's parents were from Suffolk, his father Ezekiel (b. 1816) was a farm worker and his mother was Emma (b. 1831). Ezekiel first appears in Blechingley on the 1851 census as a lodger, age 33, working as an agricultural labourer. By 1861 Ezekiel and Emma were married and living in Nutfield (one mile from Blechingley) with three children: Frederick (5), Walter (3) and Elizabeth (1). Albert was born in 1865.

In 1871 the Denny family were living at Garston Farm Cottages, the location of which is not clear. They had five children living at home, three boys and two girls, one of which was Albert, aged 6. Ezekiel was still a farm worker. Emma's widowed mother, 69-year-old Mary Groom, born in Suffolk, was also living with them. Twenty years earlier, in 1851, Mary was living with her husband Elisha, also from Suffolk, at the nearby 172-acre Coldharbour Farm (now part of South Park), where he was a bailiff. Elisha died around 1860. Thomas Fowler Wood owned Coldharbour Farm at the time. He also owned Town Farm from 1855 to 1861. Thomas was listed with his abode as Coombe, Suffolk.

Ezekiel and Emma Denny – late 1800s

By 1881 the Denny family had moved again and were living at Old Brick Kiln, Rabies Heath Road, Blechingley, with five children and Emma's mother, Mary Groom, now 79. Albert was 16 and a milkman. Ezekiel was listed as a farmer of 7 acres.

In 1891 Ezekiel and Emma were still living at Old Brick Kiln with two of their children, along with the Sexton family, who were also farm workers and had moved from Suffolk. Albert had married Kate Frances Agate (b. 1864) in January 1888 at Hope Chapel, Shaws Corner, Redhill, Surrey. The marriage certificate lists Kate's and Albert's parents as labourers, and Kate's address was Godstone. Albert's profession was hawker (selling goods in the street or door to door). Albert was known for being a wheeler-dealer and his descendants in Blechingley still have some antiques he acquired on his travels. Kate was born in West Malling, Kent. Age 7 she was living with her Agate family at Blindley Heath, Godstone, and by 17 she was in service at the home of a publisher, at Oak Lodge, Caterham (three miles from Blechingley). Perhaps Kate caught Albert's eye while he was on his rounds delivering milk. Agates had been living in Blechingley for some 350 years; Edwin Agate and family lived and farmed at Cuckseys Farm in the early 1900s.

Albert and Kate Denny with their first child, Dorothy Emma – late 1800s

Emma Denny's mother, Mary Groom, died in 1890 at 90, and Emma's husband Ezekiel passed away in 1896, at 80. Emma continued to live at Old Brick Kiln with the Sexton family. Later, her daughter Mary Murphy and son-in-law Patrick lived with her at Brick Kiln, where she resided until her death in 1917, at 86. She was buried alongside Ezekiel, in Blechingley.

Albert and Kate Denny's first child, Dorothy, was born in November 1888 at Scotts Hill, Burstow, Surrey (near Outwood). In 1891 the couple were living at Mount Pleasant, otherwise known as The Mount, a quarter of a mile from Old Brick Kiln, with their two children, Dorothy and Walter. By 1901 Albert and Kate had four children at Mount Pleasant: Dorothy Emma (12); Walter Ernest (9); Agnes Irene (8); and Kathleen Majorie (4). The family of six lived at Mount Pleasant until about 1915, when they moved and settled at Kennels Farm, Pound Hill, Outwood Lane, tenants to the Lambert family. The farm was sometimes called Pound Hill Farm in earlier days.

Mary Groom and Kate Frances Denny – late 1800s

Albert Denny, known in the family as the Guv'nor – late 1800s
L. late 1800s; R. 1930s at Kennels Farm. *Photo taken by Dorothy Emma Smith, née Denny.*

The post office moved away from Albert's building around 1913 and was taken over by the Quinlans. In 1933 he leased out his dairy store and house at 9 Outwood Lane to John Tobitt, who was still living there up to the 1980s. The Tobitt family are still farming in Blechingley (2023). Albert's occupation was variously described during his lifetime as: milkman, hawker, dairyman, farmer and purveyor of milk.

Albert Denny died in 1943, at 78; his wife Kate followed him ten years later, in 1953, at 88. They were both living at Kennels Farm at the time of their deaths and were buried in Nutfield, Surrey, Albert's birthplace. Kate and Albert's names are recorded on memorials in St Mark's Chapel, South Park, Blechingley.

Old Brick Kiln – early photo
Once home to the Denny family. It is on a site known in earlier times as Prestwell and was once part of Town Farm. *Photo from Uvedale Lambert Snr's 1921 book. Photographer Jarvis Kenrick.*

Old Brick Kiln – 2020
Now called Brick Kiln Farm, a Grade II listed house dating from the 1500s.

Mount Pleasant – c. 1930
Also known as The Mount, it was Albert Denny's dairy farm from about 1891 to 1915; the family lived in the farmhouse on the right. In earlier days Mount Pleasant was a homestead and enclosure known as Homewoods, on the open land of Rabies Heath. The farmhouse is now called Mountrath, a detached private home in Coldharbour Lane, Blechingley, on a plot of one acre (2023). There is another, larger, house on the old farm site called Highcroft, converted from or around farm buildings. *Photo taken by Dorothy Smith, née Denny.*

Albert Denny and his son Walter, advertisement – 1935

A. DENNY & SON
Cowkeepers and Dairy Farmers
KENNELS FARM, Blechingley

H. G. MASTERSON
Confectioner and Tobacconist
TOYS and FANCY GOODS
The Agent for Ingersoll Watches and Clocks
CASTLE TEA ROOMS
BLECHINGLEY
PHONE 44.

John Tobitt, The Dairy, 9 Outwood Lane, advertisement – 1940s
Tobitt was Albert Denny's tenant from 1933.

Local people and their Homes (with some Grange connections) | 255

Mountrath – 2017
Formerly Mount Pleasant farmhouse, built in the 1850s and extended in the 1950s. *Painting courtesy of local artist Jane Evered.*

Hope Chapel, Redhill– 2021
Where Albert and Kate Denny were married in 1888.

Kate and Albert Denny memorials – 2022
St Mark's Chapel, South Park, Blechingley.

The Smith Family Photo Gallery, early 1900s

Schoolteacher Dorothy Emma Smith, Albert and Kate Denny's eldest child, was a keen photographer and developed her own photos, which she neatly labelled and dated in albums. At 23 she married 33-year-old schoolmaster Herbert Basil Smith (1879–1965), who was a widower and the son of coachman John Smith. Herbert and Dorothy were married in August 1912 at St Mary's Church, Blechingley. They had two children, Ronald Herbert and Derrick Albert John. In 1939 they were living at Berrylands, Surbiton, Surrey, where Herbert was head teacher at Tolworth Junior School. In 1944 they were living at Kennels Farm, Pound Hill, Outwood Lane, they were later listed at No. 2 Parkgate Cottages, Outwood Lane, but relatives remember them living in the cottage behind Parkgate Cottages called 'The Laundry', which is still there today. Around 1960 they settled at No. 1 Bank Buildings, Outwood Lane. Their son Ronald, 'Ronny', took over the lease at Kennels Farm after Albert Denny's death in 1943. Ronald's sons, Derrick and David Smith (Dorothy's grandchildren), went on to work at Kennels Farm. They are now retired and live locally in a house built by their great-grandfather, Albert Denny.

Dorothy Emma Smith, née Denny (1888–1968)

The following is a selection of local photos taken by Dorothy and other Smith family members from 1919 to the 1930s, and another kindly supplied by the East Surrey Museum. Two of Dorothy's photos also appear in earlier sections of this book.

Kennels Farm – 1930s
Around 2010 it was converted into a small, private, gated, residential site that retained the farmhouse and some farm buildings.

Kennels Farm, haymaking– 1930s
Colourised by author.

Pound Hill Kennels – c. 1915

Built in 1903 by Uvedale Lambert Snr as a home for The Burstow Hounds (foxhounds). The Burstow Hounds moved to Felbridge, near East Grinstead, in 1908, and Pound Hill Kennels were taken over by the Old Surrey Hounds. The two packs amalgamated in 1915 to form The Old Surrey and Burstow Hounds, and the hounds at Pound Hill were moved to Felbridge. In 1999 the Old Surrey and Burstow amalgamated with the West Kent to form the Old Surrey, Burstow and West Kent Hunt. The hounds are still based at Felbridge (2023). Uvedale Lambert Snr was Master of the Burstow Hounds from 1900. Shortly after the hounds left in 1915, the site was converted to a farm known as Pound Hill or Kennels Farm and Albert Denny was probably its first tenant farmer.
From a Quinlan's Photo Series postcard, courtesy of The East Surrey Museum.

Parkgate Cottages, Outwood Lane – 1930s

Sir Henry Charles Miller Lambert built the cottages in 1903 – a stone inscription on the front reads 'H 1903 L'. They mark the main entrance to the old South Park deer hunting park. Farmer Ronny Smith and his wife Hedwige once lived here with their three children –

Rosemary, Derrick and David. David was born on the kitchen table in March 1948, delivered by Doctor Dick (James) Robertson of The Grange. David and Derrick later worked and lived with their parents at Kennels Farm. Dorothy Emma and Herbert Basil Smith lived at No. 2 Parkgate Cottages in the 1950s.

Cuckseys Farm – 1930s
When the Agate family were residents.

Cuckseys Farm – c. 1934
Photo taken by Derrick Albert John Smith (Dorothy and Herbert Smith's son).

Battling with snow in December 1927
The location is not clear, but is probably somewhere along the main road in Blechingley, the A25, possibly at White Post (junction of the A25 and Rabies Heath Road). Starting about midnight on Christmas Day 1927 and continuing into the next day, the south of England was hit by severe blizzards, with some villages cut of by 20 feet snow drifts, and central London had snow approaching 10 feet deep. When the snow thawed in early January there was widespread flooding, even in central London.

Local people and their Homes (with some Grange connections) | 261

Kate Denny and Herbert Smith on a pony and trap – 1927
Dorothy has probably hopped off the trap to take this photo.

Kennels Farm – c. September 1943
Front: Kate and Albert Denny. Rear L-R: Dorothy Emma Smith, née Denny; Derrick Albert John Smith, Flying Officer (navigator) 138 Squadron (Dorothy and Herbert's son), who was awarded the DFC (Distinguished Flying Cross); Elsa Smith (Derrick's wife); Herbert Basil Smith (Dorothy's husband). Albert Denny died shortly after this photo was taken, in November. In June of the following year Derrick was reported as missing in action, flying a mission aboard a Halifax aircraft of 138 Special Duties Squadron, Tempsford, Bedfordshire. The squadron was responsible for transporting and despatching by parachute, agents, supplies, weapons, money and so on to support the resistance movement in enemy-occupied Europe.

Herbert Smith's WWII Diary

Herbert Basil Smith (known as 'Danda' in the family), a retired school headmaster, husband to Dorothy Emma, and WWI veteran (1914–18, Mesopotamia – modern-day Iraq), kept a diary covering 12 May 1944 to 31 December 1945 on a writing pad of 88 pages. He started it after news was received that his son Derrick was missing in action. Herbert's family have allowed these very personal and poignant extracts, which have not been seen outside of the family for over 75 years, to be published.

One theme in the diary for June to October 1944 was the German V-1 flying bombs over Blechingley, en route from France to London, which the Americans named doodlebugs. They flew at a height of 2,000–3,000 feet and local air-raid sirens would sound as they flew over. Some fell short of London or were shot down by fighter planes and some landed in Blechingley. Many thousands of V-1s hit London and the southeast and, at the peak of the campaign, some 100 a day were targeted at England. The larger, more menacing, V-2 supersonic ballistic missiles/flying bombs were deployed from September 1944. One landed in nearby Westerham and one was seen to explode prematurely in the air high above White Hill, causing a vivid flash on a day of bright sunshine.

Herbert Basil Smith and Smokee

Over 2,200 bombs and 24 flying bombs were recorded as landing in district II of the ARP (Air Raid Precaution), which covered Blechingley, Nutfield, South Nutfield, Horne, Smallfield, Outwood, Godstone and South Godstone. Seven V-1 flying bombs were recorded as falling within the parish of Blechingley. Surprisingly, there were only 7 civilian deaths in district II, with 14 injured and taken to hospital and 41 slightly injured. In the whole of the Godstone Rural District 39 buildings were destroyed, 160 severely damaged and 5,600 slightly damaged.

Diary. By HB Smith. The object of keeping this diary is primarily for the edification of my son, Derrick, so that when he returns (as God grant he may do so) he shall have a chronological summary of what has transpired in his absence. With happenings around us so rapid and bewildering it is not certain that 'memory will hold the door'. I intend it to include, in addition to the facts, some reflections and observations, so that the whole shall present a sort of mirror of this family's life.

14th May 1944. Sunday Derrick and Elsa [Derrick's wife] left by taxi at 10 o'clock in the morning. They had arrived the previous Friday. It was glorious weather, Friday being the hottest day of the year. Saturday evening Ron, Derrick, Elsa and I played six games of crib, honours being even; a very happy evening.

3rd June 1944. We are all stunned by the bad news that Derrick is 'missing'. Riste [Harry Riste was the local postmaster] handed the wire to Ron in the yard [Herbert's son Ronald, in the yard at Kennels Farm], and Ron brought it into his mother [Dorothy Emma Smith], who was in the kitchen. In the morning I made a close inspection of a crashed plane in front of the White Hart, little did I dream! Oh! dear! Oh! dear! I can do nothing but pray for you, Son and do all I can to help your dear mother in this hour of trial.[1]

6th June 1944. D. Day, allied troops invaded Normandy at 6 o'clock this morning. Mrs Denny's birthday [Albert's wife, Kate Frances].

7th June 1944. Another shock, poor old Jack wrote to say his son, John, was killed in action in Italy on May 24th. What a coincidence! 3 years today that Derrick joined the RAF at Coventry.

8th June 1944. Fighter plane crashed in Tobitt's field opposite Harling's. Pilot killed: this terrible war![2]

17th June 1944. P.P.s [pilotless planes/doodlebugs] continue more or less all day and all night. One fell on Mc'Alpines in Nutfield – 9/10 soldiers killed and many houses blasted.

20th–22nd June 1944. Had a narrow escape at Sandhills from small cannon firing in sandpit. I stood near pillar box and one fell about 3 feet way and bounced past my head!

---

[1] It is presumed that the crashed plane Herbert inspected was in front of what is now The Whyte Harte Hotel, in transit, as there are no records of planes crashing in the village centre.

[2] A photo reconnaissance Spitfire XI PA929, No 16 Squadron RAF Northolt, believed to be returning from a mission. The pilot was 25-year-old Irishman Flt Lt Michael Aidan McGilligan (111245) who was buried in a Commonwealth War Grave at nearby Redstone Cemetery. The plane crashed about a mile from the village in a field on Sandhills farm, farmed by the Tobitt family. The Harling family lived in a cottage on the east side of Outwood Lane, just north of the railway bridge. In 2012 the Wings Museum (near Balcombe, West Sussex) excavated the crash site and recovered some parts of the plane.

27th June 1944. Flying bomb fell close to Water Farm, no one hurt.

28th June 1944. F.B. [flying bomb] was brought down by a Spitfire in Westerham, much damage but few hurt.

31st June 1944. Dad's 100th birthday! Thought a lot about the dear old folk. Dull mostly, but fine.

2nd July 1944. Very noisy with fly-bombs and guns. Counted over 20 F.Bs. One in sandpits near North Lodge. Tunks house uninhabitable [a local family].

9th July 1944. Saw three F.B.s from bedroom window last night. Wet day. What a summer. Wrote to Elsa.

11th July 1944. This is the worst day we have had for sirens – all day on and off, 30 to 40 times I should think.

12th July 1944. F.B. fell early today on White Hill. Flying bombs all day – none at night here. Had good rest.

14th July 1944. Derrick has been awarded the Distinguished Flying Cross for 'gallantry and devotion to duty'. Elsa sent me this news with a copy of the letter she received. I am exceedingly proud of him, but would rather have had the news that he was safe and sound a thousand times.

16th July. Summer arrives. Red hot afternoon. Watched a balloon sent up [barrage balloons with steel cables to catch flying bombs and low flying aircraft]. There is quite a lot to do in this business. There is a small parachute attached which opens when a F.B. hits the cable through a cartridge being fired. The idea being that the parachute retards the plane entangled in the cable.

21st July 1944. The balloons were all grounded today. Strange to say it is the worst day of F.B.s we have had. Does Jerry [the Germans] get to know so soon? South Park hit very badly and Mrs Lambert killed [Diana Mary Lambert, first wife of Uvedale Henry Hoare Lambert who was abroad on military service]. Her two children in a surface shelter were saved, and the dog recovered.

24th July 1944. Went to Redhill ordered wreath for Mrs Lambert on behalf of Mrs Denny.

27th July 1944. F.B. over – I dived into a ditch below Bransland Wood [Outwood Lane, near Kennels Farm]. One fell on The Mount [Mount Pleasant], below Coldharbour.

30th July 1944. Walked through Coldharbour. Lovely memories of picking blackberries with Dorothy when we were courting; don't think I've been there since.

12th August 1944. Many troops around, mainly Canadians and Poles.

15th September 1944. Heard a bomb drop at 4.10 am. Shook the House. Met Andrew. What a smart looking soldier he has become and what a good looking fellow!

14th December 1944. Three years ago Dorothy started on the milk round 'till you get someone' she told her father [Albert Denny, who died 7 November 1943]. Phew! and she's done 1,096 consecutive journeys, not had one day off.

31st December 1944. Glad this year is over – mostly a very, very unhappy one.

1st January 1945. I wonder what the coming year will disclose. Time, only, will disclose. Personally I am entering it with mixed feelings. I think that is how many people feel – uncertain and insecure. Yet well armed with Faith and Hope we will proceed.

1st February 1945. 13 years ago that I started at Tolworth, happy days. [Tolworth Junior Boys School, Surrey, where he was headmaster].

5th March 1945. Sirens went at 11.15am, bomb heard. Took Smokee [his dog] to Burstow Park. Pig which had been killed by Selmes [the butcher] arrives.

12th March. 1945. Felt unsettled all day; cannot explain why. Later heard that Westerham had a rocket.

17th March 1945. Another milestone today [his 66th birthday]. Dorothy and Ron give me a couple of packs of cigs each.

18th March 1945. Went to Westerham, had a nice day with Jack. Saw the crater and damage done by the rocket, enormous hole about 25 yards across and twenty to twenty five feet deep. 58 casualties, one fatal.[3]

8th May 1945. V.E. Day, 'Victory in Europe', celebrations. Very warm. Sat under apple tree in G's garden. I didn't go anywhere.

21st July 1945. Long letter from Mr Vick: His nephew has been to Tempsford. Squadron Leader Holdcroft told him Derrick was the best navigator in the Squadron [Mr Vick's son, Sergeant JA Vick, was one of the seven crew on Derrick's flight].

---

3 V-2 rocket is recorded hitting Westerham, Kent, on 11 March 1945, killing one.

8th August 1945. Official from Air Ministry, Derrick's plane crashed on Tholen island, Holland.

29th September 1945. Ron's birthday [Herbert's son]. Letter received from the Air Ministry about dear old Derrick. There is now no doubt. He rests in a grave on a hillside at Stavenisse Island, Tholen, Holland. There are nine of them buried there, seven crew and two civilians.[4] Your passing son leaves a void in my life that will never be filled. I was always proud of you and your achievements, and they were of no mean order. How successful you had been. And you had always been Straight – Straight as a die. Your words uttered to me on two separate occasions with reference to your Grandfather Smith should surely serve as your epitaph: 'Ah! he had guts.' Your mother's grief is very, very deep and the scar will never be eradicated. The gallantry of you and your comrades shines brightly in a sky of brilliant constellations. God rest your soul. You were swifter than eagles, you were stronger than lions, and in your death you were not divided. [Herbert is quoting from the Bible, 2 Samuel 1:23]

29th September 1945. Mrs Vincent [The mother of Flight Sergeant JKR Vincent; one of the seven crew on Derrick's flight] wrote a very nice letter in which she quotes these beautiful words:

> *He is not dead, the child of your affection,*
> *But gone into that school*
> *Where he no longer needs your poor protection,*
> *And Christ himself doth rule.*

1st October 1945. Street lamps lit in Bletchingley [after the war black-out].

3rd October 1945. Lord & Lady Munster [of Sandhills Farm] called about milk.

7th November 1945. The guv'nor [Albert Denny] died two years today.

8th December 1945. Ron married at Reigate registry office.[5]

31st December 1945. And so I conclude this record. The object was not achieved: it was not to be. Ah! me! One year and seven months – it has seemed many times as long.

---

4 Records show that Derrick's plane was shot down by German anti-aircraft fire. Two civilians onboard were Belgian military agents; a third Belgian agent, Gaston Masereel, parachuted out and was badly wounded. He wrote a letter after the war recounting how he was captured after a ground battle in which he killed four Germans. He was in very harsh solitary confinement for two and a half months, then taken to Brussels for further interrogation. Shortly afterwards Belgium was liberated and he was released.

5 Ronald Herbert Smith married Hedwige, a Swiss lady with a four-year-old daughter, Rosemary.

'Their name liveth for evermore'

Flying Officer Derrick Albert John Smith DFC 1916–1944.
His name is recorded on the village war memorial,
along with 17 others who gave their lives in WWII

Flying Officer Derrick Albert John Smith DFC and colleagues in front of a Halifax
Derrick is first left in the front row, on his first tour of duty. His plane was shot down during his second tour of duty.

The Lambert Family | South Park | Cuckseys Farm | Sandhills

The Lambert family never owned The Grange itself, but Henry Thomas Lambert JP, of Sandhills, Blechingley, purchased Town Farm after it was separated from The Grange in 1866. Henry Thomas was the father of Alfred Uvedale Miller Lambert JP, who wrote *Blechingley a Parish History; together with some account of the family of De Clare,*

Chiefly in the South of England, published in two volumes in 1921, totalling 642 pages, including photos, drawings, charts and maps. It is one of the most comprehensive parish histories ever written and is considered the 'Blechingley bible'. His son, Uvedale Henry Hoare, wrote a 44-page booklet called *Blechingley a Short History*, published in 1949 with a revised version around 1980. His booklet draws from his father's work along with other information and later developments. They both published other books, some of which are listed in the bibliography.

The family have long been involved in village civic and social affairs and organisations, including agricultural, equestrian and ecclesiastical. The family's connection with Blechingley goes back to John Lambert (d. 1533), who made his money in sheep and held land in 17 Surrey parishes, including Blechingley. Curiously, Uvedale Henry Hoare Lambert was the 35th generation in direct descent (several times through the female line) from Richard De Clare, cousin to William the Conqueror who granted him the manor in 1066. A notable member of the family, Sir Daniel Lambert (1685–1750) of Well House, Banstead, Surrey, was Lord Mayor of London in 1741 and MP for the City of London from 1741 to 1747. He held the Manor of Perrotts in Banstead and in 1738 he bought Sandhills and Mitchenhalls farms in Blechingley.

Henry Thomas Lambert JP (1818–79) was the first of the Lamberts to actually live in Blechingley. He was the son of Daniel Lambert (1776–1857) of Banstead, Surrey. He inherited Sandhills Farm from his older brother Daniel in 1858. In the same year that he purchased Town Farm, he married Georgiana Emily Miller on 3 May 1866. An article from Roger Packham's collection, in the *Reigate, Redhill, Dorking & Epsom Journal*, dated 19 June 1866 mentions:

> RETURN OF HT LAMBERT ESQ. On Thursday, the return of this respected gentleman and his lady from their recent wedding tour was a source of gratification to the inhabitants, who were determined to welcome them with honour and respect by erecting lines of evergreens and flowers across the road at several places, the first being at the western entrance (from Redhill), at which the lady was presented with a bouquet of roses of superb colour and quality by Mr AH Kent, of the grammar school, which was very affably received. In the centre of the High Street, two triumphal erections of flowers and banners with the mottos of "Welcome Home" and "Long Life & Happiness"

were conspicuously displayed over the centre of the road; further on at the White Hart Hotel the splendid silk banner of the two Friendly Societies (to both of which Mr Lambert is a liberal supporter) next met the eye, waving gracefully to the wind. The whole town was literally covered with flags and devices, the cheering was long, loud and hearty, the church bells ringing a merry peal to welcome them, Mr Lambert being highly respected by the inhabitants. In the evening the happy pair were serenaded by the band of the Surrey Rifles at their residence at Sandhill's Park, a beautiful spot recently improved and laid out with great taste, ornamented with choice shrubs and trees from Mr Ivery's celebrated nursery at Dorking.

Henry Thomas built what was probably one of the first galvanised iron houses at Sandhills, which was pulled down and replaced by the current 14-bedroom house in 1891–3. He went on to purchase South Park (formerly Fields Farm) with over 800 acres from the Clayton family in 1875.

Henry and Georgiana had two sons, the first being Sir Henry Charles Miller Lambert KCMG, CB (1868–1935) of Sandhills and Banstead, who was Senior Crown Agent for the Colonies. He had one son, Roger Uvedale Lambert MBE (1895–1985). Some of his descendants own Cuckseys Farm and some of the old Town Farm lands.

Sir Henry Charles Miller Lambert KCMG, CB
Bassano © National Portrait Gallery.

Roger Uvedale Lambert MBE
Photo courtesy of the Lambert family.

The second son of Henry Thomas and Georgiana Emily Lambert was Alfred Uvedale Miller Lambert JP, FRHS (1870–1928), who had one son: Uvedale Henry Hoare Lambert (1909–83). Some of his descendants are still at South Park.

Alfred Uvedale Miller Lambert JP, FRHS **Uvedale Henry Hoare Lambert**

Photos courtesy of the Lambert family

On 22 August 1894 Alfred Uvedale Miller Lambert married 24-year-old Violet Augusta Marshall of Patterdale, on Ullswater, Westmoreland (Lake District). She was the daughter of farmer and landowner Walter James Marshall JP, DL (High Sheriff 1890) of Patterdale Hall. The wedding took place at St Patrick's Church, Patterdale, and various reports on the day were published in newspapers, some in the 'Fashionable Marriages' sections. The *Penrith Observer* listed the details of over 100 wedding gifts, with the name of each giver. The groom's gifts to his bride were: Sultana, a dark-brown hunting mare; a pearl, diamond and sapphire pendant; and a diamond and sapphire bracelet. Other gifts to the couple included a pianoforte and a Louis XV clock. They spent their honeymoon in Windermere and Derbyshire.

The happy 24-year-olds settled at Sandhills, Blechingley, but alas, the marriage was short-lived. Violet caught a severe cold during the second week of October which developed to pleurisy with complications of inflammation and she died on 13 October 1894. She was buried on 15 October in Blechingley. It is said that Alfred walled up her wedding dress in the house and moved to a bachelor existence in the old farmhouse at South Park.

Sandhills – 1911
© *Surrey History Centre.*

In the spirit of this book, a little digression: James Norris, the owner of Castle Hill and 1,300 acres of land in the area, sender of a silver salver as a wedding gift to the bride and groom, died aged 68 the day after Violet's funeral and was buried in Blechingley the same week.

Ten years later, Alfred Uvedale Miller Lambert married Cecily, the only daughter of Gerard Hoare of Stansted House, South Godstone. The *Surrey Mirror* published two long reports on the wedding on 12 and 15 April 1904; the following are some extracts:

> On Saturday one of the most interesting marriages that have been celebrated in the old Parish Church of St. Nicholas, Godstone, took place. It was a delightful spring day, and both parties being so well known and so much respected in the village. Very large number of persons, in addition to the invited guests, assembled to witness the

ceremony. One special feature was the number of huntsmen present, Mr. Lambert being the present master of the Burstow Hounds, while the bride's father had been former master.

So great was the crowd that it was quite impossible for many of the people to be able to get into the church. The bride wore a costume of oyster white satin over chiffon, pleated underskirt of chiffon, with pearl trimming and Brussels lace; court train from the shoulders, lined with silver gauze, Brussels veil wreath of orange blossom. The bridesmaids had white cloth dresses, trimmed with white velvet and ecru lace collars with gold braid. Hats of brown straw trimmed with brown lace and pale blue satin strings.

The officiating clergy were the Rev. Gerard Hoare, brother of the bride, assisted by the Rev. G. A. Marshall, rector of Thornton-le-Dale, Yorks, brother-in-law of the bridegroom, and the Rev. C. Lambert, chaplain to the Archbishop of York, and cousin to the bridegroom. The carriages were supplied by Mr. Sam Marsh, of Redhill, who brought a large number of the guests from Caterham Station. Considering the greatly increased traffic and the crowd of people, very much of the comfort of the guests was due to the admirable arrangements made by the police.

Some of our friends covered earlier in this book were listed as givers of gifts to the couple: Mr and Mrs Bell of Pendell Court; Mr and Mrs Partridge of Castle Hill; Mr and Mrs Denny of Mount Pleasant Farm; Mr Stanley Carr Boulter of Garston Park; and Mr Edmund William Blessig of Coldharbour Farm. The newlyweds settled in the farmhouse at South Park, which Mr Lambert greatly extended and built St Mark's Chapel, which he converted from a seventeenth-century carthorse stable. It was built in thanks for the birth of his only child, Uvedale Henry Hoare Lambert, born on St Mark's Day 1909. Alfred Uvedale Miller Lambert was a Justice of the Peace, County Councillor, District Councillor, Parish Councillor, and Fellow of the Royal Historical Society.

South Park, seventeenth-century farmhouse and St Mark's Chapel – c. 1920
The farmhouse, with a Tudor chimney at the front, was built in the seventeenth century to replace the lord's hunting lodge when the park was split into farms. Behind the farmhouse are the extensions added by Alfred Uvedale Miller Lambert in 1904/05. In July 1944 a German flying bomb destroyed the old farmhouse, the chapel was severely damaged and Uvedale Henry Hoare Lambert's wife, Diana Mary, was tragically killed. *Photo from Uvedale Lambert Snr's 1921 book.*

South Park, south flank wall
The only remaining part of the seventeenth century farmhouse, built in English bond brickwork. The Latin inscriptions from Virgil, put up by Uvedale Henry Hoare Lambert above the arch, read:
Like our frail bodies, even wars are transient, but in an ancient house there is always something lasting, something ready to start anew
Arms go buzzing thru the sky, there is death, chaos and ruin But faith is our buckler and God our stronghold

South Park and St Mark's Chapel – 2019
After WWII Uvedale Henry Hoare married Melanie, an American, and they rebuilt the house with a Georgian-style front. They also repaired the damaged chapel and improved and expanded the estate. The seventeenth century farmhouse, which was located in front of the new Georgian style addition, was damaged beyond repair by the flying bomb, the south flank-wall of the old farmhouse remains, now forming part of the garden wall.

South Park from the gardens – 2019
The Georgian-style front of the house, added after the war, is on the left of the photo and the Edwardian parts (with the two gable ends) are on the right.

Uvedale Henry Hoare Lambert and his second wife Melanie at a hunt meeting – 1952
Old Surrey and Burstow Foxhounds at Blindley Heath, Surrey in January. Uvedale was joint master. Some folk in the village who knew him affectionately refer to him as 'Uvee'. Image from *The Illustrated and Dramatic News – Sport and Country*, 23 January 1952. *Image licensed by and © Illustrated London News Ltd/Mary Evans. Colourised by author.*

Excerpt from Uvedale Henry Hoare Lambert's obituary in *The Surrey Archaeological Society Bulletin*, 1983, edited by Leslie Ketteringham:

> The death of Uvedale Lambert of South Park, Blechingley, marks the passing of a well loved and respected member of the society, which he joined in 1932. Land-owning and management and caring for people were some of the characteristics of this horse-riding, farming, history-loving, teacher who was High Sheriff of Surrey 1961–2, Master of the Old Surrey and Burstow Hounds 1950–74, governor of local schools and Lord of the Manor of Blechingley since 1969–70. He served with the King's Royal Rifle Corps in the Middle East during the last war. His interest in religion led to the setting up of the

Southwark Diocesan Training Centre in Blechingley in 1971. He was also Guardian of the Shrine of Our Lady at Walsingham (Norfolk) from about 1952. Uvedale Lambert will be greatly missed by the local people amongst whom he spent so much of his life and who owe so much to him and his father for their scholarly work on local history.

Uvedale Henry Hoare Lambert also founded the Blechingley Preservation and Historical Society in 1973, today called the Blechingley Conservation and Historical Society.

Watercolour of Cuckseys Farm – 1880
By A Dickinson. *Courtesy of Michael Uvedale Lambert LVO*

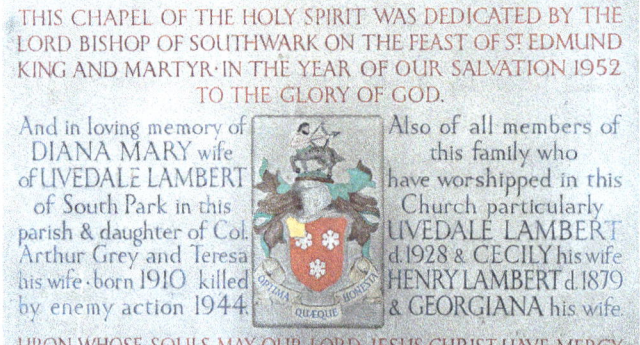

Chapel dedication and Lambert family memorial in St Mary's Church – 1952

Cuckseys Farmhouse – 2021
Built in 1695, it had 12 bedrooms when farm workers lived in the house. Interestingly, it bears some resemblance to The Grange, with its double-gabled roof, central valley and three dormer windows.

Cuckseys Farm from the air – 2024

Jarvis Kenrick IV | Pendell House

The Kenricks are related by marriage to the Clayton and Perkins families. Jarvis Kenrick IV was born in 1852, son of Jarvis Kenrick (1805–79), Rector of Caterham. His grandfather, also Jarvis Kenrick (1775–1838), was rector at St Mary's, Blechingley, from 1803 to 1838. His great-grandfather, another Jarvis Kenrick (1737–1809), was the Vicar of Chilham, Kent. Jarvis IV married Lilian Helen Jaffray (1861–1925) in 1884 at Reigate, Surrey, where their nine daughters were born. Jarvis lived at Pendell House, Blechingly, with his family from the late 1800s until about 1916, when the house was sold and they relocated to Wimbledon.

Jarvis Kenrick IV, self-portrait
Photo from Uvedale Lambert Snr's 1921 book. Colourised by author.

Jarvis Kenrick IV was a very popular man in the village. I will mention but a few of his talents, achievements and roles. He worked as a solicitor and retired in his forties. In his younger days he was a great athlete, famed for scoring the first-ever goal in an FA Cup Final, aged 19, in 1871 when he was playing for Clapham Rovers in a 3–0 victory over Upton Park. He later played for the Wanderers, when they won the FA Cup three years in a row. His talent extended to cricket and he played for Beddington Cricket Club and made one first-class appearance for Surrey County CC in 1876. He was captain of the Blechingley Rifle Club when they were the victors in the 1909 Godstone Union Association of Rifle Clubs Lord Lieutenant's Challenge Shield. In a speech after the event he said that he hoped 'next year the meeting would be at Bletchingley, and that whoever wanted the shield would have to come there to fetch it'. With his own hands he laid out his croquet lawn, which was said to be as smooth as a billiard table. He was secretary of the Croquet Association from 1904 to 1909.

It seems that he was well versed in international affairs, and perhaps a bit of a prophet. From late 1909 to 1910 he gave a series of six lectures in the village hall on the rapid increase in the size of Germany's army and navy and their fiscal policies. He was concerned about the 'almost superhuman exertion and feverish haste' with which the

German navy was expanding. The lectures were headlined in the December 1909 edition of the *Croydon Chronicle* and *East Surrey Advertiser*: 'Germany's Power – Mr Jarvis Kenrick's Theory – OUR NEXT WAR'. In *The Surrey Mirror and County Post*, an article ended with: 'All who take an interest in the fate of their country are invited to attend.'

He contributed many of the 140 photographs in Uvedale Lambert Snr's 1921 *Bletchingley a Parish History*. As a photographer he went on to document the history of Wimbledon and Surrey. In 1913 he was honorary general secretary of the Photographic Survey and Record Society of Surrey, based at Pendell. In Blechingley he was a Sunday school teacher at St Mary's and churchwarden 1909–14. He was also a parish councillor. He is remembered for giving the land on which the village hall was built in 1903. His generosity also extended to supporting the building of the new Church Hall in front of St Mary's in 1905.

Pendell House – 2021

Jarvis inherited the Grade I listed Pendell House, Blechingley. It bears a date of 1636 and is generally believed to have been designed by the famous English architect, Inigo

Jones. It was purchased by JGW Perkins in 1811 and stayed in the Perkins–Kenrick family for over 100 years. Jim Brown wrote a detailed history of the house, published in 2017, *Pendell House Blechingley 1636–2016*.

Excerpt from the obituary in the parish magazine:

> He had immense vitality and a twinkle in his eye! He pursued all church and local causes with hot intensity. He knew everybody and everybody knew him, and he gave it all to all straight from the shoulder! With equal intensity he pursued in turn one hobby after another, brought it to perfection then abandoned it. Many were the stories he told of Victorian Blechingley, and he himself became almost a legendary figure. His last years were spent at Seaford, Sussex, where two of his daughters lived. To the day of his death age 96, strikingly handsome in face and valiant in soul he might be seen every Sunday morning at the early service unassisted but slowly on two crutches making his way to the altar rail to worship Him to whom he was no stranger.

Jarvis Kenrick IV in later years (13 November 1852–29 January 1949). *Photo published in the parish magazine 1949.*

Uvedale Lambert Snr wrote in his 1919 booklet on St Mary's Church: 'Mr. Jarvis Kenrick, a name which, though no longer found among Blechingley householders, will be remembered in the parish as for many generations an influence for good in the service of it.'

Jarvis Kenrick IV memorial in St Mary's Church

The Lordship of the Manor of Blechingley | 1066–2023

In the time of William the Conqueror manors were given by the crown, usually to relatives or other favoured persons. A manor was an entire estate, not just a house. The lordship could be passed on by the lord of the manor to his descendants, unless he was unfortunate enough to fall out of favour with the monarch. Blechingley manor was seized twice by King Henry VIII, after two of the lords were executed in 1521 and 1539. In later years the lordship would be bought and sold. Many of the lords were also members of parliament. Before the electoral reforms in 1832, holding the lordship was a way into parliament via the 'rotten/pocket boroughs', among which Blechingley was numbered. Today the Lordship is usually just a legal title; however, manorial rights can still exist, for example, sporting rights, mineral or mining rights, rights to hold fairs or markets, and obligations for tenants to repair ditches, canals, etc. In 1983 High Court Judge Lord Denning (1899–1999) presented a concise summary of the manorial system:

> In medieval times the manor was the nucleus of English rural life. It was an administrative unit of an extensive area of land. The whole of it was owned originally by the lord of the manor. He lived in the big house called the manor house. Attached to it were many acres of grassland and woodlands called the park. These were the 'demesne lands', which were for the personal use of the lord of the manor. Dotted all round were the enclosed homes and land occupied by the 'tenants of the manor'.[6]

Records show only one lord and one lady of the manor of Blechingley owning Town Farm (The Grange) since 1500: John Perkins from 1835 to 1846; followed by his sister, Clara Matilda Charles Perkins. The Perkins family owned Town Farm from 1809 to 1855. Three timeline charts at the end of this section summarise from the time of the last Anglo-Saxon king, Edward the Confessor (reign 1042–66). The following is a summary of the lordship from the 1400s to today.

---

6 *Corpus Christi College Oxford* v *Gloucestershire County Council* [1983] QB 360. Wikipedia CC BY-SA 2.0.

Lord of the Manor from 1473 was Edward de Stafford, 3rd Duke of Buckingham, executed in 1521 by Henry VIII for 'plotting treason in the gallery of his palace in Blechingley'. His father, Henry de Stafford, 2nd Earl of Buckingham, also lord of the manor, was executed without trial for his role in the uprisings against King Richard III in 1483. The 2nd Earl was one of the prime suspects in the disappearance (presumed murder) of the king's nephews, the two young princes in the Tower of London. Blechingley Palace was a large house built by Edward de Stafford in the early 1500s and better known as Blechingley Place; it remained the seat of the lord of the manor for about 150 years. After Edward de Stafford's death in 1521, King Henry VIII granted the manor to his Master of Horse, Sir Nicholas Carew KG, who fell out of favour with the king and was executed in 1539.

King Henry then gave the manor to his fourth ex-wife, Anne of Cleves, in 1540. She left Blechingley Place in 1547 and kept her head to die a natural death in 1557. From 1547 Sir Thomas Cawarden took over Blechingley Place.[7] Among his many roles, he served as Master of the Revels and Tents under four Tudor monarchs, from Henry VIII to Elizabeth I. He was appointed joint Lieutenant of the Tower of London by Queen Elizabeth, where he died in 1559. His table tomb is inside St Mary's Church, Blechingley.

Anne of Cleves, Queen of England, January–July 1540
Stipple engraving printed in colour by Francesco Bartolozzi, published by John Chamberlaine in 1796, after Hans Holbein the Younger © *National Portrait Gallery*.

In 1560 the lordship passed to William Howard, 1st Baron of Effingham, Lord High Admiral, who died in 1574 and was succeeded by his more famous son, Charles Howard, cousin to Queen Elizabeth I, 2nd Baron of Effingham, 1st Earl of Nottingham and Lord High Admiral. Charles commanded the English fleet to victory against the Spanish Armada in 1588 with Vice Admiral Sir Francis Drake. Charles married his first wife, Katherine Carey, at St Mary's, Blechingley, in 1563. He gave the manor to his son William, but William died before his father, and Charles passed it to William's daughter, Elizabeth. She married Lord John Mordaunt, who was created Earl of Peterborough by Charles I. Next was Henry Mordaunt, 2nd Earl of

---

7 Sir Thomas Cawarden paid rent to Lady Anne of Cleves until her death in 1557, so perhaps he was not quite full Lord of the Manor until 1557, as one or two authors have suggested.

Peterborough, who got into debt, and in 1677 conveyed the manor to Sir Robert Clayton and his business partner John Morris.

Charles Howard, 2nd Baron Howard of Effingham, Lord High Admiral and 1st Earl of Nottingham (1536–1624)
© *National Portrait Gallery.*

SIR ROBERT CLAYTON AND MARDEN PARK

Robert (b. 1629) was Lord of the Manor of Blechingley from 1677. He married 16-year-old Martha Trott in about 1660, who was heiress to a plantation in Bermuda. He was a member of the Worshipful Company of Scriveners, and was in partnership with fellow scrivener John Morris. They formed the bank Clayton and Morris, and were scribes-notaries, land agents, bankers and brokers. John died in 1682 without an heir and willed his estate to Robert.

Among Robert's many roles, he was Lord Mayor of London for a time, MP for the City of London and Blechingley, and director of the Bank of England. He was also a benefactor of St Thomas' and Christ's Hospitals. He was thought to be one of the wealthiest men in England. His London house, which he built at 8 Old Jewry, had a banqueting hall where he entertained royalty and nobility, which was said to be more splendid than those in royal palaces. His property portfolio included Brownsea Island in Poole Harbour, Dorset.

Sir Robert Clayton
Gesturing to his Marden Park mansion in the corner. Painting by Lorenzo de Castro; the original is in the Bank of England Museum, London. *Public domain image Wikipedia.*

St Mary's Church interior – 2020
The life-size Clayton monument is on the right, erected by Sir Robert Clayton in 1705 in honour of his wife Martha (and himself). It is made of white marble, protected behind railings that are contemporary to it, and reflects the man's wealth and status. Like it or not, it is an astonishing creation, which photographs do not quite convey.

Robert and his partner John acquired the Manor of Marden near Godstone in 1672 from Mary Gittings for £4,180. Mary was the mistress of Sir John Evelyn, kinsman of diarist John Evelyn. Sir John left Marden to her in his will. She then married Edward Hoskins of Barrow Green, near Oxted. Robert transformed Marden from a farm into a grand country residence for his family. The grounds were beautifully landscaped and had a number of tree plantations and one source mentions a deer park. Marden is named on the scroll of the monument in St Mary's: 'He fixt the seat of his Family at Marden, where he hath left a remarkable instance of the politeness of his genius and how far nature may be improv'd by art.'

Henry Mordaunt, 2nd Earl of Peterborough, took out a mortgage on Bletchingly Manor from Robert and John, but by 1677 he was in financial difficulty and finally conveyed the manor to his mortgagees, in satisfaction of his debt.

There was some controversy surrounding Robert's business dealings and he received negative press from political opponents. Some imply that he acquired lands and properties somewhat ruthlessly, by foreclosure. In 1672 Morris and Clayton obtained a royal pardon 'for all usurious contracts in taking interest more than 6% … though not conscious of any ground of offence'. But, as they say in modern financial services advertisements, 'if you can't keep up the payments on a mortgage, your property may be repossessed'. In a commentary on the man and his monument English poet John Dryden wrote in *Absalom and Achitophel* (1681), in which Mr Clayton is portrayed as Ishban:

> Who was a strong Whig: Mongst these, extorting Ishban first appears, Pursued by a meagre troop of bankrupt heirs. Blest times; when Ishban, he whose occupation so long has been to cheat, reforms a nation! Ishban, of conscience suited to his trade, as good a saint as usurer ever made.

Mr Owen Manning, writing in *The History and Antiquities of the County of Surrey* (1809) painted a more positive picture of Mr Clayton, commenting that John Dryden was well known for his political motives and for 'prostituting his talent for the party'.

Uvedale Lambert Snr commented: 'Since Mr Clayton was a scrivener the bankrupt heirs might be not untrue.' He also said of the Clayton monument in his 1921 book:

> Indeed they seem to almost dominate the edifice, it is perhaps a pity that they were not provided with one to themselves somewhere else. It may certainly be subject for regret that this tremendous memorial should have been put where it is, but there seems a long step from that feeling to the drastic action of removing it. Considering how the monument was designed and put up in his own lifetime by the man whose panegyric it displays,[8] one may at least be glad to think that our own age has formed a juster estimate of such funereal pomposities, and no churchman today would desire, nor any incumbent permit, a memorial so heathenishly conceived to preside at the east end of a parish church, and, as it were, to enter into competition with the altar.

---

8 Panegyric: a speech or a written eulogy praising a person/event.

Uvedale Lambert Jnr refers to the monument in his 1981 book, *The Rectors of Blechingley*: 'A modern sermon in stone to our secular age.'

Clayton monument in St Mary's Church – 2020
The workmanship of Richard Crutcher. Robert and Martha Clayton with their only child in the centre, christened Robert, who lived but a few days.

Robert Clayton junior – 2020

I will give Uvedale Lambert Snr and John Evelyn the final say on the man himself:

> while the ostentatious magnificence of his Blechingley monument might well shew a craving for personal aggrandisement, the record of his life is an honourable and consistent one; beyond his wealth and generosity, he was a man of liberal, if not rather florid tastes, and is moreover well spoken of by the diarist John Evelyn, who wrote: 'this prince of citizens, there never having been any who, for the great

stateliness of his palace, prodigious feasting and magnificence, exceeded him. He was a discreet magistrate and, tho' envied (i.e. disliked), I think without much cause.'

Marden Park – c. 1679
Built by Sir Robert Clayton after he purchased the manor in 1672. At the very front, in the centre, is Sir Robert (wearing red stockings), with his wife Martha at his side. Martha died in 1705, followed by Robert in 1707. *From part of a portrait of Sir Robert Clayton by Lorenzo de Castro; the original painting is in the Bank of England Museum, London. From Woldingham and Marden Park, 1976, by John Greenwood, The Bourne Society.*

Marden Park – 1874
From 1821 to 1823 William Wilberforce MP (1759–1833), zealous evangelical Christian and leader of the movement which led to the abolition of slave labour, lived here as tenant to the Clayton family. It is reported that he said it was 'one of the prettiest spots that I ever saw'. Joseph Bonaparte, brother of Napoleon, was also once a tenant. This very elegant house burnt down on 9 November 1879 and was rebuilt in the style of a French chateau in 1880. The original stables survived and are still there. *Painting by M Conradi 1874. Annotated: 'Marden Park, Surrey. The property of Sir William Clayton, rented by Edward Marjoribanks 1829 – a frightfully severe winter with very deep snow'. Annotation enhanced by the author, used under Wiki Creative Commons Licence 4.0.*

The 1879 Marden Park fire story, along with some history, was published in the *Croydon Times* and the *Croydon Advertiser & East Surrey Reporter* on 15 November 1879:

> It seems that shortly before eight in the morning the nurse discovered that the contents of a cupboard in the nursery were burning, in which was kept wood, used for the purpose of lighting the fires at the top of the house. It appears that there had been a party at the mansion on the night previous to the fire, and it is supposed that a servant with

a candle had in some way set fire to the lumber, which smouldered all night, and was not discovered until the morning. The fire spread extraordinarily with alarming rapidity, the flames eventually bursting forth with volcanic fury and licking the air with their terrible fiery tongues.

A man on horseback was despatched to Croydon fire station, in Katherine Street, where Superintendent Mr Aitchison was alerted. He immediately put the horses to, and started with the steamer, this being the first time the steamer has been brought into use for a fire. Mr Aitchison had for companionship one solitary member of the brigade, but the call being promptly given, eight more men followed on with the hose cart. The brigades of Godstone and Redhill attended the scene of the fire some time after the Croydon Brigade had arrived. The services of everybody about the premises were requisitioned. Gardeners, gamekeepers, grooms, farm servants, and everybody who had been attracted to the spot and were willing to work, at once set to with a will and proceeded to remove the furniture, books, and some valuable oil paintings, which were in a picture gallery in the mansion. In this way nearly everything of great value was rescued from the flames, and placed on the large lawn in front of the house, from whence they were afterwards conveyed into the stables and other outbuildings, situated at some little distance from the scene of the actual disaster and secure from the ravaging flames. It may be mentioned that in their anxiety to save the property of their employers, the servants lost sight of their own worldly possessions, and the consequence is that all their clothes, and many other things belonging to them, are destroyed.

After some time however, the men who were employed at the pump, exhausted by their exertions, raised a cry for beer. None was, however, forthcoming, for the beer cellar was destroyed. The wine cellar was still in existence, and from this bottles of wine were brought and their contents mixed with pails of water and doled out to the thirsty men. After many hours work the triumph of water over its rival element was completed, but not until extensive damage had been done, and all that tended to make the old house interesting as a monument in the history of past ages had been destroyed for ever.

Marden Park before the 1879 fire
Photo labelled 'Trishy and Miss Woods', courtesy of Roger Packham.

The 48-room mansion was occupied by Arthur Andrews Esq., leased from Sir WR Clayton, Bart, of Great Marlow, Buckinghamshire. The broad stone steps leading to the entrance hall, over which many a man of note in English history has, perchance, wended his way, now lead to the verge of what may be almost described as an abyss. The drawing and dining room were erected in commemoration of Sir William Clayton being made Lord Mayor of London exactly 200 years ago to the very day. Napoleon II [Joseph Napoleon] spent a portion of his exiled life in Marden House, and Macaulay wrote several of his works there [Presumed to be Thomas Babington Macaulay, 1st Baron Macaulay, MP and historian].

In this abyss there was to be seen the charred remains of some of the materials that erstwhile composed the venerable fabric. Two Egyptian figures in marble stand alone as the only particle of grandeur remaining in this portion of the edifice. They were a part of a magnificent mantelpiece that adorned one of the grand halls, but, together with the stove, they are all that is left of its magnificence. On the high ground facing the house there is a statue of a member of the Clayton family, which, as the following inscription testifying his virtues indicates, at one time stood in a charitable institution: 'To Sir Robert Clayton, Esq., born in Northampton, citizen and Lord Mayor; President of this Hospital: Vice-President of the new Workhouse, and bountiful benefactor of it. A just magistrate, and brave defender of the liberty and religion of his country, who, besides many other instances of his charity to the poor, built the Girls Ward in Christ's Hospital; gave part towards rebuilding the other house (£600) and left by his will (£2,300) to the President of it. This statue was erected in his lifetime by the Governors (1701), as a monument of their esteem of so much worth, and preserve his memory after death was by beautified, 1714'.

In 1907 Sir Walpole Lloyd Greenwell, Baronet (1847–1919), purchased Marden Park, along with other local properties, from the Clayton family, having been a long-term tenant at Marden. He was High Sheriff of Surrey and His Majesty's Lieutenant of the City of London. His shire horse stud farm here was considered to be the best in the country. His son, Sir Bernard Eyre Greenwell, 2nd Baronet (1874–1939), took over Marden Park after his father's death. The Greenwell family were said to have been given land by William the Conqueror (Greenwell in County Durham). In 1946 the house became home to the Convent of the Sacred Heart, a Catholic boarding school. Today it is Woldingham School, a day and boarding school for girls aged 11–18 (2023). A blue plaque to commemorate the life of William Wilberforce MP was put up in 2021.

The Woodland Trust now own some of the Marden Park woodland, which is open to the public. The main access point to some very nice mapped country walks is via a wide gate from the car park off Gangers Hill (to the south of Woldingham). See the Woodland Trust website for more information.

The new Marden Park, now Woldingham School – 2020
Designed by Arthur Cawston, built in 1880 to replace the original house destroyed in the 1879 fire.

After Sir Robert Clayton's death in 1707 the manor was inherited by his nephew, Sir William Clayton, created baronet in 1732. William married Martha Kenrick, and was succeeded by his son, Sir Kenrick Clayton, 2nd Baronet. It then went to Sir Kenrick Clayton's son, Sir Robert Clayton, 3rd Baronet, who sold the manor in 1788 to pay off heavy debts. The three Clayton Baronets also served at times as MP for Blechingley. The Clayton family held the manor for 112 years, and for the following 70 years they were the largest landowners in the area, owning Court Lodge Farm, Place Farm and all of the South Park.

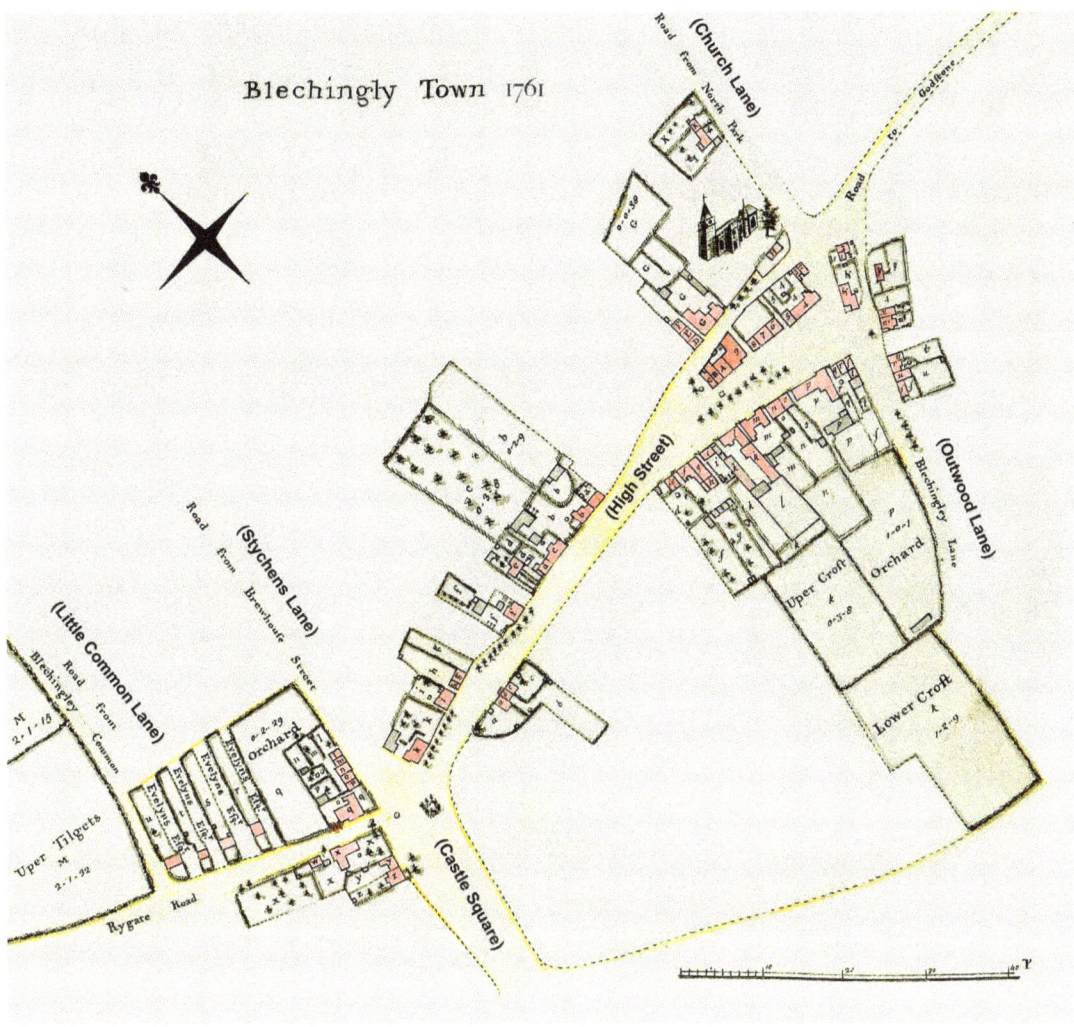

Clayton estate map of Blechingley – 1761
Of Sir Kenrick Clayton, 2nd Baronet, Lord of the Manor and MP for Blechingley. The letters and numbers on each plot refer to his tenants. The map shows only the properties owned by Mr Clayton, hence Town Farm (The Grange) and some other properties and lands are not shown. The modern road names have been added in brackets. © *Surrey History Centre*.

The buyer of the manor in 1788 was John Kenrick, cousin of Sir Robert Clayton, 3rd Baronet. John was MP for Blechingley in 1780 and 1784. The manor then passed in 1799 to John Kenrick's brother, Matthew Kenrick, the Rector of Blechingley. Matthew left it by will to his brother, Jarvis Kenrick, who for 50 years was the Vicar of Chilham, Kent. He died in 1809 and it was passed on to his son, Jarvis Kenrick, who had become the Rector of Blechingley in 1803. Mathew Russell Esq. of Brancepeth Castle, Co.

Durham, and Portland Place, London, purchased it in 1816 for £6,000,[9] and along with his son William, held the manor until 1835. The manor and the greater part of the town were put up for auction under acts of parliament on 15 September 1835, at the White Hart Inn, where John Perkins Esq., Lord of the Manor of Pendell and owner of Town Farm and its farmhouse (The Grange), purchased Blechingley Manor for £540. From this time the manors of Pendell and Blechingley were united as Blechingley Manor, and the manor went with Pendell Court. John Perkins died in 1846, and his estate went to his four sisters.

Jarvis Kenrick II

Rector of Blechingley 1803–38 and Lord of the Manor 1809–16. *Photo from Uvedale Lambert Snr's 1921 book*

Sir George Macleay, KCMG

Lord of the Manor 1878–91. *Photo from Uvedale Lambert Snr's 1921 book.*

Lieutenant-Colonel John Perkins Mayers JP

Lord of the Manor 1870–77. *Photo courtesy of descendant John Gaye.*

John's sister Clara Matilda Charles Perkins held the manor until her death in 1870, aged 78. Clara did not marry and left the manor to her niece, Margarette Mayers, who died in the same year and was succeeded by Margarette's brother, Lieutenant-Colonel John Perkins Mayers JP (1815–77). He had a home called Holbrook House in Weston-super-Mare, Somerset, where he died. His tombstone in Somerset is inscribed 'Recipient of Pendell Court, near Bletchingley, Surrey'. After John's death, the manor, along with Pendell Court, was conveyed to Sir George Macleay (1809–91) KCMG, who achieved fame as an explorer of Australia and as a statesman.

---

9 Uvedale Lambert Snr notes that author Thomas HB Oldfield in 1816 incorrectly quotes the sale price of the manor as £60,000 and the error was repeated by Edward W Brayley in 1844. Mr Lambert's information was obtained from deeds in the possession of Mr Bell (Lord of the Manor) of Pendell Court.

After the death of Sir George Macleay, his trustees sold the manor in 1893 to Doctor William Abraham Bell, who spent a lot of his time in America and, with his business partner, General William Jackson Palmer, is famed for establishing the Denver & Rio Grande Railway, along with the towns of Colorado Springs and Manitou Springs. Mr Bell's son, William Archibald Juxon Bell, inherited the manor in 1921. He sold Pendell Court (without the manor) in 1947 to The Community of St Mary the Virgin Convent, Wantage, Oxfordshire. William left the manor by will in 1970 to Uvedale Henry Hoare Lambert of South Park. Uvedale died in 1983 and his widow Melanie passed it on to her son-in-law, Timothy Francis Goad, in 1995. In 2013 Timothy passed it to his grandson, incumbent in 2023, Henrik Uvedale Hans Hoare Wetter-Sanchez (great-grandson of Uvedale Henry Hoare Lambert). Seats of the Lord of the Manor since the 1500s have been: Blechingley Place/Palace, Marden Park, Pendell Court, Pendell House, Berry House and now South Park (2023).

Uvedale Henry Hoare Lambert in front of South Park
Lord of the Manor 1970–83.

Henrik Uvedale Hans Hoare Wetter-Sanchez
Incumbent Lord of the Manor in 2024.

DESCENT OF THE MANOR OF BLECHINGLEY

The following three charts outline the history of Blechingley and the descent of the Manor from just before the Norman Conquest in 1066. They were beautifully crafted by a sister of The Community of St Mary The Virgin, Wantage, Oxfordshire, when they had a branch at Pendell Court from 1947 to 1960 (St Mary's, Pendell Court). The original charts can be seen in the bell tower at St Mary's Church, where they have suffered somewhat from the ravages of time. These are photographic reproductions that have been updated and restored to their approximate original state.

Author's amendments:

- King Charles II added
- Sir Thomas Cawarden died in 1559 not 1561
- In 1547 Lady Anne of Cleves exchanged Blechingley Place/Palace for Penshurst Place, not Hever Castle
- Blechingley Manor was sold in 1816 to Mathew Russell not William
- Added the Mayers family 1870–1877
- Death of Queen Elizabeth II added
- King Charles III added.

DESCENT OF THE MANOR OF BLECHINGLEY

DATES

Before 1066

Doomsday Book 1087

William Rufus 1089 – 1100

Henry I 1100 – 1135

Stephen and Matilda 1135 – 1154

Henry II 1154 – 1189
Richard I 1189 – 1199
John 1199 – 1216
Magna Carta 1215

Henry III 1216 – 1272

Edward I 1272 – 1307

EVENTS in Blechingley.

Norman Church built.

North Park enclosed.

Present Tower opening built c. 1170.

William de Garston buys Garston 1229

Blechingley made a Borough.
South Park enclosed.

Henry III grants bushel of wheat to Roger the Hermit of Blechingley – 1233.

The de Strangraves at Strangrave 1250–1360.
Blechingley Castle destroyed by the Royalists after the battle of Lewes 1264.

Edward I grants the Lord a fair on the eve, feast and morrow of All Saints, 1283.

In Edward the Confessor's time **Alfech**, **Alwin** and **Elnod** held it. William the Conqueror granted it to the de Clares, his cousins —
Richard the Fearless, Duke of Normandy d. 996

Richard the Good, Duke of Normandy
Robert the Devil, Duke of Normandy

Godfrey, Count of Brionne
Gilbert, Count of Brionne Murdered 1040

William the Conqueror, Duke of Normandy and King of England d. 1089

RICHARD, Lord of Clare and Tonbridge granted Blechingley by William the Conqueror. Justiciar of England 1073 d. 1090

GILBERT de Clare was with William Rufus when he was shot in New Forest d. 1115

RICHARD de Clare killed fighting for the King in Wales. 1136.

GILBERT de Clare created 1st Earl of Hertford d. 1153

ROGER de Clare 2nd Earl of Hertford Quarrelled with Thomas à Becket d. 1173

RICHARD de Clare 3rd Earl of Hertford Helped to force King John to seal Magna Carta d. 1217

GILBERT de Clare 4th Earl of Hertford 1st Earl of Gloucester also sealed Magna Carta d. 1230

RICHARD de Clare 5th Earl of Hertford 2nd Earl of Gloucester. Adviser to Henry III d. 1262

GILBERT de Clare ("The Red Earl") 6th Earl of Hertford, born 1243 3rd Earl of Gloucester Sided with Simon de Montfort, won Battle of Lewes 1264, but later joined King, died 1295.

The Royal Arms of King Edward I.

Henry III, d. 1272
Edward I, d. 1307

Edward II d. 1327

Joan of Acre 1272–1307

TABLE 2

DATES | **EVENTS in Blechingley**

"The Red Earl" (See Table 1)
1243-1295

GILBERT de CLARE
7th Earl of Hertford
4th Earl of Gloucester
1291 – 1314
Keeper of the Realm for Edward II
Killed at Bannockburn 1314

de Clare.

MARGARET
1293 – 1343
married first to
Piers Gaveston executed
1312

= Hugh d'Audley
created
Earl of Gloucester
1337. died 1347

d'Audley.

RALPH de Stafford
1299 – 1372
Created Earl of Stafford 1351
K.G. (foundation) 1348

= **MARGARET d'Audley**

HUGH de Stafford
1342 – 1386
2nd Earl of Stafford, died in Rhodes.

Edward III
— Edward, the Black Prince
— Thomas of Woodstock Duke of Gloucester

THOMAS de Stafford
1369 – 1392
3rd Earl of Stafford, O.S.P.

WILLIAM de Stafford
137– – 1395
4th Earl of Stafford, O.S.P.

EDMUND de Stafford
1378 – 1403
5th Earl of Stafford

= **Anne of Woodstock**

HUMPHREY de Stafford
1402 – 1460
6th Earl of Stafford, created
1st Duke of Buckingham 1444
Captain of Calais and Warden of the Cinque Ports
Killed at the battle of Wakefield

Humphrey de Stafford
Killed at the battle of S. Albans
1455

HENRY de Stafford
2nd Duke of Buckingham
1454 – 1483
Executed by Richard III

EDWARD de Stafford
3rd Duke of Buckingham
Executed by Henry VIII for "plotting treason in his
Palace of Blechingley"
1473 – 1521

Stafford — *Carew* — *Cleves*

HENRY VIII kept the Manor himself for a year and then granted it to his Master of Horse,
SIR NICHOLAS CAREW, K.G.
executed by Henry VIII in 1539

HENRY VIII kept the Manor himself for two years and then granted it to his fourth wife
Queen **ANNE of CLEVES**

She exchanged the Manor for Penshurst Place in 1547 and Edward VI granted Blechingley to —

SIR THOMAS CAWARDEN
Master of the Revels to Henry VIII
buried beside the High Altar here.
d. 1559
His executors sold to the Howards.

Cawarden

Dates column:
- Edward II 1307 – 1327
- Edward III 1327 – 1377 Black Death 1349
- Richard II 1377 – 1399
- Henry IV 1399 – 1413
- Henry V 1413 – 1422
- Henry VI 1422 – 1470
- Wars of the Roses Edward IV 1470 – 1483
- Richard III 1483 – 1485
- Edward V
- Henry VII 1485 – 1509
- Henry VIII 1509 – 1547
- Edward VI 1547 – 1553
- Mary 1553 – 1558
- Elizabeth 1558 – 1603

Events in Blechingley:
- 1360 – 1517 Uvedale family, lords of Pendell.
- 1460 Church remodeled in Perpendicular style by Hugh Hextall, Rector.
- William Hextall rebuilt "Brewersfield"
- 1515 The duke of Buckingham builds Blechingley Place
- Nicholas Woolmer cottages in Church Walk built 1522
- 1547 Cawarden and Rector Wakelyng "purged" the Church

TABLE 3

DATES

Elizabeth 1558 – 1603

James I 1603 – 1625

Charles I 1625 – 1649

The Commonwealth 1649 – 1660

Charles II 1660 – 1685

James II 1685 – 1688

William III and Mary II 1689 – 1701

Anne 1701 – 1714

George I 1714 – 1727

George II 1727 – 1760

George III 1760 – 1820

George IV 1820 – 1830

William IV 1830 – 1837

Victoria 1837 – 1901

Edward VII 1901 – 1910

George V 1910 – 1936

Edward VIII 1936

George VI 1936 – 1952

Elizabeth II 1952 – 2022

Charles III 2022 –

Thomas Howard
2nd Duke of Norfolk
Victor of Flodden
d. 1524

— The Dukes of Norfolk

LORD WILLIAM HOWARD
Lord Admiral 1553
Created 1st Baron Howard of Effingham
for suppressing Wyatt's rebellion 1554.
He bought the Manor from
Sir Thomas Cawarden's executors 1560.
d. 1573.

CHARLES HOWARD
1536 – 1624
2nd Baron Howard of Effingham
Lord Admiral 1585
Defeated Spanish Armada 1588
Created Earl of Nottingham 1596

Lord William Howard 1565 – 1615

Howard

JOHN MORDAUNT = **ELIZABETH HOWARD**
5th Lord Mordaunt   d. 1671
Created Earl of Peterborough 1628
He supported Parliament in the
Civil War and died of consumption
1642

Clayton   *Mordaunt*

HENRY MORDAUNT
2nd Earl of Peterborough.
Supported Charles I and tried to raise a royalist force at Dorking 1647. Sold Reigate Priory
and Blechingley to pay his debts — 1677.

SIR ROBERT CLAYTON = Martha Trott   Sarah Trott = John Kenrick   Thomas Clayton
born at Bulwick, Northants 1629, his father was a carpenter.   1655 – 1730 of
Apprenticed to his uncle "a scrivener" in London, he became   Here in Godstone.
Lord Mayor 1679, M.P. for Blechingley. He lived at Marden in
Godstone which he got from the Evelyns, as he got Blechingley,   Mathew Kenrick   Martha = **SIR WILLIAM CLAYTON**
by a mortgage. He died 1707 and was buried under the   1697 – 1752   Created 1st Baronet 1732
South Chapel.   M.P. for Blechingley 1715 – 1744

                                                                                SIR KENRICK CLAYTON
JOHN KENRICK   REV. MATTHEW KENRICK   REV. JARVIS KENRICK   2nd Bart. M.P. for Blechingley 1734 – 1769
1735 – 1799   1736 – 1803   1737 – 1809   died 1769
M.P. for Blechingley. Rector of Blechingley.   Vicar of Chitham, Kent.
O.S.P.   O.S.P.   **SIR ROBERT CLAYTON 3rd Bart.**
                                                                                M.P. for Blechingley. He sold
REV. JARVIS KENRICK = Mary **JOHN PERKINS**   **CLARA MATILDA PERKINS**   the Manor to his cousin
1775 – 1855, Rector of   of Pendell   died unmarried in 1870 —   John Kenrick 1788 and died
Blechingley, sold the Manor   1774 – 1846, who   the Manor passed to her niece without issue 1799.
in 1816 to WILLIAM RUSSELL   bought the Manor   Margarette Mayers who died
who died 1835.   in 1835. O.S.P.   in the same year & Margarette's
                                                   brother John Perkins Mayers
                                                   died in 1877.

John Perkins merged the Manor of Blechingley with that of Pendell by his purchase in 1835.
Sir George Macleay K.C.M.G. Speaker of New South Wales Parliament, 1873. His executors sold
in 1893 to William Abraham Bell whose son William Archibald Juxon Bell devised by will in 1970 to the
present Lord of the Manors of Blechingley and Pendell Uvedale Lambert of South Park in this parish.

Following the death of the said Uvedale Lambert in 1983, his widow passed the Lordship to her son-in-law,
Timothy Francis Goad in 1995. He in turn gave it to his grandson, Henrik Uvedale Hans Hoare Wetter-Sanchez of South Park in 2013.

EVENTS in Blechingley.

1566 John Whatman founds a School.

1624 George Holman built Pendell Court.

1631. John Evans restarts School.

1636. Richard Glyd built Pendell House.

1683. Ivy Millhouse built.

1704. Horne made a separate parish.

1705. Clayton Memorial put up.

1733. Drake's House becomes "White Hart."

1829 Wm. Lamb, Lord Melbourne M.P. for Blechingley.

1830 Lord Palmerston M.P. for Blechingley.

1843 Railway built.

1952 White Post Estate built.

Interesting Facts | Events | Statistics | Local Families

There have been three large property auctions in Blechingley:

1) September 1835 – The Manor of Blechingley, upwards of 100 houses and several thousand acres of land, by trustees under Acts of Parliament, the property of William Russell Esq. The auction was at the White Hart Inn and the tenant, Ralph Eldridge, purchased the freehold of the inn during the auction. Newspaper articles said the auction raised £11,000, which included the Manor, and 'that before The Reform Bill passed [electoral reform act 1832], Bletchingley must have been worth nearer £100,000 than £11,000, the difference being extracted from the pockets of the people'. Another article stated: 'to the ordinary observer the property had a most un-saleable aspect.' John Perkins Esq., Lord of the Manor of Pendell and Town Farm owner (The Grange), purchased the Manor of Blechingley for £540 – 19 years earlier it had changed hands for £6,000.

2) November 1866 – 742 acres with five farms and a number of houses, including the Castle Hill estate, Town Farm and The Grange. By order of the liquidators of Overend Gurney and Co Ltd after the financial crash of 1866 – 'Black Friday'. The 1866 auction advertisement mentions that in Blechingley: 'There is first rate Partridge and general good shooting, and several packs of foxhounds meet in the neighbourhood, offering therefore every enjoyment the gentleman can require.'

3) September 1906 – 22 cottages, the post office and bank (Bank Buildings), Berry House and two building plots (one of 10 acres). The auction was run by Harrie Stacey, by order of Henry Partridge Esq., of Castle Hill, Blechingley. Henry's name still appears on a 2016 Grange land registration regarding The Grange 'western plot' and one of Henry's cottages next to it (Bank Cottages) in a 1899 covenant between himself and Grange owner/trustee, Miss Elizabeth Mary Leslie, about the building of a wall.

Inflation. The Grange with Town Farm was sold for £5,000 in 1809 and £7,000 in 1855. The annual rent for Town Farm with the farmhouse (The Grange) in 1803 was £140. In 1866 The Grange, with three cottages, gardens, stables, coach house and the plantation plot, was sold for £2,470. Around 1952 the Marshall family purchased The Grange (in Philippa Marshall's name), without Grange Cottage, from Doctor Douglas Robertson for £4,000. In 1987 the site was sold for £160,000. In 2023 the value of The Grange and its outbuildings (Nos. 1–5 The Grange) was circa £3,000,000.

Over the last five centuries the average lifespan of the people mentioned in these pages is 70 years. The calculations are based on those whose age at death is recorded and excludes those few who died at birth or very shortly after. The youngest death in the calculation was Ellen Partridge, daughter of Henry Partridge, who died aged 15 in 1895. Hilda Wren is longest living Blechingley native that this author has found; born in 1886, daughter of blacksmith James Wren. She died a few months before reaching 108 years of age in 1993, in Canada, where she had emigrated to in 1908. Other local centenarians (perhaps not Blechingley born) were 'Slip': 'Saturday last died in the Workhouse at Bletchingley in Surry, one Slip, aged 107 Years', *The Oxford Journal*, 10 January 1778. *The Derby Mercury*, 29 January 1768, records the death of Thomas Stevens in the workhouse age 104. As far back as the seventeenth century, Charles Howard, 2nd Baron of Effingham, lived to the age of 88 in 1624.

> The days of our years are threescore years and ten and if by reason of strength they be fourscore years, yet is their strength labour and sorrow; for it is soon cut off, and we fly away. (Psalm 90:10, The Bible, King James Version.)

After 1878 women were the dominant owners of The Grange and connected properties: 1878–1924 Miss Elizabeth Mary Leslie was owner/trustee; circa 1885–1924 Miss Alicia Blakesley and her sisters were mortgagees of The Grange; 1924–32 Mrs Hope Robertson; 1952–87 Mrs Philippa Margaret Marshall. Lydia Kathleen Daws owned Grange Cottage and in 1988 and 1998 sold about two-thirds of the cottage garden to developers. Ms Victoria Granger was one of the owners at The Grange in 2023.

Local residents recall a helicopter landing in the garden at The Grange. It was Douglas Bunn, owner of Hickstead All England Jumping Course who was, for a time, Master of the Mid Surrey Farmers Draghounds. He was visiting the Marshall family and the helicopter landed next to the rose garden.

The telephone number for The Grange in 1935 was 8 and for the post office it was 1.

On 25 May 1551 an earthquake was felt in Blechingley, Godstone, Titsey, Merstham, Reigate, Croydon and other places in Surrey. *Howes' Chronicle*, London, 1611.

In 1911, 12 schools were closed for an average of three weeks in the Rural District of Godstone, which included Blechingley, due to outbreaks of whooping cough, measles, mumps and scarlet fever.

Blechingley Parish Magazine cover – 1878 First published in 1877 on one sheet of paper, folded in half as a church pamphlet and edited by the curate. It is now sold monthly for £1 as the *Blechingley Magazine* (2023). Sample covers and advertisements from the magazine up to the 1950s can be seen at either end of this book

Cinderhill Cottage, Cucksey's Lane – 2024

Blechingley whisky and wine connections. Doctor Frederick William Robertson OBE, resident at The Grange from 1909 to 1937, was the son of William Alexander Robertson, one of the leading Scottish whisky distillers. John Stein of Kilbagie and Canonmills was MP for Blechingley from 1796 to 1802. The Steins were the most important whisky distillers of their time, with distilleries in Ireland and Scotland. James Norris, who owned and lived at Castle Hill in Blechingley from 1868 to 1894, was a wealthy wine broker. John Henry Sharp JP, Grange resident 1860–3, was a director of the Brighton and Hove Wine Company Ltd.

James Norris, the owner of Castle Hill up to 1894, had a clause in his last will and testament that stated: 'if any of my daughters marries [name], their interest in this last will and testament shall cease, in lieu thereof will receive a lifetime annuity of £1,000'. Published in a newspaper after his death in 1894.

In January 1806, a 'travelling woman' of unknown name and age was buried at St Mary's.

Raymond Foster Lettings Ltd, who purchased The Grange and redeveloped the site in 1987/9, went into compulsory liquidation in May 1992.

Information and material for this book has been sourced from: England, Wales, Scotland, France, Germany, Romania, Canada, the USA and New Zealand.

Some families with long historic residential roots in the village were still living there in 2023. The following is not an exhaustive list, they are just those known to the author. Some dates were given by the families and some were found in genealogy records:

- Coppard (early eighteenth century) farm workers/tradesmen
- Maynard (early nineteenth century) carpenters/builders. Maynards are said to have been in the parish since the time of Anne of Cleves in the 1500s
- Denny-Smith (mid-nineteenth century) farm workers/farmers at Coldharbour, Mount Pleasant and Kennels Farms
- Risbridger (mid-nineteenth century) farm workers/engineers. Some Risbridgers can be found in early eighteenth-century Blechingley records; Thomas Risbridger married Elizabeth Cripps at St Mary's in 1720. The nineteenth-century family were descendants of the Betchworth/Dorking Risbridgers
- Lambert-Goad* (mid-nineteenth century) farmers at Sandhills, Town Farm, Mitchenalls, South Park, Kennels/Pound Hill and Cuckseys Farms
- Martin* (circa 1883) farmers at Pendell, Cockley, Lake and Henhaw Farms
- Osborne-Jenner (late nineteenth-century) gardeners, gamekeepers and various trades. William John Osborne (1867–1945) arrived in Blechingley in about 1890. He initially worked on the railways as a plate layer, and was later gamekeeper for Uvedale Lambert Snr on the South Park Estate, living at Cinderhill Cottage in Cuckseys Lane (built in 1899 by HCM Lambert), with his wife, Nancy (1863–1937), who was house keeper at South Park. William and Nancy are listed on memorials inside St Marks Chapel, South Park. Horace Albert Jenner (1875–1938) came to the village in about 1900, his wife was Margaret (1878–1964). The granddaughter of Horace and William (Jean Osborne) still lives in the village today (2024). There were earlier Jenners and Osbornes in the village, but not necessarily related to the aforementioned. St Mary's Church register lists the burial of widow Anne Osborne on the 26 November 1749, and several Jenners are listed throughout the 1700s
- French* (1920) farmers at Brewerstreet Farm[10]
- Miles-Greenwell (1950). Christopher and Jean Miles were farmers at North Park, Place, and Court Lodge Farms. Christopher was the great grandson of local land owner Sir Walpole Lloyd Greenwell Baronet
- Tobitt* (circa 1895) farmers at Pendell, Sandhills and Castle Hill Farms.

---

10 *Lambert-Goad, Martin, Tobitt and French are still farming locally.

George Tobitt of Castle Hill Farm – 2022
Photo taken the day before his eightieth birthday.

George Tobitt's father, Walter Hubert, in front of Sandhills
Known as Hubert. *Photo courtesy of George Tobitt.*

Chris and Sacha French of Brewerstreet Farm
Photo courtesy Chris French/Matt Weddings Photography

Michael Uvedale Lambert LVO – 2022
Of Cuckseys Farm, with Gemma. Great-grandson of Sir Henry Charles Miller Lambert KCMG, CB.

Derrick Smith and his brother David in front of Kennels Farm – 2023
The great-grandchildren of Albert and Kate Denny. In their younger days they lived and worked on the farm with their mother and father, Hedwige and Ronald Herbert.

A young Chris Martin and his father Frank
Photo courtesy of Chris Martin.

Caroline and Chris Martin of Henhaw Farm – 2022

Derrick and Ann Coppard – 2022
In front of St Mary's Church.

The Boss, Derek Moore – 2023

Chairman of Blechingley Conservation and Historical Society from 1990 for 27 years – now president, an honorary position. Born in 1936, he has been a clerk at the Bank of England and an associate member of the Inner Magic Circle. Derek published his own history book in 2023, *Moore on Blechingley*. This photo was taken in January, when his private car registration number, which he has owned for 40 years, was for sale – 'six figure offers considered'.

Gerry Risbridger (front), Managing Director/Chairman at Risbridger Ltd, and his brother Barry, Design Director
Photo courtesy Annie Risbridger Hind

Richard Miles of Court Lodge Farm – 2024
Son of Christopher and Jean Miles.

Grange | Summary of Owners and Tenants

THE GRANGE AS FARMHOUSE

1540–46 William Sackville, owner

1546–86 Gavell, owner

1586–1738 Hoskins, owner

1618–25 Henry Lovell and family, tenants

1662–? Christopher Tufen, tenant

1663–? Mrs Drake, widow of Edward Drake, possible tenant

1704–48 The Russells: 1704 John, 1738 Thomas, 1748 John, tenants

17??–1809 Benjamin Booth Esq., of Lincoln's Inn Fields, London, owner

1766–74 James Collins, tenant

1803–? Christopher Jolle, leaseholder for up to 21 years at £140 p.a., rising to £180 after seven years

1809–? Raymond or Richard Staton, tenant

1809–55 The Perkins, owners

1816–? Robert Webb, surgeon, tenant

1849–57 William Judson and family, tenants

1855–61 Thomas Fowler Wood, owner

1850s Trayton Peter Pagden, tenant

1859–62 John Henry Sharp and family, tenants

1861–67 Robert Birkbeck, owner; during which time the farmhouse (The Grange) was separated from Town Farm.

Henry Thomas Lambert JP bought Town Farm in 1866 and his descendants still own much of the old Town Farm land, incorporated into Cuckseys Farm (2023).

THE GRANGE AFTER ITS SEPARATION FROM THE FARM

1865–1924 Surgeon-General Leslie (Walter Alexander Leslie) and family, tenants/owners

1872–79 Doctor Donald William Charles Hood and family, tenants

1877–1904 Doctor Charles Edmund Oldman and family, tenants

1905–09 Doctor Charles Allen Robinson and family, tenants

1909–52 Doctor Frederick William and Mrs Hope Robertson and family, tenants/owners

1952–87 Doctor Mark and Mrs Philippa Marshall and family, owners

1987–89 Raymond Foster Lettings Ltd, owner/developer.

1989–2023 The Grange (Blechingley) Residents Ltd, freeholder with five leaseholders. Highbank Cottage was built on The Grange western garden plot in Outwood Lane and sold separately about 1992.

So we bid adieu to Blechingley, our esteemed friends, lords and ladies. Perhaps others will continue the story one day, with chapters left unwritten by this author..

These final words are from the New Testament, King James Version:

> For God so loved the world, that he gave his only begotten Son, that whosoever believeth in him should not perish, but have everlasting life. For God sent not his Son into the world to condemn the world; but that the world through him might be saved. He that believeth in him is not condemned: but he that believeth not is condemned already, because he hath not believed in the name of the only begotten Son of God. (John 3:16–18.)

The End

Acknowledgements

Dame Sarah Jane Frances Goad, née Lambert DCVO JP, daughter of Uvedale Henry Hoare Lambert: for family photos, permission to quote from and use photos from the Uvedale Lambert books, reviewing book drafts, access to the *Blechingley Magazine* archive, and for her generous time given.

Michael Uvedale Lambert LVO, son of Henry Uvedale Lambert, who was the son of Roger Uvedale Lambert MBE, who was the son of Sir Henry Charles Miller Lambert KCMG, CB: for information regarding Town Farm and his family.

Sara Macdonald, née Marshall, and David Marshall, children of Doctor Mark and Philippa Marshall: for family photos, family information and assistance with some editing and proofreading.

Antony (Tony) Percy Upton Millett (New Zealand), great-grandson of Kate Leslie (Elizabeth Mary Leslie's sister): for permission to use Leslie family photos, information from his family genealogy, and for his generous time given, which included some proofreading (and grammar lessons) and reviewing the draft.

Doctor Andrew Robertson, grandson of Doctor Frederick William Robertson OBE: for supplying and giving permission to use family photos, and for family information.

Derrick and David Smith, great-grandchildren of Albert and Kate Denny (through the line of Dorothy Smith, née Denny): for supplying and giving permission to use family photos, information, and the loan of Herbert Basil Smith's diary. In particular to Derrick for working closely with me on the Denny-Smith family, for reviewing the book draft, for sharing his experiences and recollections of life in Blechingley, and generally making a huge contribution to this book.

Ginni Beard, photographer for the Mid Surrey Farmers Draghounds: for providing Marshall family photos and information.

Peter Webb, chairman of the Mid Surrey Farmers Draghounds: for information and introduction to the Marshall family, and for permission to use an MSFD photo.

The Denny family of Blechingley 2020: for the loan of and permission to use original deeds and papers relating to The Grange and Grange Cottage. At the time of writing it was not known whether the family were related to Blechingley farmers Ezekiel Denny (1816–96) and his son Albert Denny (1865–1943).

Martin Higgins (retired 2021) and Christopher Reynolds, Historic Buildings Officers for Surrey County Council: for supplying photos, general information and advice. I am particularly indebted to Martin Higgins for his assistance, for visiting The Grange and for his patience in replying to my numerous emails.

Derek Moore (President), Richard Fowler (Chairman and Secretary) and Daphne Constable (archivist) of the Blechingley Conservation and Historical Society: for local photos and information. Special thanks to Derek for the loan of some of his Blechingley research material and artefacts going back some 30 years.

Ray Howgego who, among other things, is an independent traveller, writer and researcher. His five-volume, 4.2 million word *Encyclopedia of Exploration* (Hordern House, Sydney, 2003–13) has been cited as the longest regularly published book in the English language to have been written by a single author, unaided. He is trustee of the East Surrey Museum and the Bourne Society: for historical information and for his in-depth review and proofreading of the draft; also for his advice on the book title.

Doctor Fiona Glover: for local information and an introduction to Doctor Andrew Robertson.

The residents of Garston Park: for the loan of archive material.

Edwin Mullins, grandson of Augustus and Jean Brandt: for information on Castle Hill and the Brandt family.

Robert Trotman, Bletchingley Sports Association: for access to Grange Meadow deeds and records.

David and Anne Martin: for invaluable and comprehensive local information and for reviewing two drafts of the book in detail.

Alex Askaroff, great-great-grandson of Stanley Carr Boulter of Garston Park, author and expert/purveyor of antique sewing machines: for family information and photos, for reviewing sections of the book and for his advice and encouragement.

Paul Hyde, Doris Parker and Marian Buck: for photos and information on the history of amateur dramatics in Blechingley – bletchingleyplayers.org

Paul Cove: for information on Castle Hill, for reviewing the draft, and for his great enthusiasm, assistance, advice and encouragement.

George Tobitt: for information on Castle Hill and Sandhills Farms, and family information.

Chris French: for information on Brewerstreet Farm and local information.

Roger Packham, chairman of The Bourne Society: for generously supplying high quality scans from his comprehensive postcard and photography collections, excerpts from his collected historic newspaper and journal entries, and other valuable local information.

Mark at Lamingtons Tea Room and Gift Shop: for modelling in front of his shop and for his assistance.

Annie Risbridger Hind, managing director of Risbridger Ltd: for family information and photographs.

Mike Sutcliffe of The Leyland Society: for information on early buses.

Marcella Sant'Anna Goncalves: for assistance and editorial advice.

My thanks to the past and present folk of Blechingley who have invited me into their homes, allowed me to take photographs, and have provided historical information, documentation and photographs. You are too numerous to recall, but include: Martin Cundey, Ann Butler, Patricia Napper, John Thurston, Gordon Hall, Pam Penston, Buster and Jane Evered, Richard Coppard, Ann and Derrick Coppard, Tony Malkin, Victoria Granger, Karole Howard, Mark Rooke-Ley, Lena Townsend, Charlie Scott, Pamela and Anthony Cock, and a local retired solicitor who helped with interpreting some old legal documents.

Finally, my two children, Sarah and Jason for design advice, photographic assistance, encouragement and support.

Bibliography

BOOKS, MAGAZINES, DIARIES ETC., IN CHRONOLOGICAL ORDER

The Natural History and Antiquities of the County of Surrey, 1718, volume three, John Aubrey.

The History and Antiquities of the County of Surrey, 1809, volume two, Owen Manning & William Bray.

The Representative History of Great Britain and Ireland: being a history of the House of Commons, and of the counties, cities, and boroughs of the United Kingdom, from the earliest period. 1816, THB Oldfield.

The History of Surrey, 1844, volume four, Edward Wedlake Brayley.

Marden Park, 1874: from a book of paintings commemorating the life of Edward Marjoribanks (1776–1868) of Greenlands, Bucks, who was a partner in Coutts Bank, London.

Extracts from the *Diary, Letters, & Miscellaneous writings of Agnes Heatley Robertson*, printed for private circulation, 1895, Glasgow University Press. Courtesy of Margarete-Marie. https://whiskyundfrauen.blogspot.com

The Story of the Year, Church Missionary Society annual publication, London, 1895–6 edition.

Highways and Byways of Surrey, 1909, Eric Parker.

The Victoria History of the County of Surrey, 1912, volume four, HE Malden.

A Pilgrimage in Surrey, 1914, volume two, James S Ogilvy.

Surrey Archaeological Society, Blechingley Churchwardens' Accounts 1546–1542, 1916, Theodore Craib.

The Parish Church of St. Mary the Virgin, Blechingley, Surrey, 1919, Alfred Uvedale Miller Lambert.

Blechingley a Parish History: together with some account of the Family of De Clare, Chiefly in the South of England, 1921, volumes one and two, Alfred Uvedale Miller Lambert.

Picture Post magazine, July 1939.

Extracts from the diary of Herbert Basil Smith of Blechingley, 1944–5. Courtesy of Derrick and David Smith.

Lark Rise to Candleford, trilogy 1945, (previously published separately), Flora Thompson.

Blechingley a Short History, 1949, revised circa 1980, Uvedale Henry Hoare Lambert.

Lord Howard of Effingham 1536–1624, Lord of the Manor of Blechingley, 1952, Bruce E Money (son-in-law of Augustus and Jean Brandt of Castle Hill).

Blechingley in the World War 1939–1945, Bruce E Money. Publication date not given, presumed early 1950s

Viscount Palmerston 1784–1865, Sometime member of Parliament for the Borough of Blechingley, Bruce E Money. Publication date not given, presumed early 1950s

The History of the Blessig family of Strasbourg, St Petersburg and Liverpool, 1954, Hugh Myddleton Heyder. Courtesy of Charles Williams.

Jorrocks' Country, 1961, Uvedale Henry Hoare Lambert.

Mother Maribel of Wantage, 1972, Sister Janet, CSMV.

The Pattern of English Building, 1972, Alec Clifton-Taylor.

East Surrey, 1974, 'Bell Street'.

Blechingley Explored, 1975, Peter Grey and Kay Percy.

The Doctor's Tale 1662–1975 – Reigate and Redhill, 1976, Lawrence Dulake.

Woldingham and Marden Park, 1976, John Greenwood. The Bourne Society.

The Rectors of Blechingley, Surrey, 1981, Uvedale Henry Hoare Lambert.

Sirens, 1983, Edwin Mullins (grandson of Augustus and Jean Brandt of Castle Hill).

Blechingley Village and Parish, 1991, Peter Grey.

Bygone Godstone, 1992, Juliette Jaques.

Flings over Fences: The Ups and Downs of Gay Kindersley, 1994, Robin Rhoderick-Jones. Quiller Publishing Ltd.

Anne of Cleves, Fourth Wife of Henry VIII, 1995, Mary Saaler. Rubicon Press.

Blechingley a Village History, circa 1995, Peter Fernée.

The Buildings of England – Surrey, 1995, Ian Nairn, Nikolaus Pevsner and Bridget Cherry. Pevsner Architectural Guides.

The Robertson Trust, 2001, Charles Maclean.

Moving the Mail by Road, 2006, Julian Stray. The British Postal Museum & Archive.

Pendell House Blechingley 1636–2016, 2017, Jim Brown.

The Bourne Society Bulletins. Volumes XVI, XXIX, XV, XVIII.

St Mary's, Blechingley, parish magazine/*Blechingley Magazine*.

The Flame of Resistance: American Beauty. French Hero. British Spy. 2023, Damien Lewis

OTHER SOURCES

Askaroff, Alex – sewalot.com

Apps, Kenneth on ancestry.com for Coppard family genealogy

Arnott PhD MCIOB FRICS, Doctor Colin – The origin, purpose and properties of galleting: Theory and practice, 2017 – www.galleting.com

Automobilier, Robert Arnold – www.automobilia.com

Blechingley Conservation and Historical Society

Bletchingley Parish Council

Bletchingley Sports Association

Bonhams, London (auction house)

Bourne Society, The

British Library, The, London

British Newspaper Archive – www.britishnewspaperarchive.co.uk

Bus Museum, The, at Brooklands, Surrey

Cadbury Research Library, Special Collections, (Church Missions Society), University of Birmingham

Church Mission Society, The, Oxford

Coe, Don, FSAI, illustrator and model maker

Community of St Mary the Virgin, Wantage, Oxfordshire

Country Life Magazine Archive

de Laszlo Archive, The Catalogue Raisonné of Works by Philip de László (1869–1937) – www.delaszlocatalogueraisonne.com

Doing our Bit, Military History and Family Research – https://militaryandfamilyhistory.blog

East Surrey Museum, Caterham, Surrey

Evered, Jane, local artist, specialist in painting on bone china

findmypast.com

Francis Frith Collection, The

Gazette, The, London

HM Land Registry

Ian's Bus Stop – www.countrybus.org

Kay's Directory

Kelly's Directory

Lost Hospitals of London, The – ezitis.myzen.co.uk

Medical Directory, The

Millett, Tony, website – tonymillett.tripod.com

Mirrorpix/Reach Licensing – www.mirrorpix.com

National Archives, The, Kew, London

National Collection of Aerial Photography (NCAP), Historic Environment Scotland

National Library of Scotland Maps

National Portrait Gallery, London

Pigot's Directory

Postal Museum, The, London

Reffell family website on The Black Horse, Gomshall – www.reffell.org.uk

Sage Publishing, CA, USA – www.sagepublishing.com

Saint Mark's Chapel, South Park, Blechingley

Saint Mary the Virgin Church, Blechingley

Surrey History Centre, Woking, Surrey

    Abstract of title 1867, for the sale of a meadow on Town Farm (Grange Meadow): Robert Birkbeck Esq. to Rev Charles Fox Chawner. Uvedale Lambert Snr records, ref: 2106/2/1 – 2106/2/4

Tandridge District Council

Tarankova, Anna © 123rf.com – frame for welcome to the 'Historic Borough of Blechingley' sign.

Taylor, Will, RBA. SGFA, drawing of The Grange on About the Author page – www.willtaylorart.co.uk

UK Companies House

Village Water Pumps – www.villagepumps.org.uk

Welch, Ian (2011) The Flower Mountain Murders: a 'Missionary Case' data-base http://hdl.handle.net/1885/7273

Wellcome Library, The – catalogue.wellcomelibrary.org:
> Medical Officer of Health Reports, Godstone Rural District Council by Doctor Charles Edmund Oldman 1894–98, and Doctor Frederick William Robertson 1911, 1915, 1925
>
> The Essentials of Disinfection and Sterilisation by Steam, by Professor Sheridan Delépine. Reports on Disinfectors by Professor G. Sims-Woodhead, published by The Thresh Steam Disinfector Co., Ltd, London, June, 1909

www.ancestry.co.uk

www.geni.com

www.historyofparliamentonline.org

www.johnowensmith.co.uk on Flora Thompson

www.myheritage.com

www.olympics.com

www.scotlandspeople.gov.uk

www.suffolkartists.co.uk

www.thegenealogist.co.uk

www.thepeerage.com

www.wingsmuseum.co.uk

www.woldinghamassociation.wordpress.com

Yale Divinity School Library, Special Collections, USA

Blechingley from Grange Meadow, looking towards the North Downs - 2024

Blechingley from Castle Hill, looking towards the North Downs - 2024

Blechingley from the north, looking south 2024

About the Author

David John McCleave – 2022
Photographer Jason McCleave

David owned and lived in the converted stables at The Grange from 2014 to 2022. He was born in Croydon, Surrey, and was a car and motorcycle mechanic after sitting City and Guilds exams. He was a motorcycle enthusiast and raced at an amateur level, then established a motorcycle sales business. Always having had a fascination with photography and filming, he switched careers in the 1980s and for the next 35 years he ran sales businesses connected to the TV and film industry. He has two children, Sarah and Jason, and two grandchildren, Rosa and Cassian. He has dabbled in collecting rare books, but this is his first attempt at writing one.

www.ingramcontent.com/pod-product-compliance
Lightning Source LLC
Chambersburg PA
CBHW042356070526
44585CB00028B/2957